eu'lo·gy

[Gr. *eulogia*] A discourse, commendation of someone or something, or services of a deceased person…also, high praise; laudation.

A memoir by

Mary Bergan Blanchard

To Megan

Mary Bergan Blanchard

ABOUT THE BOOK

"People confess to the priests
if they want God's forgiveness;
they go to the nuns
when they want something done."

More than three decades ago, Catholics in general but nuns in particular were caught up in a whirlwind initiated by the Second Vatican Council. No group in America responded to its call for renewal as did the nuns.

Blanchard captures this soul-stirring period in *Eulogy*, her "memoir sprinkled with fiction" as she presents with humor and poignancy how it felt to be shaped by Catholic education and convent politics, then confronted by the social upheaval of the sixties. She weaves nature images like a fleur de lis into her sometimes gritty tale and her artistic vision delivers the quiet pleasure of a trip to a museum of Monets. Some accounts evoke pain and frustration of a lively spirit hidebound by church structures and strictures while others leave the reader smiling for days.

Eulogy also recalls early stirrings of the fierce issues of today, including feminism. Blanchard is emphatic in her stance and offers succinct, opinionated turns of phrase that will irk some and please others. She can be tough but she presents a faith anchor that makes her a respectful critic of the church and religious orders, reflecting the integrity lacking in many other books about convent life.

A quick read, *Eulogy* keeps the bedside light burning.

Reviewed by Sister Mary Ann Walsh, a Sister of Mercy for 45 years. She is Associate Director of Communications of the U. S. Catholic Conference. She has been published widely in both the secular and Catholic press.

ACKNOWLEDGMENTS

To those gone who inspired me: my mother, Winifred Mary O'Neill Bergan, and her backbone...my father, Thomas Bernard Bergan, and his spunk. To Mother Catherine McAuley RSM, Sister Mary Bertrand Degnan RSM, author of *Mercy Unto Thousands*, to Mary McMahon, my dear friend who never judged.

To my sisters, Patty Bergan O'Brien and Katie Bergan Brown, who constantly encouraged me and to my nieces, Reenie, Megan and Cailin who read first drafts, chased down correct names of places and basically cheered me on.

To the Sisters of Mercy of the Albany diocese, especially Sister Mary Martina, my teacher and mentor. Without her kindness and support, this book never would have been written.

To Sister Martha Joyce, Helen Hofmann, Sister Marion Rafferty...lifetime contributors who also did my leg work. To Sister Mary Ann Walsh, my Washington-connection and reviewer.

To Sisters Mary Agnita, Mary Anton, Rita Carr, Barbara Dudley, Jacqueline Garland, Rose Hobbs, Marilyn Murray, Rita Noonan, Amanda Schermerhorn, Rosemary Sgroi, Jane Somerville and Peggy Straney for their stories and support.

To my readers and critiquers: Leslie Blanchard, Edie Flaherty, Anna M. Green McGrath, Sydney Neill, Barbara Gossen Shelby and Ronda Sofia: also Irene Alexander, George Anderson, Virginia Cramer, Mel Eisenstadt, Eileen Fitzgerald, Sister Amy Hoey RSM, Betsy Lackmann, Val Lewis, Jan McGonaghy, Doris Stremel, Lorena Yalmokas and Mary Zerbe.

My special thanks to: Anne McGrath Sabach for her editorial and technical help, Jennifer Murphey Dye for cleaning up my typos and

Rosemary Feeley Graham for our endless telephone conversations and her unrelenting reality checks.

Thank you.

DEDICATION

To my parents and sisters, Patty O'Brien and Katie Brown who gave me a remarkable childhood, to dedicated, religious women who sacrificed their lives for others, and to you, my son, Michael, so you will know that people like this did live.

A WORD FROM THE WRITER 2000

Death prods the mind, goads the memory, unsettles the spirit.

When my mother died at ninety-four in the winter of 1992, I had prepared myself. Extraordinary spirit and health favored her during her long life but she had recently suffered through a series of strokes, and I hoped she wouldn't linger. Death is a blessing for her now, a relief, I thought. I had lived through other deaths. I was ready for hers.

But who is ever ready?

I fell into a world of memories, of my family and friends, and of the twenty years I had spent as a Sister of Mercy. The life I experienced growing up had disappeared along with the ideals that encouraged it to thrive.

So, who would tell the stories? History is being written by those who weren't there and don't know.

I began writing a novel immediately, as an observer, a commentator. Of course, that didn't work. It became a memoir, and I had to review the cost of my life's decisions. There were many because I lived through a great change in society, a change in the Catholic Church and in religious life.

I have taken liberties arranging times, changing names and combining people's characters to protect their privacy. Although not exactly accurate, *Eulogy* is a true picture of the times, my early life and a tribute to those I met along the way.

A WORD FROM THE WRITER 2011

Eulogy was first published in 2000, the year my husband became seriously ill and I did not have the time to market it properly. Through sheer neglect, it went out of print. Since I have had many requests for the book, I have decided to have it reprinted.

I had not reread it in ten years and was amazed that the message remained both current and vital. Unfortunately, the path of the Church has worsened since then. The rise of pre-Vatican II conservatives and the Vatican's current inquisition into the nuns' business and apostolates would lead one to believe that we are regressing into the Middle Ages.

Droves of American Catholics have left the Church, dismayed at the pomp and stubborn arrogance of the hierarchy who refuse to consider that all modern change is not immoral. Unfortunately, but true to form, the official Catholic Church has even abandoned dialog concerning married and women priests. Yet, for want of priests to say Mass and consecrate the Eucharist, parishes are closing, depriving the laity of its most vital sacrament.

However, history proves the authoritative Church has always slogged along, leaving change to us demanding faithful, the ones Christ came to enlighten in the first place.

PART ONE

Death prods the mind, goads the memory,
unsettles the spirit.

CHAPTER ONE

Last night, my two sisters, Pat and Katie, had picked me up at the Albany airport. My husband, Ed, had remained in Albuquerque with our son, Mike, who was to take his SAT's the next day. The flight got in at eleven-thirty and we stayed up in Katie's bedroom until after three, into our memories, talking, laughing, and weeping now and then. We had settled the funeral arrangements this morning over breakfast.

"The Motherhouse? Mom's funeral at the Motherhouse? Why?" Pat asked. "I'm curious. You haven't set foot in the place since you left the convent twenty-three years ago."

"If not from there, where?" I asked. "Our parish church? The place is cold and dark and who'd come? Her friends are all dead but the sisters remember her and besides, they'll let us arrange the funeral the way we want.

"And there's something about the Motherhouse," I trailed off. But Pat was right. Why the Motherhouse? Why did I insist mother's funeral Mass be said there? Why? What was stirring besides sheer practicality? What strange siren was drawing me back into the past? Wasn't Mom's death enough? Must I dig up graves?

"Won't it seem strange not burying her from her parish?" Katie asked, fussing at the sink. "What will the priests think?"

Pat never looked up. "Who cares? The priests didn't know her. Mary wants the Motherhouse, you want a bag piper, and I pick the hymns." She clapped her notebook shut.

"You're determined to give the eulogy, Mary?"

"Yes."

"You'll never get through it." Both of them had been so attentive last night, knowing I'd taken Mom's death hard.

"I can handle it. Her life is not going to be swept away and forgotten, barely commented upon by some stranger. Being a good, generous person should count for something." I could handle

3

anything, I thought, turn off my feelings like a light switch. Click. Gone.

"I've already called Sister Helen and she's taking care of details." Helen was the current president of the Albany Sisters of Mercy and had been my close friend since grade school days. "She'd do anything for me," I added.

The TV was on in the sunroom and sounds of some game show drifted through the French doors into the kitchen.

"I knew there was something I forgot to tell you!" Katie exclaimed. "I met Jimmy O'Neill at St. Peter's, yesterday. He felt bad about Mom. She always took such an interest in him. He was asking for you, Mary...said he'd see you at the wake." Katie's head disappeared behind the fridge door again but Pat peered at me over the newspaper, appraising my reaction. Jimmy and I had been friends forever, and just before I left the convent, our friendship had rekindled. I always wondered how much Pat guessed and how much she knew.

"I've got to run. I have some extra time so I'm going to drive through our old neighborhood. I have to meet Helen at four and we're going to dinner. I'll be back around seven-thirty." Katie walked me towards the front door where I zipped up my boots and struggled into my winter coat.

"Will you be glad to see her?" Katie's face was clueless. Since the day I left the convent, she had harbored dim thoughts, suspecting everyone in the order of foul play. Why did I leave? What had they done to me? Something had to be wrong with them! Certainly, nothing could ever have been wrong with me.

"Yes, it's been years and I'm always glad to see her. We've had good times long before and long after the two of us entered the convent. Anyway, give me your keys. I'm out of here."

* * * * *

I backed Katie's car down her driveway and into Western Avenue traffic. Sand, salt and bright January sun had cleared the roads and I could sail along. Good. My mind traveled its own routes when I drove over familiar streets.

I knew she'd die before I got here. "Oh, Mom, why didn't you wait for me?" I fumbled in my pocket for my handkerchief and blew my nose. I guess I'm not as Spartan as I thought.

Everything had turned out a quarter of a cup short...all the things I had planned when Ed and I decided to retire in Albuquerque. Mom could have spent the winter where it was warm, oohing over the red mountains and the clouds. How she loved clouds. Then she began having strokes.

Things don't always turn out.

I could hear Mom. "Mary, you can't always have what you want." Tell me about it, I thought. I remembered one Saturday, when I was about five, she went shopping and promised to bring me home a doctor's kit, the kind with those little stethoscopes. I sat all afternoon on the window seat, watching for her in the rain. I even ate lunch there. You get so caught up when you're little.

But she had completely forgotten, and came home without it. I was devastated, and the more she tried to comfort me, the harder I cried. "Mary," she finally said, "you can't always have what you want." I was sure it was the end of the world, but when I remembered the ends of the world I'd been through since then...the frustration of being human...nothing ever goes according to plan. Especially death. It comes and goes as it pleases. One morning you look up and what you had is gone.

I passed Manning Boulevard's stately homes, with their manicured firs and junipers draped in white fluff, and headed towards our old house on Academy Road. Norway maples lined New Scotland Avenue. In summer time, thick maroon leaves shaded the pavement. Today, their limbs, tucked into white snowsuits, danced with the wind and dusted the street below, beckoning me with long, woolly arms to come out and play.

Nostalgia overwhelmed me as I cruised down old roads and recollections, remembering the cocoon that enveloped my family and friends when I was young. I grew up in a dream world. It was how things were *supposed* to be then that counted. How they appeared, not how they really were. The whole country was the same way.

When I was in grade school, skating up this street to the nuns in my old clunkers that I had to tighten with a key, my biggest problem was, would the clamps that fastened the skates to the soles of my shoes loosen and send me sprawling? In the meantime, nineteen year-old boys were fighting a war and being maimed and torn apart and killed. Despite that reality, the war was romanticized. Society was determined to cultivate a simple and safe milieu for its children, truthful or not. For me, growing up during the early war years had been one big marshmallow.

I caught the green light at Cardinal Avenue and noticed the rambling old private homes below St. Peter's Hospital were now doctors' or lawyers' offices. I remembered walking towards the Motherhouse with the nuns, on my way to piano lessons, carrying some favorite sister's book-bag. In the old days it was common to see nuns, always in pairs, walking somewhere, wrapped in curious habits designed over a hundred years ago. Protected only by crocheted shawls, with veils flowing, they were seemingly unaware of the biting winter winds that blew across the fields chilling their bones…their simple presence proclaimed to the entire world that God was worth it. A total enigma to most and perceived as more angel than human, they appeared to hover between heaven and earth.

Those 'angels' had been a prime ingredient in my fairy tale world…human beings leading supernatural lives, piquing my imagination and desires until finally I could resist their message no longer.

Twenty years later, following the revolutionary changes proclaimed by Vatican II, I left the community. The decision had been excruciating. I felt the way fervent Jews must have felt at the time of Christ, called away from the Old Testament, its pomp and rituals and its devotion to trivial detail and into the new gospel of love of neighbor.

I rarely reviewed the past. To what purpose? But today, it banged on my doors and rattled my windows. This was crazy. Here I am, a counselor, forever cajoling clients to air out used bedding, find peace with old decisions. Was something still unsettled (something I was sure I had put to rest years ago) or was I simply grieving, missing people I had lost? Maybe my youth? What was it?

Cutting over Lawnridge Avenue to Academy Road, I took the old route I had walked on my way home from St. Teresa's School. The area had changed. Brick buildings had crawled up New Scotland Avenue, swallowing up the blocks, tarring over the killdeers' nests, and driving away the quail. No one hunted rabbits with B B guns anymore or sledded down the hill across from our gray house. Those fields were now a parking lot.

On summer nights, we had played 'Red Light' and 'Giant Steps'; in the fall, we had run down those hills, flushing out pheasants. Today, I was flushing out memories. Reserved signs dotted the parking lot, but I found a spot that faced our old house with its twenty-nine windows and cozy sun porch. I turned off the engine and settled myself. My heavy coat and fur-lined boots would keep me warm.

A sweet sadness overcame me; I felt as if I were watching soup simmering on a cold November day, comforting and nostalgic, its contents slowly bubbling to the surface. I closed my eyes and thought, Dad and Mom, you're both gone. The sweet life you wrapped around us, the fun, the pizzazz, the honor, the innocence, the optimism, the sheer goodness. I hadn't thought about these things in years. I observed the rose bushes Mom had planted by the front door, bare and dormant, gathering strength for the demanding spring ahead. Against many odds, my religious vocation took root and blossomed in this house. I settled down in the car and began to deal with my memories.

CHAPTER TWO

We were a moral family, not a strongly religious one…not typically Irish Catholic if such a thing exists. Dad came from a long line of disgruntled Catholics. "The closer you are to the Church, the further you are from God." I'd heard that one enough. In 1904, when he was considering attending Union College, the parish priest had arrived with his wisdom. "Send him to work," he told my grandmother. "He's had high school, more than most. Send him to the foundry and let him support you." She showed him the door. "You have your nerve," said she. "Education is good enough for the likes of you but not for the likes of us," and off Dad went to Union College to become an engineer. He had more respect for his country than the Church, he said. "What had the Church ever done for me except give orders?"

However, the subject of religion came to a head when we moved to Albany from Utica on the Monday during spring vacation in April 1940. Dad had flourished in business during the twenties and Mom and he were planning a trip on the Queen Mary when the Depression wiped him out. He returned to civil engineering and ran the Works Project Administration in five counties in upper New York State, building roads, bridges and swimming pools. But the economy was improving, the bureau was closing and he needed to find work. Dad took a Civil Service exam for Assistant Commissioner of the State Department of Corrections, got the job and here we were.

The next Saturday afternoon, Mom stood in our big kitchen over the huge porcelain sink, dropping peeled vegetables into a bowl of cold water. Dad stared out the window at the fields and I sat on the radiator. A pot roast was simmering and I could smell the dark juices and sweet onions.

Dad and Mom had sauntered in and out of this conversation for days. P.S. 19 or St. Teresa's? Dad liked the idea of public school and wanted us enrolled there, especially me. I had attended John F. Hughes in Utica. He claimed that Our Lady of Lourdes where Pat

8

went was too far for me to walk. Now, Mom wanted us in Catholic school together.

I had loved public school, especially kindergarten. There was music and art all day, a totally creative program: stories, dramatics, swathed in an invisible routine. Despite this gossamer regimentation, my report card read, "Delightful child, imaginative, *but does not like to do what she is told.*"

Dad could not see me in St. Teresa's. The fact that all Catholic children were supposed to be in Catholic school meant nothing to him.

In those days, the Church was so definite. "I speak," it said. "You believe." Dad feared its subtle and not-so-subtle codes would lean against our choices. We needed room, he said, not a web. But my mother, for all her seeming compliance, was determined that we go to Catholic school and she met him head on.

I was naive enough to believe my parents were of one mind, since they never argued; they just talked and talked, and gave reasons that they were right until one of them wore down.

"Why pay money for books and uniforms when there's a perfectly good public school one block closer?"

"As far as uniforms go, they'll still have to wear clothes," Mom answered, "and they can resell their books." She always futzed during a serious discussion, and today, she pared carrots and scrubbed little potatoes. I sensed uniforms and books weren't the issue.

"The classes are overcrowded"

Mom countered it didn't matter, that the nuns could handle an army. Their whole life was devoted to their work. They taught discipline and ideals and stressed written English. The Sisters of Mercy were an Irish order, weren't they? Some of the old nuns still had brogues. Was there a soul on earth who spun the English language as well as an educated Irishman? Look at Shaw and O'Connor, she said.

"Now Winnie, be reasonable," Dad complained, staring out the window. "It's too strict, too narrow, too confining."

"Where else will they learn about their religion, if not in Catholic school? We don't know enough to teach them."

He continued, addressing the glittering windowpane. "If they go to Catholic school, I admit they'll get a hell of an education but they won't learn a thing about life." He received no comment from Mother, who didn't seem to care what we knew about life. He was licked and he knew it.

"I don't know about Mary and Catholic school." Jingling his change, he disappeared into the living room and behind his copy of *The Knickerbocker News*. What was the difference? I thought. The schools were both brick and only a block away from each other. St. Teresa's did appear more inviting, flanked by the church, the rectory's front lawn dotted with evergreens, while down the street stood P.S. 19, stranded in concrete, barren and dismal. Was it the way they looked?

But it was something else that made the difference because I soon learned Catholic school was the way you dressed, where you went and with whom, what you did on weekends, what you read, what you mocked, what you thought or refused to think. It was truths you couldn't escape.

Catholic school was a way of life.

* * * * *

The following Monday, off we went to join others in brown and tan uniforms, to *The Baltimore Catechism*, the small green paperback that synthesized our religion, and to the mysterious nuns, clothed in yards of black serge, with flowing see-through veils and long clacking beads...to seemingly heavenly beings. Did they fall out of another world?

Dad decided it was his duty to enroll us and made his one appearance at St. Teresa's that day. After a few words of greeting to the principal, a pupil ushered Pat into sixth grade, but Katie and I remained behind. Katie grasped Dad's hand while I stared up at the face of the nun. He kept talking, Katie kept clinging and I kept staring.

Katie looked scared to death.

I was fascinated.

I hadn't seen creatures like this before. My First Communion nun had worn a blue gown and big white wings on her head and had a neck. This one had only a face. The starched white cotton that held up her veil had a hole in it where she peeked out. Dad had prepared me.

"They're only people, Mary. Just look at their faces." Sister Boniface was beautiful, just like the Blessed Virgin and eventually became my fourth grade teacher.

Every morning after prayers and 'I Pledge Allegiance', we would sit transfixed for an hour. As Sister Boniface leaned against the front edge of her desk, her eyes found a spot between the back wall and heaven. Then, she described St. Sebastian with all the arrows in him and the Christians eaten by lions and St. Joan, gone in the fire. I sat there shuddering inside. I was terrified of fire.

St. Elizabeth's husband was furious at her for giving bread to the poor and when he caught her, God changed the bread to roses. Finally, he believed her and saw she was a saint. What was wrong with him? I was only eight but I could tell something was going on.

Sister assured us later that he turned out all right.

But most saints' lives were frightening. How about St. Peter who was crucified upside down and some English priest who had his insides torn out when he was still breathing? Being a martyr scared me and I kept telling God I wouldn't be good at it. Sister Boniface, however, made it clear we should keep "our minds open for that grand consideration and special crown of martyrdom."

I wasn't sure, but she mesmerized me.

I was thriving. But poor Katie! Because she was shy and behaved well, she sat in the back of her classroom, even though her name began with B. All the troublemakers were in front. She tried becoming an A student. It did her some good and it did her no good. She led her class but felt little approval because her nun was too busy, too overworked by sixty-four second graders, only seventeen of them girls. Katie never recovered from her original terror, and the worst of it?

She was afraid to make her First Communion!

We shared the back bedroom, a four poster and our deepest secrets. Saturday mornings, lounging in bed, we reviewed the week.

"Why don't you want to make your First Communion? Don't you like your dress?" I couldn't understand it. First Communion was big time.

In second grade, the nuns decided children knew right from wrong, and taught them everything in *The Baltimore Catechism*. Well, not everything, but the basics anyway. Then, they sent them to the priests who heard their 'sins' and forgave them in the name of God. They said it was God who really did it…forgive the sins, that is. On a special Sunday, usually Mother's Day, the girls dressed like brides in short white dresses, and the boys wore white suits. Everything was white, and the whole class received Communion at a Mass the priest said especially for them.

Presents, relatives, friends, pictures, parties! First Communion. Definitely big time.

"I'm scared I'm going to be sick," Katie confided, eyes brimming.

"You're not going to be sick."

"I am too. I'm going to be sick." Clearly, Katie was upset.

"Why?"

"I can't eat somebody's body and blood, even God's." I pushed myself up on one elbow.

"Oh, is that all?" I sank back on the bed. "Don't worry. It tastes like bread. The host tastes like bread. But it serves you right for reading all those awful comic books where everybody gets cut up, and all that blood." She was close to tears. "I'm only kidding," I said. "There's no blood, there's NO BLOOD."

"I'm scared I'm going to be sick," Katie persisted. "Sister Gerald told us it was the body and blood of Christ." This was serious. I got up on my elbow again.

"Now, listen. It's not the way it sounds. The host tastes like dry bread, like cardboard. Save up a lot of spit, let the host melt in your mouth and it will go right down." Since I had made my First Communion two years ago, I was an authority.

"Sister says it's the body and blood of Jesus. I'm going to be sick." Katie looked so white and upset, I thought she was going to be sick right here in the middle of our bed. She was still trying to get used to the nuns, who scared her speechless. And now, this, this body and blood stuff. I sighed. What was wrong with Katie's nun? How could she miss a point this big? Why couldn't she do it right? Why didn't Sister Gerald do what my First Communion nun did? When it came to getting people ready for First Communion, my nun with the white winged hat had it all over her nun.

She had smiley lines around her eyes. I used to stare at a brown mole on her neck and at her square hands and nails. Not polished like my mother's. But when my nun talked to us, she bent down and made her voice low and we thought we had a joke together that nobody knew about except us.

One afternoon after school, she led us from her classroom, through the church and into the sacristy, where the priest dressed. We were the 'publics' and had special lessons, because we didn't know as much as Catholic-schoolers. They had religion every day.

"You can talk in here because this is not the church. It's like a back hall." She opened a drawer and pulled out a small box of white wafers and put it in her bag.

"These are not Jesus yet. The priest hasn't made them Jesus. He does that when the bells ring at Mass and everyone bows his head." I never bowed my head. I always kept it up. Something was going on and I didn't want to miss it. Maybe someday I'd see it happen, like Jesus coming down from heaven and disappearing into the round flat piece of bread the priest held up.

SHAZAM! And I'd see it because I kept looking. But I didn't tell her I looked.

She pulled up a straight backed chair and the eight of us settled at her feet, wondering what else she had in her bag and what she was going to do next. Would she make it happen right here in the sacristy?

Could she?

"Look at your hand, and make a fist. Spread out your fingers. Isn't that a miracle?"

We weren't sure. We'd never thought about it, but we went along.

"All the things inside your hand that have to move so you can close it." She sat there, opening and closing her hand and I could tell by looking at her she thought it was something. Her face sort of lit up.

"And you can see me!"

"And you can hear me!"

"God makes it all happen. Think of all that He can do. How smart God is! He can think up anything. He can do anything, anything."

We agreed. She brought out a picture book.

"Now close your eyes and think of an elephant and a bee."

We did.

"Think of how big one of them is and how small the other is. Think of all the different things they can do. Each one is a miracle.

"An elephant can feel things with the end of her trunk, feel things the way you feel with your fingers, and pick things up. And as big as she is, she never steps on her baby, even though her baby likes to walk under her." We all looked at the picture of the mother and baby elephant.

"And the bee is tiny and goes to work every day just the way your fathers do. He comes home and puts all his honey into a wax box and seals it up. No matter where the bees live, they do the same thing." She showed us the picture. We had been creeping up, some of us on our knees, and we looked again. We liked being close to her. She smelled like Ivory soap.

"Sit down, now. I have a surprise for you." She pulled a jar of honey out of her bag and said, "Who would like some honey?"

We all wanted some. It was messy but as we sat in the sacristy eating crackers and honey, I thought I must be in heaven. The sun sprinkled through the colored windows. Confetti light fell around my nun and any minute, I thought she'd rise right off the chair and disappear before our eyes. "God knows that children like to eat," she began, "and since He wants to be part of you..." she held out her hands, palms up, eyebrows lifted, and waited for our answer.

"He turns Himself into something we can eat!" we chorused.

"Yes." There we sat, munching on our snacks in a dusky sacristy, learning how miracles happened. Made sense to me. It seemed to make sense to everybody else, too.

Then, we ate the dry hosts and she told us how to melt them and swallow them. We knew what they tasted like and that the priest hadn't changed them into Jesus yet. We figured she knew everything, and that we weren't far behind.

So why was Katie stuck on thinking gory thoughts about something so wonderful, such a miracle? She deserved better than that. I told her the stories my nun had told me and she seemed a little better. Then, I said, "I have an idea."

"What?"

"Let's go."

Mom was doing the laundry in the cellar and Pat was still asleep so we had the run of the house. We threw off the covers and padded barefoot downstairs into the kitchen where I took out a slice of bread and cut a hole in it with the top of an orange juice glass.

"There." I pushed my hand on the bread, flattening it out. "Come on upstairs. We can't do anything here." When we got back to our room, I shut the door, just in case Pat woke up. "Okay. Now you kneel on the chair." I put my bathrobe on backwards, wrapped a handkerchief around my neck and stood behind the chair.

"I'm the priest and it's your turn to go to Communion. All the kids will be kneeling with their heads down. You keep looking at the priest out of the side of your eye." I moved to her right and watched her eyes. "When you see him coming, maybe two kids away, fill your mouth with spit as much as you can. The bread will taste like cardboard, but you can get it down. Remember, let it melt. It's just bread."

Katie knelt on the chair and looked at me solemnly.

"He holds it up and says, 'Core puss dummy knee' or something like that and puts it on your tongue, all right? Don't lose your spit, all right?"

"All right."

"Close your eyes, and open your mouth."

"All right."

"You're not going to get sick!"

"No." It went off well. She swished it around and down it went. Too bad Daddy had sent Katie to Catholic school. If she had been a 'public,' maybe she would have had what I had. I guess her nun couldn't do it with sixty-four kids in the room.

"How about confession? Want to practice?"

"Yes." There was a closet in the middle of the wall in our bedroom with a door that frequently came in handy. Pat hid behind it Saturday mornings when Mom came upstairs to give us the deuce for raising hell on the beds, and knocking out slats. She never did see Pat making faces at us from behind the door and Pat got us into terrible trouble with Mom more than once. Today, we used the door for a confessional. I sat on a chair in the closet and Katie who seemed terrified still, knelt on a chair on the other side.

"Bless me, Father, for I have sinned. This is my first confession." She grabbed the doorknob and stuck her head around the corner.

"Now, what'll I say?"

I sat there, thinking. "What'd you do?"

"Nothing."

"You can't say that."

"Okay." We thought for awhile. She pulled herself back and said, "I lied a' hundred times." I jerked my head around the door.

"Really?" Katie never lied.

"No." I retreated and then stuck my head around again. "You can't tell him that…you didn't do it. What about stealing?"

"No."

"Talking back?"

"No."

"Did you disobey or commit adultery?"

"No." I flipped through *The Baltimore Catechism*. This job was proving harder than I thought.

"What's a dull tree?"

"I don't know but it's here." I shut the book in disgust. No help at all.

"What about not picking up your dirty clothes? Mom doesn't like it when we don't pick up our dirty clothes."

"Is that a sin?"

"I don't know but you have to say something."

"You sure about a dull tree?"

"You can't use it."

She kept looking at me hopefully, so I went back to the book. "It doesn't fit. It means marrying someone else's wife. It doesn't fit."

Katie sighed, "I didn't pick up my dirty clothes a hundred times." She leaned around the door again. "Can you think of anything else?"

"No."

"For your penance say five Our Fathers and five Hail Marys and say the Act of Contrition."

"Oh, my God, I am hard'ly sorry for having offended Thee and I detest all my sins…"

We lived in an age of innocence.

CHAPTER THREE

School might have been a pain for Katie but we loved our new house and neighborhood, our own private Sherwood Forest. Academy Road was wide enough for street games and all the backyards ran together and there were lots of kids our age. We could play in the fields with Sally Anne Clinton, build straw huts and weave cattails into mats. Katie scrounged a wooden sign from the cellar and waterproofed our hut. When it rained, the three of us would squeeze in, our heads nearly out the door, and we'd listen to the patter in the fields. One Saturday afternoon in late winter, we were out back near the brook, roasting potatoes, sitting close to the fire and talking, cozy in our snow suits with hoods, hand-knit scarves and mittens. Sally Ann Clinton wanted to play again tomorrow morning. She was Protestant and didn't have to go to church every Sunday but we did or we'd end up in hell.

"You're Catholic," she sniffed, "and you have to do what the pope says."

"Says who?" I asked.

"My mother," she sassed back.

"I don't know the pope and anyway, all he does is take care of pagan babies."

"What are pagan babies?"

"During Lent," Katie answered, "we give up candy and ice cream. We buy pagan babies. Chinese are pagans and they kill their babies."

"How come?"

"They haven't got any food," she continued. "They'd starve anyway. They cost five dollars apiece and Catholics buy 'em. I put in my birthday money and saved the most so I got to name her Rose Marie."

"We're not Catholic and we don't kill babies!" Sally Ann protested.

"You're not Chinese, either, and you're not pagan." So there, I thought. "They only kill the girls." That made it worse.

_eu'lo·gy_

"What does the pope do with the babies?" Sally Ann wanted to know.

"He doesn't buy them. He sends the nuns the money. They take care of 'em." We stared at our potatoes for a while.

"Mom says your church is dark and scary," Sally Ann ventured.

"Want to come see it? You can see ours but we can't go into yours," I said.

"Why not?"

"The nuns are afraid we'll lose our religion."

"Just by going in?"

"I guess so. What's yours like?" I asked. "It must be something if we can't even go in!"

"It's a big white hall with pews. The choir stands in front where Mr. Turner talks." Katie and I waited.

"Anything else? Do you go to Communion?"

"Yes. They pass Communion around."

"Wow! In our church, no one touches Communion except the priest. Do you go to confession?"

"No. My mother says you shouldn't tell anybody except God what you do wrong."

"No kidding! The nuns bring us to confession once a month whether we need it or not. What do you do in church? Do you have Mass?"

"What's Mass?"

"If you don't know, you don't have it. There must be something we do the same."

"We sing hymns." Sally Ann stood right up, shook her straight blond hair out of her hood and in a sweet, clear voice began,

" '_Jesus loves me this I know,_
For the Bible tells me so.
Little ones to Him belong.
They are weak but He is strong.
Yes, Jesus loves me.
Yes, Jesus loves me.
Yes, Jesus loves me.

19

The Bible tells me so.' "

I coughed, smothering my laughs. We never sang stuff like that in church. Old ladies with high voices warbled from upstairs with the organ, and they didn't sing in English. But they never sang about the Bible. The Catholic Church was never big on the Bible. We had *The Baltimore Catechism* and the pope. I didn't want her to know what I was thinking so I said, "I want to see your church. Do you think we'd get into trouble?" Katie thought we would but Sally Ann and I made plans over her head and decided to sign a pact in 'blood' by each chipping in a nickel and walking up to Abrams Drugstore for a small scoop of strawberry ice cream.

We never did see her church.

* * * * *

Mom thought I was getting too old to play in the fields. She had vainly hoped the nuns might transform me into a lady, but finally decided she would tame me herself. "There is more to life than building tree huts, creating straw villages and declaring war on those boys from Grove Avenue."

For my tenth birthday, she promised to buy me a pretty dress, grown up pumps, stockings with seams, and throw me a big party. I'd even get a pair of black racers, but I must act the part of a lady, just for that one day.

It was a deal.

She taught me how to sit, my back not quite touching the chair, how to cross my ankles and bend my knees ever so slightly to the left. She showed me where my hands belonged, and, above all, how not to fidget. I bore up because I was getting a McCall's mannequin with removable arms and real sewing patterns out of this, plus the ice skates.

At last came the day to buy my dress. Mother, as usual called The Young Folks Shop in advance so the owners would lay out the right size and colors. I had to wear my best clothes: leggings and a coat with a velvet collar. Gloves even. I'd made the bargain. There was no escaping.

We took the bus downtown to Pearl Street, and it was unusually crowded. All the men were standing and when another woman got on, Mom signaled me to give her my seat. As we reached Madison Avenue, a young black and very pregnant woman boarded the bus and as she waddled past us joggling for space, Mom rose and insisted she take her seat. She protested but finally did.

"I remember how I felt the last month I carried my oldest one," Mom remarked. "It was summer and my ankles used to swell." They chatted like neighbors about children and the woman said she had two more home. I kept watching because no grown-up I knew talked to a Negro woman like she was a person.

When we got off the bus and began walking towards The Little Folk's Shop, I asked Mom why she stood up for another lady. "She wasn't older than you. She was young and she was a cleaning lady," I insisted. In my eyes, my mother was royalty. Why should she stand up for anyone?

"Should that make a difference? She was pregnant and she was tired and people should think of someone besides themselves. Please open the door for me, Mary. We're here."

Sylvia and Rose, the two elderly maiden ladies who owned the store had long, very black hair, tied in neat buns on the top of their heads. There, the similarity ended. Sylvia was tiny, sharp, well groomed, and ran the show. "Mrs. Bergan," she cooed, sweeping towards her with arms thrown out in welcome, "we're all ready for you." She jerked her head towards the silent Rose, who smiled sweetly at Mother and shooed me into the dressing rooms off the back corridor.

While Mom sipped tea and nibbled homemade cookies, Rose dressed me. "Where is your sister today?" she asked. I told her the birthday story and how I cut a deal and she smiled.

"But I hate this dress!" I moaned. It was plain navy blue, like all the others Sylvia chose for me. But, I hated every dress because I was so skinny, and nothing looked good, just hung there.

"So, you hate this dress," and she winked at me and stepped out of the dressing room for a minute, returning with a pretty light turquoise thing with a swishy skirt and little brick red flowers on it. Rose made me bite my lips and lick them, and pinch my cheeks and twirl around. She combed my hair, fluffed it out and said, "Now, walk out slowly and turn and smile at your mother."

Sylvia's eyebrows flew into her hair when I made my entrance, but good old Mom! She saw me standing there, smiling, and she saw Rose, half hidden by curtains, smiling, and I got the dress. I thought, if I had to look like a girl, I might as well do it in this dress.

On my birthday, it was pouring rain and I was in a panic that no one would come. But they all did. I sat on one of the straight-backed dining room chairs Mom had moved into the living room. The girls gathered around and gave me presents. I looked right at them as if they were lovely strangers and said, "Thank you very much."

All the other mothers were there; it was quite elegant and formal. I helped serve the ice cream and cake and never spilled a thing. I was a lady at last! Lady Mary. I liked it, and never forgot it. My mother battled dragons to teach me manners and poise, which she thought was her gift to me on my tenth birthday. But what stuck with me was that she gave up her seat on the bus for a tired Negro cleaning lady.

CHAPTER FOUR

No matter how much fun we had at home or in the neighborhood, my life still revolved around school. After a year of hands folded on the desk and ankles crossed, we met Sister Stanislaus Mary who taught fifth grade, was ten years older than God, bulky, and a bona fide Indian who had a Ph.D. and emigrated from Canada from some French order of nuns.

She wore flat men's shoes, pulled her skirt up in the front when she taught us dancing and loved teaching. Activity, activity, both physical and mental! Stanislaus Mary nearly drowned us in both.

Helen, my new friend, had moved from Catskill in August and minded her little brother. After school, at her house, we helped each other memorize the presidents in order and all the county seats in New York plus the forty-eight states and their capitals and major products. We knew the geography of the whole earth: mountain ranges, deserts, trade winds, oceans, currents, major rivers and how come they could flow up on the map. While I asked questions, Helen started dinner. She was keen and seemed much older than I. Stopped smoking last year, she said.

Our fifth grade teacher did not please her, however, as she had pointed out to me in school last week. "Sister Stanislaus Mary never gives us a minute's peace," she complained, because Helen hated dancing and liked everything neat. "How can we hang up another project? Just look at this place!"

Our classroom was jammed with projects past, present and in progress. Cellophane-straw bird cage mobiles dangled at odd levels, peppering the ceiling with riots of color. From the floor up were posters, and product maps of our country by states. Spelling papers, compositions, geography tests, history reports and math quizzes, all corrected and starred, concealed everything except one tiny piece of the blackboard. The walls were hidden by multiplication tables, health charts and the four food groups.

On high corkboards, along with the Palmer Method cards, Sister had tacked constellations, planets and rules for good posture. Birds' nests, rock collections, and empty beehives cluttered the radiator, leaving little room for our pet goldfish, Doolittle, who swam around in a huge bowl.

Helen sighed. "If there were any room left in here, she'd probably keep horses."

But what fun! I thought I was back in public school.

We pushed the chairs and desks around the room, danced, acted out stories and sang in three languages, all forty-six of us. Sister Stanislaus Mary gave us candy if we could recite long poems and orations like 'The Gettysburg Address', or Longfellow's 'Under the Spreading Chestnut Tree'. We made messy elevation maps with salt and flour and water right on oil cloth on the floor, and I still know rain forests and deserts worldwide and how everything got that way. I never had a teacher like her before or since.

My luck held in sixth grade. Before the bell and prayers in the morning, we'd vie for a place in line where, armed with her stopwatch, Sister Francina or 'Lister', as we nicknamed her because of her interminable lists, heard us gallop through the times tables. Then, she checked off our names. The first one to diagram the complicated sentence on the board could read a comic book for fifteen minutes.

Jimmy O'Neill whizzed through the tables and helped other kids with arithmetic, but I corrected his English papers and heard his reading because he had trouble and Lister knew Jimmy wouldn't let anyone help him except me.

We were pals. In fourth grade, he and Jake Redmond had jumped over the fence into the convent back yard and saw the nuns' frozen underwear, blowing as stiff as panes of glass in the bitter wind. Sister Stanislaus Mary caught them and the boys swore she beat them over their heads with long johns but Jimmy loved to kid. So who knew? We pushed boxes of books around the cloakroom and set up a couple of chairs by the door so Lister could see us from her desk.

"You're her pet," I'd hiss at him. If I had been a boy, he would have punched me.

But instead, Jimmy just grinned.

"How come you always pass things out and get to shovel snow with the janitor? And open all those cartons of books, and bring stuff around to the other grades? No wonder you have trouble with reading. You're never here."

"She takes me after school to make it up."

"Don't you mind?"

"Naw, it's easier."

What a wonderful age that was, dangling over the abyss of adolescence, peering into that unpredictable chasm from the safety of childhood, but still friends with boys, real friends.

* * * * *

The bishop was coming to confirm us that May, to give us the grace to lead good lives when we got old enough to have bad temptations. Lister had given us a list of questions that she cautioned us to answer honestly.

So, over Easter vacation, Jimmy, Jake Redmond and I went fishing at Norman's Kill and did our list there. We rode our bikes out past the Municipal Golf Course and Walley's truck farm. The spring rains had been heavy and we heard the water rushing before we saw it. The skunk cabbages were up and the ground smelled dank, but finally, we slumped on the grass under the willow trees that lined the creek, and spied on the Baltimore orioles building teardrop nests in branches that drooped over the water.

We caught three bullheads with sharp whiskers, one seven inches long. I knew how to take them off the hook but I made Jake do it because it made him feel important.

Eventually, I pulled a pencil box and tablet out of my canvas knapsack, sat cross-legged and began checking off the Commandments. Did I obey them? I glanced at the works of mercy. Did I practice them?

"What's the worst sin?" I asked and when no one responded, I answered the question myself. "I think the worst sin is being mean and making fun of kids who wear knickers or knee socks because their mothers make them."

"Ummmm."

"…and repeating gossip and secret, bad things about people. That's clearly awful." I understood detraction because my mother told me it was evil and worse, beneath one's dignity. Lying was a gray area, though. I loved making up stories and seeing how far I could go. I put a star next to the eighth commandment, and I didn't tell the boys, either.

"What do you think?" I asked them. "What's the worst sin?" Jimmy was lying on his back, his hands behind his head, his gangling knees bent and pointed heavenward.

"I think being a bully. Yeah, being a bully."

"Stealing and talking back to your mother is pretty bad…" and we became lost in our own thoughts.

'Thou shalt not kill'. I kept looking at that one. "Hey, Jake, did you ever want to kill your older brother?"

"Once in a while, not lately." It was known Jake and his brother had terrible fights, right on their living room floor, and Jimmy told me one time their mother threw a glass of water over them, and the three of them ended up laughing so hard that Jake nearly choked, and their mother laughed harder because Jake was wearing the water, and couldn't drink it. There must be something about water.

I wanted to kill Pat once, really kill her, her and her whole gang. They had lured us younger kids into a neighbor's cellar to tease us. They blindfolded me and made me tiptoe around in my bare feet until I stepped into a pail of cold water. Everyone laughed and I felt like a fool, and the heat rose in my head and I exploded and threw the whole pail of water at them, and then the pail.

I scared myself because I saw red and white lights, and I felt like breaking a piece of iron over their heads. I ran howling down the street, gulping for air, the crowd of them who dared, following me at a safe distance. I was out of control. Mom made me suck an ice cube and hold a cool wash cloth on my head. She shooed away Pat, who looked anxious, and as I paced back and forth across the living room, Mom soothed me until my rage was spent.

After I settled down, she listened while I blubbered out my story and finally cautioned me quietly, "Mary, you're too old to have tantrums. You must learn to control your temper. If you don't, someday you might kill someone."

She was right. This hadn't been the first time. The summer I was eight, I fell into a rage and kicked apart an iron bed, and when I was really little, I'd have tantrums and throw myself on the living floor and kick and carry on and Mom would ignore me and move around me until I got so tired, I'd just stand up and walk away.

I was eleven now and grown up. I tried never to get mad after I threw that pail, no matter what anyone said to me. I turned off a switch and I went blank. Then I'd think and then I'd answer. It worked so far. I circled 'Thou shalt not kill' and glanced down the list. Envy wasn't a problem. After all, I had everything. That took care of the tenth commandment. I sat back, breathing in the beautiful spring afternoon. It all seemed so simple. I loved God and He loved me. I was lucky, because some kids feared God a lot.

"Are you afraid of God?" I asked Jimmy.

"I have a healthy respect."

"Ummm," I agreed. "The nuns always say God will not be mocked. Sodom and Gomorra and the flood and all."

Jimmy added, "I'm not about to step out of line."

Jake, who was standing near the water with the fish lines, asked, "Mary, are you ever afraid of going to hell?"

"No," I answered, "I don't expect to do a terrible, bad thing, you know, like face God down and stick out my tongue at Him. Or worse, think I'm as good as God, or better than Him, even, like the fallen angels. Sister says that's the bottom of it all, thinking you're better than God. I'm never going to be that bad." Jimmy and Jake knew I meant it.

"You haven't said anything yet, Jake. What do you think?"

"I think the hardest part is going to be girls."

"You think girls are a *sin*?"

Jake laid a rock on the fish strings, and sank down, squatting on his heels. "Look, Mary, you're a girl. What do girls think when they look at me? They think, 'There's Jake'. But, what do I think when I

27

see girls? I can't even tell you what I think. Even I shouldn't think what I think," Jake concluded.

"Aw, c'mon, Jake," I teased.

"I'm telling you, you're a girl and you wouldn't get it." Jimmy was glaring at Jake. Drat Jimmy! He was so protective.

"Well, I'd get it if you told me," but Jimmy was already packing up. "Damn it, Jimmy, you're not the only one in the world who has to know everything, you know." We threw the fish back and I soon forgot our argument.

On our way home on our bikes, we bought a can of sardines from Dominic's and strung them, oil and all, so it looked as if we had caught something. I made my mother take our picture with the box camera. It came out great; the two of them, Jake with his dark good looks, and Jimmy, his forehead covered by waves of sandy hair, splashing over his eyebrows, elbows slouched on my shoulders. We owned the world.

But it changed. In seventh grade, Jake Redmond kicked me into adolescence.

* * * * *

I was sitting on the edge of our bathtub, smoking, and thinking about Jake. The door was locked, the window, open. The cheek of it! I never smoked cigarettes. And in the house, unheard of!

"Mary, are you smoking in there?"

"Mom, you know I'd never smoke in the bathroom."

"Well, I smell cigarettes."

"Maybe the Filkins are burning leaves." After all, it was the fall. I pulled out another cigarette and knelt on the toilet seat, my head out the window. I hoped Dad wouldn't drive into the driveway. Me, with my head hanging out the second story window.

"What are you doing in there?"

"I fell skating and I'm cleaning up."

"I still smell smoke." Mumble, mumble...footsteps down the stairs. I did fall skating last Thursday and I was cleaning up now, but not from last Thursday's fall. I had a wrestling match with Jake at school today and he had won. I used to be a furious fighter and the boys regarded me with respect because I wasn't afraid of them. I was small, but I could win...terrible intensity. He had pinned me down and I kept trying not to get mad. No matter how hard I struggled, I couldn't move, and I couldn't lose my temper because I had promised myself I never would again. So I cried because I knew he was stronger and it would always be this way. Jake and I had tussled for ages, but my crying was new.

He was alarmed. "Did I hurt you?"

"No."

"I didn't hurt her," he told the onlookers. But I ran home and took refuge in the bathroom with the cigarettes.

Things were happening too fast and I needed time to adjust. In sixth grade, I was the class leader and collected nickels for Hershey bars and Cokes for the Friday afternoon parties Lister gave us for doing good work. Some boys tried to wiggle out of their fair share but I'd take them on, eye to eye. Even when they hid in the cloakroom, I'd find them and collect all the money. They knew they couldn't escape.

I was their equal.

But the boys didn't like being pushed around. One day last year in late February, on my way home from school, seven of them lay in wait for me with blackboard erasers full of chalk dust. They cornered kids and dusted their coats white for the fun of it, and it was the devil to brush off.

They were the same kids that dipped Johnie Donovan's head in vinegar last week and he had to come to school smelling like a salad and I thought they were a bunch of bullies because there were seven of them and they were big and Johnie Donovan was small, like me.

"Well, what do you want?" No answer. They waved their erasers and danced around. I wouldn't fight. I just stood there and glared at them, folding my arms across my chest. After a few claps at my coat, the spirit of it was gone.

"Aw, leave her alone."

"Yeah, she's no fun." They lost interest and backed away. I wouldn't amuse them by getting scared or fighting, and I think some of them felt sorry for me, too.

"C'mon, let's go." I stood perfectly still, my blue pea coat, chalky, and I, shaky, but I stood there until they left. I was so angry, I started to cry. I always cried when I got mad, and got madder because I cried. The next day, I glared and sniffed at them and they didn't know which way to look. If I had told Jimmy, he would have beaten them up, but I felt I could fend for myself. But now, it was different.

Anna Maria Delisa came to school the first day of seventh grade wearing a sheer blouse and white bra and Jake sat and looked and smacked his lips. We didn't wear uniforms until the third week of September, opaque cotton blouses and brown jumpers, the color of the Carmelite habit of St. Teresa of Avila, all lip-smacking areas discreetly covered.

"Gosh, Jake, what's wrong with you? You're drooling."

"She looks so pretty…"

"She looks the same as she did last year," I snapped. Anna Maria had the personality of a cereal box, a smiling poster, last year's exams.

"She's sitting there in her see-through blouse and, and she's bursting all over the place and..."

"Well," I clowned, posing with hands on hips, and imaginary chest thrust forward, "where does this leave me? Muscle-less Mary?" Jake looked so embarrassed, we both laughed, but I was dying inside. Oh! Jake! So that's what we've come to? A padded bra? What about me, Jake?

Oh! Jake.

I sighed and shoved the cigarette down the toilet.

I was feeling a loss that I knew I was right about and I didn't need anybody, especially my mother, to nag me for smoking in the bathroom. I knew I was on to a big change that would affect me for the rest of my life. From now on, all my dealings with boys were going to be different. I had thought we would frolic and wrestle like cubs forever but today was the end of it. From now on, I'd have to look pretty and sit and listen to the boys talk about themselves, like the girl's magazine said, and smile and ask the right questions. They'd hold open doors for me, but it was all a game and I hated it because I was losing them and it would never, never be the same.

And it never was.

CHAPTER FIVE

The boy-girl parties began. We'd play 'Lights Out' and 'Spin the Bottle' in remodeled cellars and parents would pop in and out with food and Cokes or pretend to fold laundry next door. I didn't enjoy necking but I wasn't about to be left out. The excitement! Eluding discovery! The nuns decided to monitor our social activities and scheduled dances for Saturday afternoons. Loaded with soda, cookies, and our favorite 78's, we gathered in the school hall. The parents taught us to waltz and we taught the young sisters to jitterbug.

I had a terrific crush on Sister Carolus and spent hours in front of the mirror, trying to raise my right eyebrow, one of her many attributes. Imagine controlling a class with a right eyebrow. What a move! I watched her and Lister chatting in the halls as we marched out to the tunes of John Philip Sousa. On Halloween, I went out begging dressed as a nun.

What was it about the nuns? They laughed and talked together like real friends, seemed happy to teach us, but at Mass, looked like statues with heavenly smiles. They fascinated me, and I stuck my nose into their lives. During recess, I'd bring Sister Agnes, who now taught fifth grade, a cup of hot tea. A wisp of a thing, no bigger than I, she had sunken cheeks and wore wire rimmed glasses a half an inch thick. When her little voice rasped, "God bless you, dearie," I felt like a saint.

Helen and I cleaned the black boards, ran errands and hung around while we strained to overhear what the nuns said and did. We discovered they were held together by hooks and pins and that in minutes, they could be ready to wash walls and floors and in minutes, ready for the classroom or church.

A Sister of Mercy dressed in a long black pleated habit, with a yoke and fitted sleeves. She wore a leather cincture, or belt, around her waist that looped through an ebony ring and fell to the hem. A large rosary hung from the ring with an ebony cross on the end that wasn't a crucifix. Sister slipped her crucifix around her neck before she put on the top part, tucking it safely into her cincture. Every sister wore an elaborate headdress of four different pieces. A long sheer veil, pleated in the back, was pinned to a short one, the domino, that in turn was pinned to a white linen starched coif, fitted snugly around her head and face.

The fourth piece, a starched coif front lined with blotters, was also pinned to the top of the coif. The sheer veil rested neatly over the coif front, because of a veil board, skillfully shaped and eased through the wide hem of the veil. I learned later, that at night, the sister slipped out of the entire headgear and hung it on the pole end of her door mop to keep it from wrinkling.

In the old days, the sisters wore a starched linen wimple or guimpe tied with strings around their necks under the coif. It covered their chests but left enough room to reveal the crucifix fastened in the cincture. Later on, the guimpes were made of plastic, a godsend because they could be removed in seconds and scrubbed with a brush and cleanser in case of a spill.

But the first time I saw Sister Lister shed her nonessentials to clean the classroom, I was stunned. Two days before school opened, Helen and I were delivering textbooks when Lister asked us to give her a hand with a ladder. Off came the big sleeves, unhooked from large buttons sewn on the shoulders of the habit. Off came the guimpe, revealing a neat row of assorted safety and straight black-headed pins, woven into the upper right yoke. Off came the outer veil, unfastened by two black headed pins that were then stored on the yoke with the others. Off came the cincture and beads and up went the habit, which she pinned in back with one of her huge safety pins, revealing a heavy black sateen petticoat.

It was a balmy September afternoon, and Helen commented, "You must get hot in there."

"Today is a paloozer," Lister said, "and so humid," and she struggled up the ladder with a pail and sponge, eyeing grimy windows. We continued off to another classroom.

"Gee, Helen, she's like a real person."

"You knew that."

"I suppose."

But a nun in her habit was awesome. She could stand at the head of the stairs, and settle down the wild boys from School 19 who stomped up to the second floor for religious instructions. She silenced a class with a flick of an eyebrow. Older people addressed her in high tone English, as if she were God or something, and stood back and treated her better than the priest. Her feet never moved; she glided up and down the aisles and streets on some invisible belt built into the ground just for her, while all the rest of us bustled about, heading hard into the wind.

Now here was Lister taking off her habit and washing windows. Nuns were two things at once. Mysterious.

What was it about the nuns?

"Do you ever think about being a nun?" I asked Helen as we plowed through the boxes of books in the dark corridor, sorting out which ones went where.

"Yes."

"What about it?"

"I've got to."

"What do you mean?"

"I mean I'm stuck with it. I have no choice. I ask myself all the time, 'Why me?' But there it is."

"I don't get it," I said.

"No, I suppose not."

"Don't talk to me like that. I'm not stupid."

"I *know* you're not stupid, but if I can't explain it to myself, how do you expect me to explain it to you?"

"Are you really going to be a nun? I mean, I know you like Lister, but, gee, Helen, that's taking it too far."

"She has nothing to do with it."

"Well, then, tell me, what does?"

"I've got to do it."

"Why?"

"I've got to."

"It's God, isn't it?"

"It's God."

I sighed. "Sometimes, I feel the same way, but I'm not, you know, suited. And I love to talk. They have to keep quiet in the convent and pray all the time. I don't go to Mass every morning during Lent and Advent, and receive Communion the way you do. And I don't like rules and I'm not holy, like you. You like to pray. I'm not holy at all."

"It's something different. You know you've got to do it. Oh, GOD!"

"Exactly," Helen said, and we began hauling books and didn't discuss it again for five years.

* * * * *

Eighth grade was different. When I turned twelve, sweet little me disappeared. The fifty-one in our class were four handfuls, and too much for one teacher. On the first day of school, the principal lined us up in the hall according to gender and height. The last thirteen in each line, the tall ones, went to Sister Grace, a willowy nun with a droll sense of humor and quiet voice who played the violin with hands and fingers a foot long. The rest of us filed into the room next door with Sister Rosanne, physically opposite in every way except for the voice.

"I can't believe it! I want to be in Grace's class with you and Helen and Jake," I complained to Jimmy. "How can they do this to me? Who's in charge? Who do I see?"

"Come on, Mary. They'll never change your class," and Jimmy laughed. "But you'll think of something. You always do." I griped. I fumed. I plotted. Sister Rosanne was the placid, kindly type, a pushover. If I were uncontrollable, the principal might send me to Grace who was known for control.

I turned brat overnight.

Our room was equipped for forty and I hid my books in the empty desks in the back, pretended I'd lost them and practiced 'sullen'. Being good hearted, Sister Rosanne let me sit with one of my girl friends, and each time she called on her to read, I'd slap my hand over the text. My friend would have a coughing fit; we'd fight over the pages and stifle laughs and then, trouble. I was relegated to the back seat. No more sharing a desk.

I decided Sister Rosanne was hard to beat down so I became more defiant. When the pastor came in to hand out report cards, he observed my isolation and asked, "Sister, what do we have here? One of the Solomon Islands?" I received my first F in deportment and neither Father nor I were amused. That afternoon, I chose my moment and threw a pile of books on the floor. Bull's eye! Rosanne's face turned as red as her hair. She was furious.

"Young lady, how dare you? You've been trying to disrupt this class since September. You want attention? Then come right up here where everyone can see you! Kneel before that crucifix and extend your arms and ask God to forgive your miserable ways." I wasn't embarrassed and I wasn't ready to die. It was a fair fight. Sauntering up to the front of the class, I ignored the embarrassed looks on the other girls' faces. I knelt, extended my arms in front of the crucifix and remained a bold piece. Get ready, Sister Grace, here I come.

But Rosanne did something I hadn't counted on, something she should have done the first time I stepped out of line.

She called my father.

* * * * *

Dinner was over and the dishes cleared away from the dining room table. When the phone rang, Katie, who was folding up the linen tablecloth, answered it.

"Dad, it's for you. It's Sister Rosanne."

Oh, God! I thought, what am I going to do? Very slowly, I headed for the stairs that were exactly opposite the phone. I heard a string of, "Yes, Sister, yes…is that right? Yes, Sister, certainly, Sister. I understand. And thank you for calling." My father was staring at me, freezing me in my tracks, pointing to a spot at the foot of the stairs where he expected me to glue my feet.

I was a dead man, a dead man.

"Young lady, I want to talk to you."

I was dead, dead. Katie had fled, sensing eminent danger. I was frozen, staring at him.

A dead man.

"I don't know or care what has caused this behavior. You are to have every book in your desk tomorrow. You're to address this nun by, 'Yes, Sister,' and, 'No, Sister'." Dad might not have liked Catholic schools but the nuns who taught us were a different matter entirely. "Whatever she asks you to do, you are to do. I never want to be notified again about your behavior by any teacher. Ever! This nun owes you nothing. You owe her everything. No daughter of mine will ever disobey a nun. Do you understand?"

"Yes."

He had not taken his eyes off me from the time he answered the phone. "I will sign your report card, now."

Hooray! I was going to live! God love you, Rosanne. She didn't tell him about kneeling in front of the room. He would have killed me for sure. It was funny the way the three of us girls behaved with my father. He never touched us, never raised his voice, rarely corrected us. But his word was law. We adored him and were terrified of a wrath we never saw, which I later learned never existed.

CHAPTER SIX

After my eighth grade fiasco with Sister Roseanne, I took stock. I wasn't like any other girl in my class. Embarrassment would have deterred them from taking that stand. Why didn't I care? Where was I coming from? When I wanted to, I could fit in, but my heart wasn't in it. I was twelve years old. Why should I act thirty? Did I resent growing up or did I hate some rules because I thought I could make better ones?

Even my interests were different from my friends. I took the war seriously. Two of my cousins were Marines, island hopping in the Pacific and Dad would talk in hushed tones to their mothers long distance and nobody talked long distance unless things were bad. Pictures of atrocities, Russian women the Germans hung from trees for no reason, began to appear regularly in the newspaper and *Life* magazine; Mom couldn't protect us from them anymore…they were everywhere.

What could *I* do? I had outgrown saving tin foil and collecting old tires and hauling them to the gas station in wagons. I wanted to *do* something. Before Thanksgiving, a woman in a sort-of nurse's uniform came to our eighth grade and told us about wounded men in the war. Wouldn't anyone want to roll bandages for those poor boys? I'd have to give up roller skating with the gang at the Four Corners in Delmar but why not? It sounded perfect for me so on Saturday morning, I rode my bike to St. Peter's Hospital and met Sister Clarissa.

"You're the youngest volunteer we've ever had," she said, smiling down at me, measuring me with her eyes.

"I thought I'd do something for the war effort," I mumbled. "I'm too young to join the WACS." But she wasn't listening anymore. A group of old, dirty men in rumpled clothes, slouched at tables in the back corner of the room, absorbed her attention. Hustling me next door, she introduced me to ladies who cooed and told her how cute I was. Oh, nuts! I thought, how did I let myself get talked into this? I cursed Helen for having to baby-sit with her brother Saturday mornings. Shrinking down in my seat, I smiled meekly and rolled bandages.

I didn't like some of the ladies. They made fun of Sister Clarissa, starting with her name. I admit it didn't fit but it wasn't her fault and my mother always said nobody could help the way she looked, that she could keep clean, and stand up straight, but looks came from God. Clarissa was a hulk of a woman with bushy eyebrows. She wore corrective shoes and had little physical grace to redeem her, nothing except her eyes, which were crinkled and navy blue and looked straight through me and everything else. I could have kicked myself for laughing at what some of the ladies said, but they were funny.

The one with long red fingernails and a jet-black pompadour noticed me, and jerked her head in my direction, so they sent me off with a tray of cups for coffee. As I neared the elevator, an old man I'd seen before came out of the men's room, and just stood there, eyeing me. I would have had to knock him over to get by.

I didn't like this.

We were working on the basement floor. Even though there was light from the thin windows near the ceiling, it was still dim and deserted. The hospital was scary enough, huge with winding corridors and green doors that said DO NOT ENTER leading who knows where. Now this smelly old man was standing there, looking me over. I did the only thing I knew how. I glared back, and figured I'd throw the tray at him if he tried to rob me.

He was lank and bent and mussed and shabby. His hair was straggly, and the bald place above his forehead, freckled. His nails were dirty. Yuck, I thought, yuck, yuck, yuck! He wiped his nose on his sleeve and tugged at his trousers and sniffed and said, "So, you're working with all the biddies, eh?" What was I going to do? He was talking to me.

"Yes."

"And what do they say about Clarissa?"

I kept staring at him defending 'us'. I felt faithful, because I was now one of the ladies and who was he? I must have looked a little scared, because he softened.

"Oh! I 'eard 'em." He sniffed again. "I tidy up in there and I 'ear 'em. Some of 'em talk about her like she was dirt." He faked this high falsetto. "And 'er shoes, my dear, 'er shoes. And all those dirty old men.'

"Well, let me tell you this, young lady, let me tell you this." He leaned his face down and breathed stale beer at me. "She's got a heart as big as she is, so don't let me catch you saying nothin' ag'inst her," and he turned and ambled away to the room he was in before. I stood still until the door closed behind him and I was safe and then I asked aloud, "How are you going to know what I say, anyway?"

Now I was curious. The following Monday, I cornered Jimmy O'Neill on the playground. The hospital was shorthanded and he worked in the laundry on Saturdays and knew what was going on.

"Quit walking that yo-yo and listen to me. What about these old men with Clarissa?"

"How do you know about them?" I told him about last Saturday.

"That was probably Smitty. He thinks Clarissa's a saint. He goes on and on, but never to her face." Jimmy smiled. "She puts all the old guys to work in the laundry."

"Do you work with them? In the laundry, I mean?" "Yeah."

"But they look awful."

"Naw, those were the new ones. She cleans them up. Everybody except Smitty. He's a stubborn old coot. She's got these clothes she gives them and she takes their old clothes and washes them or throws them out. She keeps her eyes on them, makes sure they're clean, and they're afraid of her, afraid to step out of line, afraid they won't have a bed that night."

"You mean, they sleep there?"

"Yeah, she's fixed up a place in the attic. Nobody talks about it but it's there, okay. She got some of her boys to fix the broken hospital beds. I saw it myself. Smitty sneaked me up."

"Where do they come from?"

"The streets, the trains. Most of them are drunks, Mary. They're drunks, trying to get off the sauce, with nowhere to go and she needs them. The men are gone and there's no one left to work in the laundry. The women are working at the Arsenal or in factories. The sisters do what they can on their days off, but they still need help." I stood there, staring at him. How could he know so much when I knew so little and we were both in the same grade?

"How come you know so much?"

"I'm older than you, and I get around." It was true. He was fourteen and drove his father's trucks in the auto yard.

"Well, what does the place look like?"

"It's this long, low room. It's an attic filled with beds. Like, lined up on either side and backed up against the wall, with a space in the middle. And there's a hook on the wall behind each bed for clothes and things.

"And Smitty told me," he started to laugh, "wait'll you hear this...Smitty told me Clarissa has this big baseball bat. Every morning at seven o'clock, after she goes to Mass, she takes that damned thing and walks up and down that aisle and slams each one of those beds, and does that ever get them moving."

"She won't go in there unless Smitty's with her. She pays them Sunday morning so they can't buy liquor and makes them go to Mass Saturday and Sunday, makes them get up early so they won't tie one on the night before. She's a corker." I could tell Jimmy liked her.

"What else?"

"Oh, yeah, she's got a kid."

"C'mon, Jimmy, she can't have a kid. She's a nun!"

"I'm telling you, she's got a kid. She takes care of this kid, and he's a little soft, talks all the time. He's not all there, but in some ways, he's smart as hell." He stopped playing with the yoyo and looked at me.

"You'll see him. He's dressed nice. She buys his clothes and he knows his way around the hospital better than anybody. She sends him on messages. The doctors and nurses use him. They know everything, Smitty and him, everything about the place, like what's going on all the time."

"What's his name?"

"Bobby."

"Where does he live?"

"Upstairs on the seventh floor. He does model airplanes on this big table. He can't read much so he reads the pictures. The models are perfect."

"He's got his own room in the attic?"

"Um hum, she fixed it up for him. Not near the old guys, though. No one goes near him but Smitty. He keeps his eye on him. He's always around, he's a regular."

"How come she can't clean up Smitty?"

"Smitty's stubborn. He won't leave and she won't kick him out. She's not finished with him yet, and he's not finished here either." Jimmy started to grin. "You should hear them in the laundry. She lays him out if he's late and he sulks around and sasses her under his breath. He says what he wants but God help anybody else who does. He keeps his eye on Bobby, too." He trailed off, thinking, "and believe it or not, Clarissa's started to take Smitty with her when she goes out, when the nursing nuns can't go with her. He's like, he's like their bodyguard, hers and Bobby's."

A nun with a bodyguard and a kid in the attic!

"Hey, Jimmy, I'm going back next Saturday. Those ladies know everything and they talk. I'll find out where Bobby came from."

"You and Clarissa will get along just fine, the two of you, always taking in the strays. But, watch your step. Bobby's Clarissa's kid and she carries a bat," and he snapped his yo-yo back into his hand, tightening the string.

That next Saturday, I rolled bandages again. I introduced myself to the new group and held their chairs for them and never said anything for about an hour. Pompadour, the only one there from last week, was strangely silent. The new ladies really admired Clarissa and during a lull, I mentioned that my friend from school worked in the laundry on Saturdays and sometimes ran the elevator and that he knew Bobby. Then I kept still and listened.

It turned out Bobby wasn't a kid at all, just looked like one. He was old, nineteen, and had lived in the hospital for three years. Pompadour, with the red nails, was delighted I had mentioned him and rattled on and on, details and details.

"He was from St. John's Home. His parents didn't want him, and no one wanted to adopt him because, well, he's not all there, you know, and so Sister Rosari kept him at the Home until he was sixteen. People like that should be in an institution!"

"...but the nuns didn't think so and they were determined to place him," continued a nice lady with blue hair who I could tell was Sister's friend. "Sister Clarissa found out, took him in and gave him a job, so now he's here." And she smiled at me.

"Well, he should have ended up in some institution!" added Pompadour as if she were put out. As if we all would have been better off if Bobby were in an institution. Why did Clarissa put up with Pompadour? And yet, she was nicer to her than anybody. I couldn't figure it out.

Next Monday, I cornered Jimmy at school, and stuck out my chin. "He's nobody. His parents didn't want him. He's not her real kid."

"I never said he was."

"Oh, you're so smart!" I huffed and stalked off.

I stayed on for months at the hospital; because I was the youngest volunteer, my picture with Clarissa was on their Christmas card. We found out they bribed her to pose, promising to give her beds for her old men. Bobby and I became friends, not the kind you take home, but friends of a place, work friends. The doctors and nurses and young students got used to us: running all over the hospital, eating in the cafeteria, being big business, owning the place, carrying our trays and ducking in line in front of them.

Smitty kept his eye on us, though, because nobody went near Bobby without passing by Smitty.

* * * * *

I still wanted to see the men's attic in the worst way and one afternoon when Clarissa and Smitty were out, Bobby invited Jimmy and me to his room to peek in. It was so exciting.

"I've seen it all before," Jimmy said. "But watch out for Clarissa and her bat." Bobby and I sneaked up the seven floors, climbed the stairs, giggling and laughing. We hugged the walls with our backs and the palms of our hands, like spies. And then, the big moment. Bobby put his finger over his lips and we crept down the hall, pushed open the door at the other end, and tiptoed around the men's dormitory. It was just as Jimmy said and I was disappointed. Bobby could sense it, so, he began running around and laughing and banging on the beds and then we were both carrying on and, Oh, God, there she was, standing there, in the doorway, staring at the two of us.

Clarissa.

Bobby wasn't upset. "M-Mary came up to see my mmmodels," he said. "It's okay. No one's in here. I'm Ss-sorry if we're m-making noise." But she kept looking at me and into me and right through me. If she yelled at Bobby, I'd die. He'd pick up bad feelings, a look, a pause. She knew that. My eyes pleaded with her. Leave him alone.

She did. She sent us downstairs, and told me later never to go up there again. The old men deserved their privacy. Then she smiled at me like a friend, like someone she knew, that warm, heavenly smile. "I appreciate that you spend your time with Bobby. He doesn't have many friends. But you have to understand that his judgment is young, that when you're with him, he would do anything to please you, to keep you." Her face became more serious. "Why Bobby, Mary? Why don't you spend your time with Jimmy?"

Lord! She expects me to say something grown up! "Bobby doesn't have anybody to talk to and people shove him away, and treat him as if he were nobody and he really likes people and he likes to talk and…I see Jimmy all the time at school." I ran out of ideas.

"Yes, I understand. You're an unusual little girl," and she immediately retreated into that pleasant detachment where she appeared to live her entire life.

Little girl, little girl! Why does everyone think I'm a little girl? Phooey, I thought. I just look like one. But I must admit, sometimes it paid off.

Bobby and I floated around the hospital like invisible ears. The staff chatted away, simply ignoring us and he knew just about everything that went on and I found out my share.

eu'lo·gy

Sister Esther, the head nun at St. Peter's, was a bigwig with vision and knew important people and had her way, even against the bishop. She was responsible for moving the hospital uptown to a piece of land that had been donated to the community. Since it wasn't the bishop's idea, he shook his fist at her and told her she would never do it and that he would never set foot in the place if she did. (But he knew she would no matter what he said.)

Her friends and admirers, the Glavins and Farrells, had money that the diocese needed and "he might enjoy bullying Esther but wouldn't dare harass benefactors." (Dr. Cowan said that.) The staff knew Esther and Clarissa were great pals and that Clarissa's niche depended upon Esther who conveniently ignored her odd arrangements and old men in the attic. Esther did what she pleased.

She hired Philippino doctors which was unheard of in those days and everyone complained. Did she care? No. "They're trained, competent and they're here." Who dared argue?

These nuns worked undercover as much as Bobby and I.

I loved what the hospital taught me, and St. Teresa's, and the intriguing sisters I'd met in both places. In my heart, I knew I'd be one of them someday. It was a decision that had crept up on me. Not one incident, not a moment I could pinpoint. I woke up one morning and couldn't see myself doing anything else.

Imagine, knowing at twelve years old, what you want to do with your life.

CHAPTER SEVEN

In the spring of my sophomore year, I had decided to approach my father who was standing in the living room, jingling his change and staring out the window at the barren fields and trees across the street. My stomach and throat tightened, but I stood straight and tried to look calm. I knew how he felt about the Church, and this bomb had no lead-in.

"Dad?"

"Ummm?"

"I want to be a nun."

He turned and said, without any emotion at all, "I don't think so. No daughter of mine is going to be a nun." I didn't move. Was the conversation over? "No, Mary, it's a phase. Time will change your mind," and he dismissed me and my life's plans with a flick, by turning towards the window, continuing to jingle his change.

That's it, I thought? Just like that? I had been thinking about my vocation since the day Helen and I had seen Lister climbing that ladder, probably since First Communion. Ordinary life and riding new waves did not satisfy me. A strong yearning for God and dedication to His work lingered and its consistency impressed me. God had given me so much and I wanted to give back.

However, my father had an accurate insight into my character and besides, I was not going to throw my life away. I had never been a fool or a rebel for the sake of being a fool or rebel, and I did not intend to play those roles now. I decided to reexamine my motives, convincing Katie that helping ourselves to the nun pamphlets in the back of the church was not stealing. Mom was answering phones at the Red Cross and Pat was rehearsing for the spring concert so we had the house to ourselves. We plopped down and spread the pamphlets over our bed. *A Woman Becomes a Nun.* Woman. Hmmmm. Serious.

"Are you disappointed in love? They say that's an archaic rumor and no reason to enter a convent." The two of us collapsed, giggling. I dropped the pamphlet on the bed.

"How can I be disappointed in love at fifteen? I've never been in love." I lay on my back, hands folded under my head. I didn't consider myself weird. I wasn't ready for whatever the boys were after and I was protecting my virtue. It was also a matter of honesty. Having just anyone's arms around me disgusted me. Kissing games in seventh grade had been one thing.

This was different. I listened to the nuns in school. One of them was pretty graphic about petting and the occasions of sin and how boys are weak and how we're *not* supposed to indulge them. But I was sure I *could* fall in love. My whole body tingled with heat when I read about Rhett carrying Scarlett upstairs. Wow! Someday, I knew I could meet somebody and, lah di dah! There *he* would be. But now, I'd never find out.

I was going with God.

"I don't know what I'm going to do about Jimmy," I confided. "He thinks he's going to marry me."

"Oh, come on!"

"I mean it. He's protective like he owns me, when we go to the movies, or a dance, but Jimmy wants something from me I can't give him."

"He doesn't want to marry you. You're both too young!"

"But he does! He's planning to work after high school. He's saving for a house and bought his own car. His father didn't give him a penny." Lately, Jimmy's future plans included me.

"Mom says his father's mean. He won't send him to college, and they have all that money." I ignored her.

"I can't lead him on. I'll break up with him this summer, and that's final."

I toyed with the pamphlets, flipping the pages of the ones nearest me that littered the white chenille spread and spotted a picture of a Sister of Charity, all in white, smiling lovingly at a baby she held.

"You know, not having children will be the killer. A nun doesn't physically have her own children. She has everyone's. I'll have to accept it. I can't have it both ways." I couldn't explain this strong calling. God was real to me, always around, ever since First Communion, when I sat with my white and gold Book of Prayers, and

47

the bitty rosary that came with the First Communion paraphernalia. When we sang *Little White Guest*, as young as I was, I understood that He had come to claim me.

"If He wants me, it's okay."

* * * * *

But it wasn't okay with my family.
"Those nuns are influencing her."
"One more of her crazy notions."
"She'll get over it."
I didn't, though, and Dad became concerned. HIS daughter, a servant?
Never!
Provide cheap labor for the Church?
Never!
He respected the nuns, yes, but not me as one of them. In a weak moment, he murmured, "Too bad you can't become a priest." They played golf, drank wine at the country clubs, said Mass, toured Europe and became pastors with housekeepers. He wanted me comfortable, not relegated to housekeeper status. Besides, my father saw a mistake, a square peg seeking the round hole and knew I was determined enough to try to make them fit.
Mom asked would I be happy.
That came when you did something right. God was calling me! I *had* to enter the convent. I knew I wasn't doing what my parents wanted, but could God be wrong?

* * * * *

One Thursday evening in the May of my senior year, Dad summoned me downstairs. I sat next to Mom on the couch, twisting a loose thread on the sofa cushion while Dad paced the floor, occasionally jingling his change and pausing to think of the precise word. Finality loomed tonight.

"Your mother and I have decided that we will not stand in your way if you want to join the convent. We only ask you to finish college first."

"But I'm still in high school!" Four years! Wait four years! I was thwarted, bursting, my blood, racing!

"If you want to lead this life, get your degree. Be a principal or a college professor. Don't end up washing windows and scrubbing floors. Wouldn't you be of more use to the order if you were educated?" Those were worldly ideas. Washing windows and scrubbing floors for God would be fine. I squirmed on the couch, barely contained, my verbal sword drawn.

"Don't interrupt me now, Mary. You'll have your turn." He looked at my mother, who was ashen and stroking my hand. "How do you expect to teach girls if you don't have any discernment, any experience?"

"I have to go. I have a *vocation*!" I gulped. "I have five years to make up my mind. I can come home any time. It isn't as if I want to run away with the circus..."

"Mary, why make a mistake? You're uncertain, too young." He pulled himself up to his full height. "We'd never let you get married now so how can you expect us to let you do this?"

"I'd never *think* of getting married now!" I gulped between sobs. "Marriage is between two people, it's a sacrament. Being a nun is different. It's between you and God. It's not the same."

Mom called a halt. "Mary, there is nothing in your nature compatible to convent life. You're enthusiastic and full of ideas. The regimentation will crush you. Why would God call you to a life so foreign to your nature?"

"Don't you think I've thought about that? How can I explain the ways of God? I don't expect my spirit to drop dead. It's supposed to come alive in the convent," I insisted. "Besides," I added, complacently, "God will give me the grace."

They both sighed. It was no use. My father believed in action. He spoke to the Reverend Mother; he spoke to the parish priest; he spoke to his friends in high places. Then, he spoke to me. If I were to leave his house before the age of eighteen, he would have to issue a warrant for my arrest and have me removed physically from the entrance ceremony. Despite all considerations, he could not agree with my choice and he was my legal guardian until I was eighteen.

That was it.

* * * * *

"He'll do it," Pat said. "He doesn't bluff. I know him." It was early September and my two sisters and I were in Pat's bedroom. She sat at her desk, Katie sat on her bed, and I slumped against the wall. "They won't let you go," Pat said, tapping her pencil and staring at me. "What are you going to do?"

"Get a job at the Telephone Company. I'm interviewing next week."

"You won't get a job, either. Dad will see to that."

"At the Telephone Company? How can he stop me?"

"Dipper Mahoney's father is the president. He and Dad play golf." She kept staring at me, and tapping her pencil. "What have you got against going to college? You'll have to go anyway. Are you afraid if you start, you'll like it too much and won't be a nun?" It cut me short. Was she right? Did I really know what I was doing? Another fad? Was I giving myself a chance?

And if I were right about my vocation, why was I the only one who thought so?

* * * * *

It didn't make sense to tangle with Dad anymore. The following Monday, I walked over to the College of St. Rose on Madison Avenue, enrolled as a freshman and threw myself into everything I could. I made friends: was elected to student council, wrote the freshman play, sat for hours with the other girls in the smoker while they knit argyle socks, or played bridge and talked about sex.

Sex in all its glory was new to me. I didn't read much because I never sat still that long, but I was glib and acted streetwise, so who knew how much I knew? Besides, the nuns had pounded into my head forever that sex was reserved for marriage and I concluded if I couldn't reach the end of the road, there was no reason to start walking down it. The summer after I graduated from high school, I threw a slumber party and Pat and a couple of her friends determined that none of us was going into any convent without knowing the facts of life. I pretended it was meant for everybody else, but as I sat there smugly, trying to mask my shock, I thought, "I'm seventeen years old. I've seen dogs do it on the street. I can't believe I'm so dense."

"Learn about life, Mary." Is this what Dad meant?

The Albany area abounded in colleges and universities and every football game, every bonfire, every mixer, every wild party, I was there, including the Saturday night Union College held its first frat bash. Two of my friends were sick in the bathroom, some bodies were flopped on the floor and a few were draped on the couches, or nestled somewhere else up to no good. By one a.m., the only two able to navigate were the piano player and myself, because we didn't drink.

A joker had stuck thumbtacks on the piano key felts and as he rinky-dinked a few numbers, we sang together. As I hung over the piano the two of us moved into a few Frank Sinatra hits. This was my first frat party and I had spent hours 'dolling up'. As he looked me over, I felt flattered. I could get used to this, I thought, but it all was about to end.

On January 3, I received a formal letter from the Sisters of Mercy. They would accept postulants on February 2nd, which was quite extraordinary because the nuns hadn't had a February class in over twenty years. It seemed like a personal call, like God was watching, could see me straying. I remembered thinking, "You don't fool around, do you?"

* * * * *

The next Sunday, I remained in church after the eleven o'clock Mass. What am I going to do?

It wasn't that I was devout. I wasn't. Daily Mass during Lent and Advent were Pat's choices, walking a mile in bitter cold, dry winds whipping fine snow across her face. She fasted so she could receive Communion in the de Paul Grotto, so no hot steaming coffee warmed her blood. I heard her rustling around her room before daylight and I snuggled deeper into my warm bed, feeling a little guilty but not guilty enough to join her. Pat took religion seriously. On Friday nights, her current boyfriend would cool his heels outside the Grotto until after she attended Benediction. It was different with me, but I couldn't grasp how, couldn't define it.

If I entered the convent, I would belong to God. He would design my life, give me specific tasks. He would move me around, use me to do His work, arrange things so I would meet people who needed me, even though I didn't understand why or how. I could not explain this calling to myself, this divine, mystical voice beckoning me to His service. I was under no illusions what it would cost me to have no family, but I'd never have this opportunity again. I knew myself. If I were going at all, I couldn't wait four years.

It was now or never, a clear choice.

Could I put my life into the hands of God and be off on a great adventure?

Yes.

"Here I am, God. I'm all yours."

* * * * *

My romp through my memories ended abruptly. The shadows in the parking lot were lengthening, the sun, waning. I scrunched around in Katie's car, trying to get comfortable in the bucket seat. My feet were cold. I blew my nose, checked my mascara and lipstick, and stretched out my legs. Time had slipped by…only twenty minutes to reach the Motherhouse and meet Helen. I turned on the ignition and slowly backed the car out, storing forever all my sweet, cloying memories.

Good-bye my youth, good-bye my old house and street and fields and games and backyards that were one big backyard. Good-bye you neighbors who ate summer suppers together on makeshift tables and chatted quietly under big leafy trees. When we caught fireflies in jars, you made us let them go.

Good-bye brown and tan uniforms, and First Fridays, and nuns in long habits, herding us into heaven.

Good-bye Mom and Dad, and all your friends who smoked fat cigars and kept us awake on Saturday nights arguing politics, and rocking our house with laughter. I hope you're all playing poker up there.

Good-bye young girl, cantering through the neighborhood, mane streaming behind, caught in a gentle wind, tossing a curious head and sniffing new experiences tugging, always tugging at the reins...anxious, always anxious, for the next run.

Good-bye.

Good-bye.

Good-bye.

CHAPTER EIGHT

On my way to the Motherhouse at last, heading towards upper New Scotland Avenue, drenched with memories…driving into Holy Row…St. Peter's Hospital, the Motherhouse, Maria College, the old Dominican monastery, now a dormitory, still cloistered by ivied walls. I felt nervous and blamed my unease on the sight of the old Motherhouse. Why? The whole thing was over, history! Washed, ironed, folded and neatly tucked into a drawer.

Rats, nearly ran a red light. I pulled to a jerky stop and kept mulling, tapping my fingers on the dash. By this time I was talking out loud. The light stayed red but my mind raced, twirling around the past, resurrecting buried decisions, airing them out, examining their cost. Oh God! Tightening my grip on the wheel, I heaved a deep sigh.

Death prods the mind.

There I sat, stone-faced, watching the pedestrians leaving St. Peter's Hospital, wrapped in scarves and breathing puffs of ice, headed for the neighborhood stores across the street. I tapped the wheel some more, momentarily stalled, unable to shake my mood. I felt as if some strong spirit were lurking inside the Motherhouse, ready to rattle my decisions and grab me by the bones. Straightening myself in the seat of my car, I stared belligerently through the bare branches of trees that screened the old building. "You've got your nerve, rustling around. You had me once and you didn't want me. So now what do you want?" And then I laughed. "This is ridiculous."

Tapping, tapping. Would this light ever change?

It did. Get hold of yourself, I thought, and viciously jerked out of the sedate traffic, jarring the sensibilities of some white haired woman one car over who had been regarding me with interest. "You're bound to have feelings. You're no robot, Lady Mary. You learned that long ago."

Cruising half a block, I took a left, drove slowly into the circular driveway and there she was…the rambling old brick matriarch, three stories high, sprawling across the front of her six acres. Mature maples and bare pricker-bushes dotted with frozen red berries screened the barely visible west wing that housed the refectory. Old shrubbery hugged the walls and the neatly clipped green, drizzled with snow, hid nine inches of gnarled trunks. Squashed against the building, the roots nibbled at the foundation. Huge oaks thrust out their bare determined branches, jostling for space with the third floor and attic.

A newer addition on the opposite corner, the forty-year-old chapel jutted out towards the street and hospital. Despite the fact that the builders used the same antique bricks, the chapel added the architectural allure of an oversized cracker box tacked onto a tastefully wrapped Christmas present.

God bless the Catholic Church. Did it ever have a plan?

In spite of herself, though, the Motherhouse had its charm; the blue slate roof, interrupted only by the huge bell tower, marched, piece by piece, across the entire structure like the unending army of nuns who lived and died within its sturdy walls. I marveled at its stability, its link to the past. The same, it's the same, maybe more cars parked in the driveway, but the same, after all these years! I found an empty parking space that wasn't reserved, locked the car through habit, then climbed the wide staircase.

Am I out of my mind? I shifted my weight to my other foot. Too late. Well, here goes, and I rang the bell.

The pleasant woman who answered the door informed me she wasn't a nun, only the receptionist. As we walked down the long corridor to the superior's visiting parlor, I looked at the linoleum. The pattern gasped for breath, buried under myriad layers of wax, some of those layers applied by me, on hands and knees, with other young novices, tee-heeing our way through drudgery, supposedly in silence.

I barely had time to settle myself on a comfortable couch when Helen glided into the room. Helen always glided, and here again, nothing had changed: the same figure, one size too big for the bones, and flawless olive skin, enhancing brown eyes and subtle smiles. A white streak flowed across her dark hair that fell into natural waves; her rose silk blouse complimented the gray suit that had a simple silver cross pinned to the lapel. She looked like everybody's mother, like the picture on a box of frozen pizza or homemade pie. We hugged and I stood back, grasping her by the upper arms as we exchanged knowing looks.

"You've gained weight since I last saw you," she began. "It becomes you."

"You're being kind, my dear."

"Well, at least you don't look scrawny. And I like your hair. It looks wild."

"It's supposed to. The new wind-blown look, that takes an hour to fix. So much for the casual nineties."

"I'm sorry about your mother."

"I know. I'll be fine as long as you don't say anything." She nodded as we sat down. Within minutes, we had settled all the funeral arrangements: the readers, the hymns, the piper and the eulogy.

"Are you sure you're up for the eulogy?" she asked.

"Yes. I have to do it."

"All right. We're done. Time to chat. Where shall we start? Your turn or my turn?" she sing-songed, just the way we did when we were twelve.

"Your turn. It's been a long time. Catch me up on the news." We were off: the people who had left, the people who stuck, the people the community was glad to be rid of, the people it was sorry to see go, the possibilities of the people who stayed, the effect of the exodus on them, the ones who had died…all the losses. Sister Boniface, my fourth grade teacher, was gone with cancer, refusing all 'extraordinary means', no operations, no chemo, no radiation.

"She had her wish, Helen. She always wanted to be a martyr, to suffer."

"She went fast, Mary, two, three months. Never told anyone. She was so far gone before they found out." We sat quietly a while; then Helen continued, her voice light and cheerful, trying to break the mood. "Sister Edmund works in the hospital office. Would you believe she's over eighty? Had a knee replacement but she's going strong. Living in an apartment on New Scotland, down near St. Teresa's with Lister and another nun you don't know. You remember Sister Edmund, our old high school principal?"

"Of course. I just passed St. Teresa's. It's still a grade school, isn't it?" She nodded. "Helen, remember?" Years melted and we rehashed the good old days, grade school, high school, our days as young nuns in the novitiate. "How did we live through the novitiate? All the demands? All the formality? All the severity of those first few years?" I asked.

"We were young, and we laughed…made the best of it."

"The superiors were either wringing their hands or laughing behind them. Sometimes we acted like a bunch of college kids."

"That's just what we were, a bunch of college kids. Think of the strain of trying to adjust to the life, of trying to make sense of it. We were only seventeen and treated like children. What could they expect? Remember the bird cage?" Helen smiled, looking innocent.

"Oh, no, the bird cage." I moaned.

"That was your bright idea," she added. I had discovered it on the fourth floor in the trunk room, an ornate wire hourglass as big as a breadbox, huge stand and all. I smuggled it down to the novices' floor and plunked it in one of their cells for fun. There was no place to hide a birdcage. Cells were small, identical, the furnishings, sparse: a single bed with a white chenille spread, a small press protected by a white linen scarf where a mirror should have been, a crucifix on the beige wall above the bed. Desperate novices slunk through the corridors during the great silence at night, trying to dispose of…the birdcage.

Worse, if a novice vacated her cell before morning prayers to finish a chore and returned to make her bed, she found…the birdcage. Anyone of us could have returned it to the trunk room but, the intrigue, the intrigue.

Of course I was caught and called on the carpet. I could remember standing there, a contrite postulant, trying to remain serious and explain to the stone-faced Mistress of Novices…the birdcage. We sat in silence for a moment. A thin, white shaft of light pierced the curtain and fell between us. Patterns danced on the Oriental rug, demanding to be included.

"Remember the time Edna and I were cleaning the dining room," Helen asked. I wondered how long it would be before Edna's name came up. "And she was supposed to be dusting, but she was standing at the lectern, giving the Gettysburg Address in cockney, and Reverend Mother came in?"

"All that pent-up energy, Helen. It had to go somewhere." I leaned way back on the couch. "It seems a lifetime ago."

"It was. I have more pressing problems now."

"Oh?"

"I'm sort of in a pickle," Helen mused. "The Motherhouse needs renovation and I'm not certain what to do. Eventually, we have to consider an east wing. If we go ahead, the new building will be an assisted living unit for seniors, lay people, and priests who could say Mass in our chapel. We may have to lease the wing in the future."

"That sounds perfect. St. Peter's would snap it up. Why the indecision?"

"Well, if we redo the Motherhouse, we face serious decisions and consequences. Simply sprucing it up won't work. It's impractical…wiring installed in the twenties, community lavs. The architects want to expand the cells into small suites and add private bathrooms. It would end up a great assisted living facility if we need to sell it in the future. So many sisters today are living in apartments."

"Wouldn't the building be more comfortable for the retired nuns living here now? What's the problem?"

"It's the end of the Motherhouse per se. The architects will use the first floor parlor and community room for suites. They'll change the refectory into a cafeteria. No room for community meetings, feast days. It will end an era. The Motherhouse and all that it signifies will be gone."

"Helen, twenty-five years ago, you knew the sisters' roles would change. It seems to me that renovating the old building would be to everyone's advantage. The location is perfect. Look at all the ministries available to the retired sisters here. Visiting the sick in St. Peter's, dealing with the young children in day care, pastoral work, all within walking distance of this building. You're practical and I'm sure the rest of the brass has pointed this out to you. What's really holding you up?"

"Nostalgia, maybe, on the part of the sisters. The Motherhouse is symbolic. It wouldn't be the same."

"No, it wouldn't. That's a grim thought. I can't think of a world without the Motherhouse either. But, it's all in the past, Helen."

A knock on the door, and the portress stuck her head in. "Sister Helen, telephone. Father wants to know about the funeral, Monday." She looked at me sympathetically. I stood up as Helen left, which she noted with a raised eyebrow and a slight smile.

I don't stand up for everybody.

* * * * *

Helen would be a while. Her secretary would snatch her and make her sign papers and answer calls. I peered out the door. No one in sight, so I crossed the corridor to the window, where I stared at the cloisters and grounds. When I was a novice I had planted a sprig of my mother's forsythia at the very end of that cloister. One visiting Sunday, when I was a postulant, she had objected to the abrupt end of the building, the bare space patiently awaiting the east wing. Rooting a large branch, Mom wrapped it in wet shredded newspaper and told me how to plant it.

I had argued politely with the gardener about his clipping it into a huge ball, explaining flow and natural form and the weeping willow effect and eventually, I won. It was over ten feet tall now, and the bare branches the sun pulled upward, fell gracefully from their own weight and trailed along the ground, the tips buried by the light snow.

In the distance, I could see the hospital that had expanded every way it could…up, back and flush with the synagogue's parking lot on New Scotland Avenue. The land behind it, strewn with ugly brick Diocesan boxes, housed computers and people in suits, administrators of God knows what. I stood there, anchoring my elbows on the high windowsill and recalled the stories the older nuns had told us about the grounds, because all the land as far as I could see once belonged to the Sisters of Mercy.

59

Years ago, after the sisters had moved up from downtown into the new hospital, a young nursing sister had wandered onto the adjacent property to say her rosary, and fell in love with the Queen Anne's lace and views and slopes and the lone deer she saw near the woods.

"What a beautiful place for our Motherhouse," she thought, and buried blessed medals there. Within the year, an unknown benefactress donated the land to the sisters and it surprised no one because that was the way things happened then. The nuns built their new Motherhouse among the Queen Anne's lace, the very Motherhouse I was standing in right now.

The tale was romantic but nursing nuns were romantic. Even though they were business-like practical people, licensed professionals, there was something idyllic about them. Maybe because they wore white...more likely because they played major parts in dramatic situations, like birth, sickness and death. I continued leaning my elbows on the windowsill, my chin in my hands and recalled the history we had learned as novices.

The Sisters of Mercy were nurses since the day they were founded in 1832 in Dublin, Ireland, by Catherine McAuley. Fondly called 'walking nuns', they were among the first to visit the sick and poor in their homes and move outside the cloister, one of the first orders of sisters to be 'let out'.

To this day, it infuriated me that throughout history, the Church was always so determined to stow nuns inside the cloister, no matter how great the need outside. It wasn't that women didn't know what they wanted or know what others needed; since Adam and Eve, they had been squelched. Mother McAuley had fought like a tiger against the confines of the cloister, but she ended up saddled with those restrictions plus the responsibilities of her apostolate, her mission outside the convent.

In March 1832, a cholera epidemic broke out in Dublin. The ignorant hid their sick and dying in their hovels, since rumors spread that the hospitals were death traps, and that the poor were poisoned or buried alive with the corpses to halt the plague.

But word moved around that the 'walking nuns' were in the hospital, so they brought in their ailing and dying. The nuns went from bed to bed on their knees, exhausted, saving lives and preparing souls to meet their God. They became so proficient in their work that the death rate at the Townsend Street Hospital was one of the lowest on record. Sister Mary Clare Moore later used the nuns' methods with Florence Nightingale during the Crimean War.

The Irish are great for their fancies and the nuns became saints on the spot. The nursing sisters themselves began to believe they had extraordinary obligations and powers to save not only bodies but souls. Legend grew. Protestants would rather die unattended from cholera than risk being nursed by a sister, for fear of deathbed conversion, brought about only by her presence.

No one can overestimate the value Irish Catholics placed upon their faith in those days: the fervor, the tenacity, as avid as the Christians in the catacombs. It became part of the spirit of the Mercy Order.

A thirst for souls.

In the 1930's, Sister Immaculata was stationed at the old hospital on Broadway in Albany. Times weren't good. She met the trains, and collected the tramps who hung around the station and the ones who had arrived hidden in box cars and whisked them away right under the officials' noses, bringing them back to the hospital. She washed their clothes and cleaned them up, and after their hot meal, made them go to confession. The chaplain, Father Jordan, was newly ordained and scrupulous. She'd corner him each time and ask, "Father, did he tell you everything?" He was scandalized.

"Really, Sister, I can't tell you The seal of confession!"

"But, Father," she'd say, "I know it's sacred but his soul, his immortal soul! If he didn't tell you everything, he won't go to heaven and he won't get his swig!" Poor Father Jordan. Caught in the middle. The sacred seal of confession! But how could he deprive those poor men of the good whiskey that sister provided to those who claimed to have told the priest all?

"God knows," he'd say, "they didn't have much else."

So it became a gigantic game: the tramps wanted their whiskey, the priest wanted their confidence, the nun wanted their souls. Father

Jordan got around it. "Sister, I'm sure they did." And he'd pause. "Tell me everything."

I laughed to myself, recalling the old sisters' tales. What does God think about us all, I wondered, as I stared out at the hospital? All our antics, our good deeds with bad reasoning or worse, our bad deeds with good reasoning? Is He up there holding His head, watching our daily show, and looking like an ad for aspirin?

And the people the nuns dealt with? What did they think? Maybe one or two of the tramps understood, that someone cared whether they lived or died...whether they went to heaven or hell. I shifted my position but continued gazing into space. Religious women are probably the most misunderstood group of people in the world. Their critics can not conceive of their motives so they misjudge them, ridicule them, and try to ignore the true meaning of their lives. I rarely told anyone I had been in the convent because I wanted to know what people really thought. Most people's opinions of nuns were unenlightened and ungrateful.

I didn't judge the sisters much differently now than I had when they first taught me at St. Teresa's. They were people; some appealed to me and others did not. But the sacrifice of their entire lives...family, husband, and the children they would never have, impressed me more now because I could judge from experience. Although I had left the ranks after twenty years, I had done so with great respect for the sisters' good will.

For hundreds of years, religious women have been the backbone of the Church: the lowly workers, the teachers, the nurses, the comforters, the humble, the exploited, the unappreciated, the true saints. The fact that I hadn't remained a nun, never lessened my admiration for their sacrifices. Where would the Church be now without them? Who would take care of business if they completely disappeared?

For centuries, religious orders had wandered in and out of history, increasing and decreasing, meeting the needs of the times. The Mercies weren't the same as they had been when I entered. The sisters had aged; so many had left; there were so few vocations. The thrust was different. Most of the trappings had changed radically and some said religious life was dying out altogether.

The past was gone, certainly, old customs cleaned out, but didn't the spirit remain, ready for a rebirth, a new creation? People were more needy now than ever. How will the young deal with their challenges?

I watched the sun busily painting the hospital windows, gold and rose and red and purple glitter from top to bottom, its final chore of the day, a glorious finish to an uneventful journey through clear blue skies. On a whim, it siphoned the paint from the windows and tossed it over the edge of the horizon, leaving the hospital a glowing teal blue.

The end of a day.

The end of many days.

The Motherhouse corridors were deserted and dusky, nothing moving but the twilight, quietly retreating into the glowing silence. I felt more at home than I thought I would, as old comforts enveloped me in strange, honeyed ways.

Taking a few steps into the hall, I stared down past the front entrance and all the parlor doors. There, framed by an elaborate archway, glowed the jeweled stained glass window of Our Lady of Mercy.

The sisters had been adamant about its being above the side altar instead of over the main one, so it would be visible when they entered the front door of the convent. They visited the chapel every time they entered the Motherhouse and insisted that the window welcome them.

I had time for a visit so I began walking towards the chapel. This is a dream. I'm in a dream. The entire building was submerged in silence. In my mind, I could hear the din of the Motherhouse in full swing, overrun by postulants and novices and visitors and piano students and violins squeaking behind doors...goings and comings and exciting ceremony day...now, deathly still. Helen told me Saturday evening was a free night. Most of the sisters went to visit friends or family or for a quick supper and an early movie. Since there were no formal prayers anymore, the ones at home picked up whatever they wanted in the kitchen, but I didn't think many were here.

I passed the statue of St. Anthony recessed in its niche, where years ago, old Sister James, in her ill-fitting linens, would stand with one hand on the statue's feet and say her rosary, murmuring away, as if to a lover.

I went in through the back door behind the sisters' choir, genuflected, and sat in the front pew. The chapel always astounded me: three stories high and no pillar...so different from the old makeshift attic that we used when I entered. Italian marble walls and terrazzo floors gleamed as usual. All the familiar saints peered down at me and I smiled back at them. How long has it been, I thought, since I had made the Stations of the Cross? Today the chapel was empty. I closed my eyes and remembered its being full of exhausted school sisters, of white-veiled novices and bright-eyed postulants, chanting the Office and tittering at the wrong times, amusing all the old sisters in the back pews.

The infirm nuns on the second floor had taken over the choir where the pipe organ used to be. The balcony overlooked the main altar of the chapel and as I settled in, I heard dishes clattering and distant voices floating from the nuns' infirmary...calm voices, some forced and patronizing, voices that talk to children and old people. Helen had said lay nurses tended the sick sisters now since there were so few left in the community to care for the old and infirm.

I stared at the altar and even at a distance, I recognized Clarissa's delicate tatting that edged the linens. I thought about the sisters who had influenced me to join their ranks, not by words, but by being alive under those habits, witnessing a life I couldn't resist.

I could see them now, like specters, moving in and out of their stalls, chanting the Office, or praying at odd hours. I thought about my entering the community as a young girl and leading the life with my friends. As I sat looking at the tabernacle, I was amazed I felt so peaceful.

CHAPTER NINE

I had entered the convent forty years ago and that day still remains an emotional hodge-podge with good reason. My father didn't come to the ceremony, just hugged me hard when he went to work that morning. He said absolutely nothing and I kept hugging him and wouldn't let go. I thought I'd never see him again. A neighbor drove Mom and me to the Motherhouse where we met Pat, Katie and nearly thirty of my college friends who had just heard about my entering. I vaguely remember entertaining everyone, clowning around in my postulant's outfit with its little black cape and white cuffs. Mom graciously held up as always but I knew she was grief-stricken. I don't remember saying good-bye to my sisters but I remember Katie crying through the whole thing.

The previous night, I had gone to dinner with Jimmy, who had never completely disappeared and wanted to take me out on my eighteenth birthday. Knowing I'd be in the convent by then, I moved up the date.

"Haven't you told Jimmy yet that you're entering the convent tomorrow?" my mother asked.

"He knows it's in the back of my mind. We're not engaged or anything. I haven't told anybody."

"Mary, be fair. He thinks a great deal of you."

"I know."

Jimmy and I went to Keeler's, then danced and drank wine at the Hotel Ten Eyck and I wore the flowers he sent me and kept putting off telling him until the very end of the evening. "Don't feel bad, Mary. I thought you were going. It's my loss but at least it's to a better Man."

When we do something we're supposed to do, how do we handle it and why is there so much pain? How could I do this to myself, to my family, to Jimmy and act lighthearted, nearly frivolous, as if nothing mattered?

But it's always been in Irish blood to dance through the black hours.

* * * * *

On my entrance day, the new chapel I was sitting in right now had been under construction. The old chapel in use at the time, an attic on the fourth floor of the Motherhouse, was jammed with friends and nuns I had never met. The girl entering with me cried all through the brief ceremony. "What's wrong?" I whispered out of the side of my mouth.

"Later," she mumbled back.

Her name was Edna but we couldn't talk much since we were the center of attention. I thought fast. I had taken piano lessons here for years and I knew the first floor lav. Visitors locked the door, especially during a ceremony day when everyone was nervous and wanted a smoke. The nuns expected it.

"I'll meet you in the visitor's lav at four," I whispered to her as family and friends swept us down corridors and into parlors. We broke away from the crowd, feigning necessity, and began our enduring friendship over a last drag on a Lucky Strike.

"I'm not sad, I'm mad. I don't know how I got myself into this fix," she moaned, sitting on the john seat.

"What do you mean?" Here I was, delighted and relieved to be in and she was already crying to get out.

"You just got here. Why do you want to go home?"

"I don't."

"What's wrong, then?"

She looked up at me, sparkling in front of her, my enthusiasm gushing out, threatening to drown her right here on the spot. She sighed.

"How can you be so cheerful?"

"I'm happy. Aren't you happy?"

"Not exactly. Look, we don't have time. We'll talk about it later."
So began our unique friendship, the kind that only death dares
interrupt.

The hubbub faded as the bells and Mistress of Novices shooed the
crowds away and the Motherhouse settled back to normal. Choked
good-byes completed, friends and family slowly floated of...the
friends, back to their same lives...the families, back to lives disrupted
forever.

Some novice came and led Edna and me upstairs to the chapel, to
our new stalls filled with pious books. The sisters were sitting
meditating when the first chimes of the 'Angelus' rang. I sneaked a
look behind me, spotting the tall novice standing solemnly with long
rope in hand, controlling the huge bell that informed the faithful for
miles around that it was six o'clock, the nuns were praying for their
souls, and it was time to eat dinner.

Bong, bong, bong. Pause. Bong, bong, bong. Pause.

I'm in Heaven, I thought. Heaven! I bowed my head and took a
stab at the Latin words I knew of the prayer. Suddenly, the bell began
a wild clanging, and the rope, worn and shredded, broke, sliding
noisily through the tower and landing with several unceremonious
thuds at the feet of the astounded novice.

Clang, clang, clang, clang, clang, diddy clang, diddy clang,
d i d d y c l a n g, c l a n g, c l a n g, c l a n g, d i d d y c l a n g,
c l a n g, c l a n g.

I guess everyone should have known right then.

Anyway, they talked about it for years.

* * * * *

Edna and I were inseparable. I had learned early to pick my own
friends. That way, no one would be disappointed. I rarely allowed
anyone to pick me, because people's first impression was flash and
dazzle, and flashes wane, leaving the ordinary to stand on its own.
Those looking for continuous flash didn't find it and went off, and
worse, blamed me for their disappointment.

But Edna and I picked each other, and she had a special feeling for me and I for her, the same feeling I had for Helen and Jimmy…that she knew me so well and understood what I was about and even if she didn't, she accepted me and my doings. Even better, she didn't want to rearrange what she knew.

Rub this off here, add this there. I found friendship most people would kill for.

Everyone loved Edna. She had no enemies and although magnetic, she was not especially pretty. Apparently shy, mild, and good-natured, people at first underestimated her emotional depth and intelligence. Those washed blue eyes set in a childlike heart-shaped face saw so much more than the rest of her implied. She had something, a viewpoint, an understanding of human nature that drew people to her.

I could never understand what drew her to me.

Edna was not shallow, so it wasn't my glitz but her friendship was the greatest compliment ever paid me. However, I was a total mystery to her. Why was I so happy? During the first weeks of my postulancy, I felt and acted like a puppy in new surroundings, taking stairs two at a time, skipping down the long corridors when no one was looking, swirling around and dancing in my new long skirts.

The sophistication of my brief college life blew away and I felt ten years old again, playing in the fields. A few days after we arrived, it snowed for two days and the Mistress of Novices sent the novitiate out in groups to shovel snow. I had always walked three miles a day back and forth to school, so I welcomed the exercise and as I shoveled away, all but whistling, I could feel the cold stares of the second year novices, who were not so thrilled.

"Do you really enjoy this?" Edna hissed out of the side of her mouth. One look at my face told her the answer.

She sighed.

The nuns loved the story about the 'Angelus' and the broken rope and following our dramatic entrance, most of the community smiled at us and dubbed us 'the twins'. Unusual, because religious orders forbade close friendships. 'Particular friendships' were to be avoided at all costs. But no one ever explained what 'particular friendships' meant, so I asked Edna.

Were we breaking the rules? We talked incessantly and were together constantly, sometimes in the tiny bathroom off the kitchen. We'd duck in and hash things over until Sister Karl caught us.

"Look, are we 'particular friends'?"

"How can you be friends and not be particular?" Edna answered. "It doesn't refer to us."

"Well, who are they talking about?"

"Not us. I've been looking around. Mother Patricia and Reverend Mother have been close friends for years, since they were novices together, but they're not 'particular friends'. It's all on the up and up."

"What do you mean, up and up?" How could the term, up and up, apply to those two? They were above approach.

She gave me a long, hard look.

"Don't you ever read any books?" Edna asked.

"Not too many. I can't read gory stuff, or racy stuff. It's too, too…it sticks in my mind." I could remember Lister telling us not to read anything we might want to forget, because once we invited a book into our mind, it would find a home and live there forever. "I'm so visual, I read discriminately for protection."

"You should read some good novels." Edna had been reading Henry James at twelve, the same year I read *Ramona.*

"What do books have to do with this?"

She shook her head in disbelief. "How did you ever get to be eighteen? All life's experiences are laid out in books. If you want to find out about life, read a good novel."

"Hey, don't be mean," I retorted. "All right," and she explained. "Mother Patricia and Reverend Mother are two good friends, like us. They're not jealous, and they're not possessive."

"All right, I get it." But, of course, I didn't. My friendships with girls had an innocence about them: affectionate, loving, intimate, giddy and childlike. We slept in the same bed and never thought a thing about it; Katie and I cuddled when it was cold, the way a person would with a teddy bear or pet dog.

"We are going to be friends like Mother Patricia and Reverend Mother," Edna told me. I sat back and wondered if we would ever look holy like they did when we were old. All that wisdom and serenity.

"Edna, can you imagine the two of us at that age? I can't." "We're looking at hard work," she mused, "but it's a promise."

CHAPTER TEN

No wonder Edna thought it would be hard work. It was.

A clanging bell awoke us at five-thirty when the novice gave the call. "Benedicamus Domino" (Let us bless the Lord), she advised, knocking at each door. We replied, "Deo gratias." (Thanks be to God.)

A mad rush began to the huge, white-tiled bathrooms. No privacy. The four showers and four toilets had swinging doors, open at the top and bottom like the dressing rooms at the Young Folks Shop.

Each cell had a sink so we could wash our face and brush our teeth in our rooms. Both morning and night, we dressed in the dark, utilizing whatever glow came through windows. Dressing took the pros about eight minutes, and took us postulants longer, because we were still involved with bobby pins and curlers.

When the chapel bell rang at five-fifty-five, the novices in charge of the refectory had dragged up wooden milk cases from the mudroom, put out fruit and cereal, and switched on the coffee urn. The laundresses had emptied the chutes and set major washing machines in motion and the sacristans had collected water and wine from the fridge and laid out vestments for the priests. School sisters had either dust mopped, vacuumed, dusted, cleaned sinks and floors in the lavs or in some other way, begun their daily chores.

At six, the 'Angelus' rang; we prayed aloud, then meditated until six-thirty, when we chanted the Office. Mass was celebrated at seven, breakfast at seven-forty. The school sisters tore around finishing their duties and left, abandoning the Motherhouse to the postulants, novices, sick, elderly and Mother Superiors.

On Mondays, we did laundry downstairs and since there were eighty sisters living in the convent, it took us all day. The entire bottom floor of the Motherhouse was a musty, dark cellar, poorly ventilated by high cantankerous windows too stubborn to open wide or close tight. In hot weather, thick shrubs swallowed the few gentle breezes that stirred near the outer foundations, and in winter, cold drafts sneaked in to warm themselves under our sweaters.

The laundry that lay beneath the refectory was the largest room downstairs. Neither poles nor pillars interrupted its dreary expanse. To the right of the double door entrance, hugging the wall, a mammoth cylindrical oak tub chugged away four days out of seven. Two large mangles flanked its right side and next to those stood a huge, unpredictable dryer, which either spewed out sheets too hot to handle or stubbornly refused to dry towels that had whirled around for hours.

We hot starched and rubbed the sister's coifs Monday nights. Tuesday nights, the linens were cold starched, rubbed and put into the fridge to be ironed on Wednesdays. A few professed sisters were assigned to teach us the tricks, which was unusual because it was against rules to talk with professed sisters.

Actually, we weren't supposed to talk, period. Except for big Feast days, the rule was silence until four. But the novices and postulants took classes then, while the school sisters prepared their lesson plans.

We all prayed in chapel at five until dinner at six. Recreation that consisted of sitting and chatting and mending, hands never idle, extended from seven until seven-thirty. We then studied until eight-thirty when the great silence bell rang. Everyone was supposed to be in bed at nine-thirty.

It was an austere life.

Once a month, on Sunday afternoons except during Advent, Lent, and summer, the postulants and second year novices could see their families and friends from two to four. If a family member were unable to come for any reason, she lost her visit. The sisters couldn't go home. Sister Rebecca's mother broke her foot in September and was laid up until after Thanksgiving. Sister 'offered it up'…accepted her disappointment as a penance…and never told Mother Patricia. No visiting during Advent, and her parents missed the Christmas visit because of ice. Her mother came down with a bad cold during January and died of pneumonia. Rebecca had not seen her since the previous June and never had a chance to say good-bye.

When we heard about it, we were all devastated and that afternoon I had slipped into Edna's cell to tell her the news. She was sitting on her straight-backed chair, reading, and had already heard. "How about Rebecca's mother? Why didn't they let her go home, Edna? What's wrong with these people? Haven't they any heart?" I observed her blank face. "Aren't you mad?"

"Are you?"

"Of course I am but I can't afford to be. I have to accept all this if I'm going to stay. But I don't understand their attitude, Edna. If I had wanted a cloistered order, I could have gone next door to the Dominicans. This is an active order of sisters. Why all these cloistered rules? The sisters who taught us in high school were so human and full of fun." I threw up my hands and shrugged.

"I don't know. The superiors must have known. They take all the calls and read our mail, when we get any. Somebody must have called and told them the mother was ill."

"Why are they like this, Edna? Mother McAuley was kind and compassionate, always nursing some member of her family. Severity was never up her alley. Why can't we be more like her? Bertrand doesn't paint her a severe person." Sister Bertrand, a community scholar, reviewed the history of our order on Friday nights in the refectory. The Sisters of Mercy were bent on having the Mother Foundress, Mother Catherine McAuley, canonized and our present Reverend Mother had sent Bertrand to Ireland and England to gather information for Mother McAuley's biography.

Bertrand: tall, regal, a stunner, a woman aware of herself and her gifts, prominent nose and bones, nearly haughty, but a nun, nevertheless, although I could picture her playing Medea. An accurate historian, a humorist, and a holy woman, she wore her job of a hagiographer like a neatly tailored suit.

Bertrand was clearly enjoying herself, though, as the first nun to fly Pan Am and travel around Europe after the war. A riveting speaker with perfect diction, she drew us in flocks to listen to her stories every Friday night. I couldn't wait to read her book. She wouldn't burden us with another syrupy account about a saint, denuding, then candy coating an honest and admirable life.

73

Last week, she had explained the state of Ireland during the mid-eighteenth through the nineteenth century, because without that background, she felt we'd never understand the roots of our Order. The next Friday night, Edna whispered at me. "Do you have the notes Bertrand handed out last week? I've misplaced mine."

"Yes. Pull your chair over. We can both look at them."

"The full misery of a people under tyranny and persecution eludes both historian and biographer. The historian can do little more than suggest wretchedness accumulating with event and legislation, and the biographer can expose only the measure of human woes at some focal point. Consequently, suffering visited on any nation year after year, century after century, remains largely unrevealed though registered in a library of biographies and histories.

Such is the case of Ireland.

The persecution the Penal Laws set in motion attacked the most sensitive features of Irish nationality: the right of land tenure, love of learning, tenacity of Faith. It was against the Faith that the Penal Laws leveled their particular genius, and it was through limitations on land tenure and prohibitions on education that they aimed to coerce or subjugate the faithful."

She opened her book, *Mercy Unto Thousands*, with those two paragraphs. Of course, Bertrand was Irish, as were most of us, second and third generation and this section was old hat to me. Dad had filled my head with stories about his mother who loved learning, but wasn't allowed to attend school in Ireland. It was a bitter pill, since her family came from a long line of scholars. After she immigrated, my grandmother was employed as a maid, and the family, sensing her intelligence, taught her to read and write and lent her the classics. It always amused Dad that the family was English.

"Into this state of wretchedness hardly paralleled in Europe, was born 'James Mc(G)auley, gentleman,' a man who became an

architect, a contractor, and a realestate dealer, because this was a profession left open to Catholics. He grew up in Georgian Dublin where the government allowed one 'registered priest' to a parish, so at least he had some Catholic education. The man was well off, and devoted to the poor. As much as he prospered, so did the poor because his wealth flowed through his hands into theirs. Disregarding his young wife's complaints, on Sundays, he ministered to their needs and taught them their religion.

"His young daughter, Catherine, never forgot what he did although in later life, she could not describe him, could not remember the color of his eyes. But one certainty alone would stay with her; her father had needed these people about him; he was under some compulsion that flowed in his words and filled her soul, words she could never closely recall though she would always remember their spell upon her and feel their force within her.

"He died when Catherine was young, leaving her to a Protestant upbringing . . . but besides a material legacy, he passed on to his daughter, Catherine, a kernel of faith and the vast fortune of a compelling pity for the miserable.

"Later, in the 1820's in Dublin, Catherine McAuley, now a grown and wealthy, warm-hearted woman, inherited a great deal of money from her Protestant guardian, and decided to put both her legacies to work."

Bertrand handed Edna and me new sheets of notes to pass out to the other sisters as we began to study the origins of the congregation.

"She had already gathered some orphans right off the street, including a baby abandoned on the curb, and brought them home to live with her. But she yearned to open schools for the poor and a house to shelter servant girls of good character, whose lot she thought appalling.

"The girls had no recourse, no place to go. Pursued by masters young and old, masters with other things on their minds besides character, the girls were paid little and exploited much. Practically speaking, they were no better than slaves, receiving room and board and not much else.

"She decided to build a House of Mercy, a social service center and staff it with ladies of like mind.

"However, her relatives were doctors and socially well placed, and were embarrassed as her Baggot Street house was constructed, and in a residential district, too. 'Kitty's Folly' they called it, and begged her to come to her senses and get married, for she never lacked suitors.

"She'd have none of it.

"Other women joined her, many of them young socialites from the best families, Louise Costello and Miss O'Connell, her father being the famous Daniel O'Connell, organizer of The Catholic Association. They became the poor's salvation.

"The country, devastated by prejudice and confiscation, famine and cholera, opened its arms to these angels of mercy. The women who joined her spent long hours nursing the sick and burying the dead and because their good works mirrored those of religious orders, the Church prevailed upon Catherine McAuley to found one herself, something she dreaded.

"She feared and detested the rules and rigors of religious life and the clutches of the organized Church. Although she was born a Catholic, she had been reared in Protestant surroundings, and harbored grim feelings about the Catholic Church's prejudices and inner workings."

(Which proved prophetic. Bertrand's aside.)

"But the Church Fathers were accustomed to having their own way, and she was completely open to what she thought was the spirit of God. Gravely reluctant, she succumbed to the prodding of the clergy and established the first congregation of sisters to take simple vows, vows originated to accommodate this group of women who wished to be active in the 'world'. Up to this point, religious sisters had remained in the cloister.

"The hierarchy established rules for the community and these rules mirrored the thinking of the day: puritanical piety, religious discipline and the insignificant place of women in society. The rules have never changed, but are basically the same today as they were in 1830.

"But the thousands of women who opted to follow these rules were products of their times: wealthy Irish ladies, Victorian women, American-Irish immigrants, flappers, children of the Depression, and the jitterbuggers of the forties. The trappings of the order might have become obsolete, such as the habit which was the conservative dress of women in the 1820s, but underneath all the voluminous yards of black serge, the spirit lived; the spirit of the Foundress, the spirit of the current age and the spirit of the community that Mother McAuley had in mind before the priests began to meddle."

Bertrand went on and on about the interplay of the Holy Spirit and the rules of the community as interpreted by the sisters who were living at the time. She'd say it over and over; "The spirit of the rule lives in the sisters." I wasn't so sure I agreed.

* * * * *

Saturday morning, Edna and I took a walk on the back cloisters. We had a few minutes before class and we were still hepped up about Bertrand's talk. March was hurling its bitter gray winds, clawing at our shawls, piercing our sweaters and leaving us stamping our feet. Turning backwards, we walked against the wind.

"It will be spring soon," I noted.

"Sure, Pollyanna."

"No, really. See the little green daffodil leaves and the crocuses peeking out down there?" But Edna wasn't looking.

"I admire Bertrand's honesty. She spares no one. She certainly has no love for most of those parish priests."

"Why should she? Some of them were petty and jealous and rotten to Mother McAuley. They couldn't stand her because she was wealthy. She traveled in the best circles, a real lady."

"But the Church made her do things she didn't want to," Edna persisted. "What a dilemma. That must have cost her. Bertrand makes her so human."

"Ummmmm. I liked the part about the spirit of the community, you know, the interplay between the sisters and the times and the rule. We're the sisters she's talking about, Edna. We're the sisters living at the time. It's us. And when I'm old enough and respected enough, I'll change the rules and let all the Rebecca's go home to see their mothers."

"You haven't gotten over that, have you?"

"No."

The bell rang, clanging away, calling us to ceramics class.

"What did you finally make?" I asked Edna, as I stamped my feet and folded up my shawl.

"A fisherman. You?"

"A fencer."

* * * * *

In the art room, Sister Anita smiled as she carefully drew the figurines out of the kiln. I loved free flow sculpture, one of the aspects of art she had taught me when I had been her pupil at de Paul's. She had respected my talent and had been gathering material for my scholarship to Rhode Island School of Design when I told her I was going to enter. I thought about that as I looked at our work.

Edna had rounded arms and legs out of her ball of clay and suggested a slumped head sheltered by a cap. The figure sagged over a rock, fat hands covering a fatter stomach, total repose. As she began examining the tiny hole she had poked through for the fishing pole, I compared our statues.

My fencer, skinny and vibrant, was on its toes with knees bent, legs spread and set. Its arms thrust out, its long blouse flowing. It would lunge forever at some enemy or other.

No wonder Sister Anita was smiling.

CHAPTER ELEVEN

We had no time to ourselves. As postulants, we finished our second semester of college, tasted our new circumstances and considered if they were to our liking. In six months, we could decide if we had a true vocation, if we wanted to stay. If so, we would be received into the community, dressed as a bride, the 'Bride of Christ', and then wear the same habits as the other nuns except for our veils, which would be white. In the meantime, the community was looking us over. Did we fit in? Could we obey the rules?

There were plenty. The Holy Rule said, "The Sisters are always to bear in mind that, by the Vow of Obedience, they have forever renounced their own will and resigned it to the direction of their Superiors."

Even the professed sisters could do little without permission: use the phone, send a letter, receive candy from parents, dispose of a worn-out sweater. And no matter what the superior told a sister to do, she had to believe it was the will of God for her.

All congregations worked on the principle of blind obedience, that God could make good come from anything one was told to do. He would give the religious grace to do it and it was His business to see everything turned out all right.

God should work through us, the convent said, like water flowing from a pitcher (the pitcher contributing nothing, of course). So communities contrived to make subjects feel humble and dependent using, among other things, the Chapter of Faults. Once a month, each nun knelt before all the sisters and recited her foibles. The professed sisters had their group; the novitiate was separate.

Everyone had a prepared list and picked out three appropriate faults. The recitation began with the junior sister. The first time I walked up in front of the novitiate and knelt before the crucifix, I felt as blasé as I did that day in eighth grade. "I accuse myself of all the faults I have committed in the discharge of my duties especially: talking about my family, talking in times of silence and talking in the corridors (in short, talking) for which I humbly beg the pardon of God and the prayers of the sisters."

It didn't faze me a bit. But it wasn't true about the others; it fazed some of the novices quite a bit. Five of them wrote every word and I could see the paper shaking in their hands and hear their breathless voices. True, the rules were antiquated, the customs, questionable. Many felt the same as I but, since this was the route we had chosen, we accepted the whole package. Some laughingly compared it to boot camp, especially those of us who were more impressed by the call to action rather than the call to contemplation. We were where we wanted to be, surrounded by God and people who talked about godly things. Still...

"What's the real purpose of this show?" I asked Edna, curiously. "What is it supposed to do?"

"The reason for the Chapter of Faults is to make you humble, curb your pride."

"It's medieval!

"Of course," Edna replied, expressing surprise that the fact had just dawned on me, "the whole thing is medieval. We decided that when Rebecca's mother died and she couldn't go home. Monastic life hasn't changed in centuries. Have you stopped listening to Bertrand? As much as Mother McAuley resisted these customs, the hierarchy wouldn't let her get around them. They swallowed her up." I sighed. Edna lacked my enthusiasm but she definitely felt the same way about rules being strange. However there were those who took them more seriously than Edna and I, the Mistress of Novices, for example. My spirit didn't escape her, because obviously, I was throwing myself into the life.

Mother Patricia, who found good will but little else to recommend me, felt a shade skeptical of this whirlwind who blew in against everyone's better judgment. I was born talking and silence was the rule. Creativity was my strong point; conforming was expected. Why walk up stairs if I could run, but decorum was preferred. The Holy Rule, chapter 25 read, "They (meaning us) shall never be seen running giddily through the Convent."

What to do?

I worked at it and so did Mother Patricia, no easy task for either of us. I admired her, saddled with the responsibility of distinguishing 'spiritual mirage from stable vocation'. She, too, was one of those who fastened her eye on some far off vision when she spoke, like Sister Boniface, leaving the ones she spoke to feeling as if her words had come directly from Above. I must convince her I belonged, because I sensed there were some who didn't think so.

Mother St. Michael, a tall commanding person with an impenetrable expression, a high mucky-muck in the community, was Mother Assistant, one of four discreets in charge of the Order. The day I entered, as I stood talking and entertaining my college friends in the front corridor, my eyes caught a cold and calculating stare. I asked myself, "Who was the poor slob she was appraising?" and turned around, but no one was there.

That stare was for me.

Brrrr. Well, I thought, at least she isn't the Mistress of Novices. A few days later, I asked Edna, "Who is she?"

"They elected her Assistant. Rumors are she never takes off her good habit, that she scrubs floors in it and sleeps in it. One of the novices saw her smile once. The corners of her mouth rose an eighth of an inch and nothing else moved. They call her 'Dead Eye'. If she catches your eye, you're dead," Edna contributed, and I told her about my first day.

"You're dead," she quipped, and I fell to the floor of the priests' parlor, clutching an imagined wound, gasping for air, only to hear that soft voice of Mother Patricia, inquiring from the doorway, "Sister, is something wrong?"

Oh, God! Caught again. How did nuns learn to sneak around on cotton feet and where did they get those melodic, soft voices? I tried to lower mine, to no avail. To this day, it would crack chalk. But I kept thinking, maybe if I walked a little slower, maybe a little less drama. I was sure I could do it, be like all the others.

One morning, in the priests' parlor, Edna and I talked as we dusted the heavy Victorian furniture. We, too, had chores and even though we weren't supposed to, we'd help each other; it reminded me of the times Helen and I would walk each other half way home and I talked about Helen. She had been received into the community the previous January and was a canonical novice studying canon law, Tanquerey's *The Spiritual Life*, and listening to Father Phelan, the priest Mother Patricia engaged to speak to the novices occasionally. Everyone who entered the novitiate spent a canonical year after she received the habit, and the postulants didn't see much of them. Canonicals were allowed to study only college subjects that weren't profane, but at least we had instructions together once a week.

One Tuesday morning, Mother Patricia was late. The rule was: all stand waiting until the Mistress enters the room and is seated. Helen must have been tired because, after ten minutes, she sat down, but stood when she heard Patricia getting off the elevator. But Patricia had spotted her.

"Are you that tired, Sister?" and she made a big deal out of it and sent her to bed at eleven o'clock in the morning! Just like a naughty child! I was furious and snapped at Patricia in my mind. "Why should Helen be humiliated that way? She wasn't the one who was late. YOU were." I hadn't been this angry in years. She proceeded to give instructions about silence and cited the wise old owl, supposedly kind, brilliant and wise because it never spoke, just observed. My biggest fault was talking and Patricia sensed I was steaming in my seat, so she called on me. I stood calmly and told her the owl was stealthy, sly and flew silently to stalk its prey. It was headstrong, practically untrainable, more cunning than wise, and anything but kind. (My mother studied birds so I knew birds.) Besides, intelligent conversation distinguished man from animal. I could see nothing wise about interminable silence, especially if a person had something worthwhile to say. A silent person might simply be stupid.

I wasn't rude, but was definitely on the verge.

"Then, what happened?" Helen asked. I had torn down to her cell the minute instructions were over, and was sitting on her bedspread, carefully folded at the foot of her bed. Absentmindedly, I picked at the tiny white chenille balls.

"It was strange. She wasn't upset. She listened carefully, then went on. I felt she baited me, as if she were conducting a study. I thought I'd be out on my ear."

"We're different from the other novices, Mary, a new generation and she knows it. All the superiors entered the convent before the First World War, the Victorian Age, everything reserve and manners. But we're the brassy products of the Second World War. "People are changing," Helen continued, "and so are the new postulants. They're questioning. Patricia doesn't like it but she knows it. Father Phelan just came back from Collegeville, from the Benedictines who are studying liturgy reforms, and it's a good thing Patricia doesn't stay to hear him speak. He's really avant garde."

"Then how does *she* know him?"

"She taught him in high school when he was a 'dear sweet boy'." Helen rolled her huge brown eyes, and went on. "You know Dr. Phelan, the cancer specialist at St. Peter's. He's his uncle." I shook my head, no.

"No matter," she continued. "Anyway, he's fired up about the new theologians, about liturgy, scripture study, and ecumenism. He's bringing in books by Guardini and Jacques Maritain, and articles about other religions. He'll talk to us again next month. You'll be impressed." She reached under her pillow, where she had shoved a magazine when I came in, and handed it to me. *The New Catholic.* I flipped through the pages.

"Read the article on page sixteen. The war has caused all kinds of rumblings in the Church. Theologians are questioning its true spirit. Is blind obedience its major tenet or is there more?"

I was annoyed. "You always accuse me of going off on tangents, Helen. What has this got to do with your being sent to bed?"

"Everything. Don't you see? Everything."

"Are you saying that blind obedience is crazy?"

"Mainly outdated."

The noon prayer bell rang, and I stood and Helen quoted solemnly, "They shall obey the call of the bell as the voice of God."

"Helen, I wonder who thought it all up? Edna and I were talking about it just the other day. Maybe you and she will get to know each other when we're received and become novices."

* * * * *

That evening, after we had chanted the Little Office of the Blessed Virgin and said the litanies, I reached into my stall and pulled out Helen's magazine, carefully opening to the article she had selected. Our mistress assigned us our reading matter, always books, so secrecy was expedient.

"...but the Church is in desperate need of an overhaul. Unfortunately, the idea of the Catholic Church, the moral rock of Gibraltar, altering its positions or viewpoints is unthinkable to most Catholics. However, the activities of Germany, and other Christian countries during World War II are more unthinkable.

The Holocaust was appalling! How did it happen? Theologians are stunned and ashamed of the ancient reaction of Christians to Jews during the war, and are urging the Church to shake off its aristocratic trappings, fortress mentality and general torpor and reexamine its position.

"What has the Church become? Where is the Christian message?

"1950 offers a ripe opportunity to the Catholic Church to be the leader it was destined by Christ to be. Few historians dispute its influence on the course of western civilization, for better or for worse.

"This could be its hour.

"The situation has been hopeful. In 1943, the Pope promoted ecumenism by encouraging scholars of all faiths to share their knowledge of Biblical studies, something they had been doing unobtrusively for decades without much reassurance from Rome.

"To reexamine the Bible and the message of God, together, Jews, Catholics, Protestants, as one people...to shed pomp and ceremony

and explore the possibilities...to recognize women in their rightful place in the New Testament...exhilarating!

"But for reasons uncertain, the Papacy seems to be turning its tail, pulling up the drawbridge, returning to its conservative ways, and again, withdrawing its support for simple, honest dialogue and intellectual exploration with all the people of God.

"Let us pray for the Light of the Holy Spirit and for the Hand of God in our lives and in the life of the Church."

The Holocaust section had hit me. I had followed the Nuremberg trials, and individual responsibility seemed tremendously important. I never recovered from that part of the war, committing atrocities because you were told to. When I was in eighth grade, I remembered the horror I felt when I first saw concentration camps. I stared at those pictures in the morning as my father read the paper and I ate cereal with cream, in a bright warm kitchen, as my mother squeezed my fresh orange juice. I stared at bodies of children my age, piles of naked men and women. It was horrible, sickening. My mother would say, "Tom, don't let Mary see those. She'll have nightmares."

Nightmares! This was no dream. It really happened! In high school, I had paid close attention to the trials and we talked about them in ethics class. If I had been a war criminal, what would I say to God? He made me do it! Could I honor obedience before my conscience? Obedience never had set well with me, but since it was the convent directing, I must swallow it.

The 'Angelus' began to toll, terminating our spiritual reading and calling us to dinner. Maybe these ideas will flower in the future, I thought, but can I afford to adopt them now? Life here was confusing enough and if the sisters were going to receive me into the community, I'd better give blind obedience a whirl.

CHAPTER TWELVE

In the imposed isolation of the novitiate, we were expected to pour out our worldly selves, our judgments, our old ways and refill our lives with lofty thoughts and personal decisions the community thought appropriate. Since my life was on the line, and I wanted to be a spiritual person, I prayed devoutly during Mass and tried to stay awake through morning meditation. I loved the Office, and although some of the Latin escaped me, the monotonous chant that praised the Lord through the psalms calmed my spirit. When I walked the cloisters, saying my rosary, I cast my eyes down. The least I could do was *look* like the wise old owl. Meanwhile, Edna and I scouted around, noting how others led their lives. Hidden in all this float, who was who and why?

Our interplay with professed sisters was limited to observation only. The rule forbade us to talk with them without very special permission, depriving us of making knowledgeable judgments about their sanctity and basic beliefs. Edna and I watched carefully and some appeared to attain serenity, even holiness, by following the rules. Their presence exuded an unearthly quality and the administration stationed these types in the Motherhouse for our edification. Most of the 'live wires' were stationed in branch houses.

Many novices turned towards the retired sisters who in turn kept their eyes open towards them. That group was beyond correction from superiors and wise enough to know which rules were important so the discreets practiced benign neglect in their regard.

The novices and postulants wheeled them around and brought them their tea and soaked up their wisdom and learned the difference between the dried up bitter old sticks, who existed, but were much in the minority, and the sisters whose dealings with their lives had made them holy.

Fortunately, on feast days, jubilees and community celebrations, every one of the three hundred professed sisters able to pour into the Motherhouse injected it with the kind of life that originally had attracted most of us. Nuns chatted in doorways, since talking in corridors was taboo. Clusters of friends gathered everywhere; all parlors were congested with small lively groups.

Old Sister Annunciation would seek out some postulant or novice who looked especially lonely and ask, "Could you take me to chapel?" The delighted sister would saunter down the front corridor, snailing past the bustle, smiling and waving on the sly at all the teachers who had taught her in school. We all hoped a professed sister might ask permission to spend a few minutes with us on feast days, but those opportunities were nearly non-existent.

So we turned to each other.

The senior novices were an especially sweet and thoughtful group. Determined we were lonely, bewildered, and confused, they would stick a little holy card in our Office books or leave an appropriate spiritual poem or a quotation from scripture on our press in our cell. Four of them, my sister Pat's classmates, had been to our house for cookouts. I knew them when. But now, they treated me tenderly, and appointed themselves Edna's and my babysitters; they clucked away, resolved to shelter us from the severity of questionable customs. We were grateful, though we didn't quite understand them.

* * * * *

The sisters were using the new chapel occasionally even though it hadn't been officially dedicated yet. The altar stone would be laid the day the bishop performed the ceremony, the same morning that Edna and I would be received. In the meantime, Father used a small cloth containing relics of martyrs, which he laid on the altar, a requisite for saying Mass.

The previous week, I had been appointed as junior sacristan to assist Sister Bryand in the new chapel. She was the senior novice, Pat's old friend, high school class officer and appointed by the business teacher as the principal's personal secretary. She had worked for the State Department of Taxation a year before she entered and was so organized and practical, I was in awe. Bryand intrigued me because she seemed to sail blissfully along as if daily demands were tacked to the top of her life. What had happened to her? Didn't she care? Was she real? The way Edna and I were when we were together? Or was her reality reserved only for members of her own set?

Could I sneak in?

Late one Saturday afternoon, we were both mending. I had put my foot through my petticoat and Bryand was stitching hems on altar cloths. "You know," she complained good-naturedly, "the trouble with this place is the minute anyone walks in the door, the brass thinks she can do everything...as if the habit turns a nun into a magician. Imagine! Me, sewing." The machine jumped along erratically as she gently tried to prod the foot pedal.

The seven machines were turned the same way so I did an about face on my stool and watched her as she argued with a stubborn bobbin. "There, I think that's it," and she tentatively began to stitch again. "Check the tension," I said. "My Singer at home is just like the one you're using and it slips sometimes." She did and the machine perked up.

"Bryand, if you can't sew, how are you going to make your Profession habit?"

"I'll swap jobs with somebody."

"Swap with me. I can sew. You can edit my term papers."

"Are you sure? You've only been here a little over a month. Can you make a habit?"

"Sure. I watched the novices lay theirs out during recreation. The whole shebang is based on math, measuring and pleating four widths of material. I sew it at the selvage," I began gesturing, "pleat, and then attach the tube to the yoke and sleeves. I'm a good seamstress and a rotten typist. You're vice versa. Let's swap." We were alone in the novices' sewing room, a dismal spot. Long and narrow, it was painted hospital green and graced by an ugly, large crucifix, rejected by every other room upstairs. Dim light filtered through the high windows, windows the novices cranked open and closed, standing tiptoe on a solid oak, slat back chair.

This room and the laundry, the only usable space in the cellar, were connected by a long corridor, aptly named the Catacombs. Dark, dusty and dank, only bodies were missing and we weren't so sure they weren't buried down here somewhere. Mr. Shoultz, the handyman, swept it up occasionally but no one claimed the Catacombs as a duty, not even a novice. The old sisters said the Catacombs were haunted but the old sisters said everything was haunted; they lived in another world anyway. But, when I was here alone, I thought about it, and today, I was glad Bryand was with me.

"This place is creepy, Bryand. Why don't they paint it?"

"No money for frills. Haven't you noticed that the only windows with curtains face the front of the building? Shades make do for the rest of the rooms."

"True, convent life is tight. All the week's left-overs end up in Tuesday's meatloaf!"

She started to laugh. "This habit you're making me will last at least ten years. Pull apart, repleat, pull apart, repleat. The sisters really don't have any money. Occasionally, I do the R.M.'s bookkeeping for her. Believe me, we're poor."

"I don't mind that, do you?"

"No. It's part of it."

"Some things I don't understand, though." I had finished my petticoat, neatened my mess and was sitting facing her, waiting for her to finish. "Can I ask you something? What did you think about the Chapter of Faults, I mean, the first time you did it? You know, what did you think?" I was nervous, wondering if she'd tell me, if she'd be honest. I knew we'd be crossing a line, moving into friendship, where a person reveals the truth about herself, no matter how small the truth. Our eyes met and I felt she was sizing me up.

She started to laugh. "I thought it was weird, WEIRD, the only time I doubted whether or not I belonged here. I rehearsed my lines to Mother Patricia, that the Chapter of Faults was not of this century, that I thought it was obscene, not for me, that I was a healthy American girl and there was no place in my life for this kind of nonsense.

"But, would you believe it? When I knocked on Mother's door, all ready to sound off, she had gone out. The only night I can ever remember her out of the Motherhouse, and the next day, I thought, this has been going on for hundreds of years and *I'm* questioning it?"

I knew what she meant and the two of us mimicked simultaneously, "It goes with the territory."

Sister Bryand had flaming red hair that never stayed put under her linens; the curls danced out when she was excited and she was always tucking them back in as she was now. As senior novice, when Mother Patricia was at a meeting, Bryand said prayers, read the litanies and gave Instructions, reading from a book Mother had left. She was also a clip could get the group roaring during recreation, write a parody in a flash, and entertain us when things were tight. But no one pushed her around. She took her role seriously.

Helen had told me that when Bryand was a postulant, one of the second year novices took issue with Sister Timothy, a member of Bryand's set. Timmy was a brilliant research scientist who had 'heard the call' and entered our community. She was a misfit, a Ph.D. among high school graduates and Sister Dionysius, a second year novice, was jealous. She purposely skipped Timothy when she put out the butter and poured the milk and water in the refectory. Poor Timothy, who hadn't expected mean-spirited people in the convent, was crushed by her inability to fit in.

Bryand cornered Dionysius right in front of her friends in the refectory. "You're acting like a silly adolescent."

"It's none of your business. Stay out of it," she said.

"I'm making it my business," Bryand told her. "There's a vocation at stake here. If you want to pick on someone, pick on me or would you dare? I'm warning you, if you don't stop pushing Timmy, I'm going to Mother Patricia." And she stared her down. It stopped. I loved the story and loved knowing something about Bryand that she didn't know I knew.

* * * * *

I didn't do my spiritual reading that night. I plunked a book on my lap and went through the motions of reading, but I was thinking. I had known this was a strange life when I entered. Poverty, chastity and obedience and the service of the poor, sick and ignorant. Those were the vows. The sisters had lived through the Depression and didn't complain about poverty, about writing on backs of envelopes and wearing clothes so long they were worthless, even as dusters. They understood it. Chastity was never discussed. You didn't marry. That was it, and service came after a sister left the novitiate.

But obedience! The endless lists of rules that confined every thought and action? Did anyone understand the interminable directives? Yet the sisters accepted them whether they made sense or not, offering them up. Whether they respected them was moot. It all went with the territory, they said.

So now I know SOMETHING, I told myself. There's a whole body of customs (some worthwhile, some not) that everyone accepts that is basically unimportant. I wonder if I'll ever find out which body of customs is which?

I wonder if I'm supposed to try?

* * * * *

Right after dinner, I skipped down the stairs to the Catacombs, and made myself walk slowly through the dim corridors to the sewing room. When I was little, I had been petrified of the dark, imagining six-foot spiders with leering grins and ferocious eyebrows lurking in the bathroom or behind chairs or in the bushes near our front door. The Catacombs didn't thrill me but I had to learn control. No skipping. This was a good exercise.

Bryand and I settled in and she sat mumbling at her crooked hems and spots where the needle slid. She had brought her habit material and I measured out the four pieces and sewed up the tube.

"You'll be out of the Motherhouse soon, won't you? Has anyone told you where you'll be sent after Profession?"

She shook her head, no, her mouth full of pins. Bryand would take temporary vows and receive her black veil next month, then teach in a branch house. She'd be a junior professed and we wouldn't be able to talk to each other for the next two years, until I was professed. What a dunce I am, I thought, making a new friend who's leaving the novitiate in a month.

"It's not easy making friends here, is it? We can't talk to the professed sisters, we're really not supposed to talk to the old sisters and you second year novices will be out of here in two months and we won't be able to talk to you either." I dropped my thread into my sewing box as the bell rang.

"You won't be in the novitiate forever."

* * * * *

Recreation was especially noisy that night. A few novices were giving Edna and me the business about being the first set to be received in the new chapel.

"Think about it," Bryand pointed out, "You were the last two who entered as postulants in the old chapel and you'll be the first two to receive the veil in the new one."

"It isn't as if WE had anything to do with it," we protested. (Good-natured oohs and ahhhs and um hummms)

"Well, it makes sense, doesn't it?" I asked. "There are twelve of you and only two of us. It would take them all day to dedicate the chapel and profess the dozen of you."

"Whatever is the will of God," Sister Rebecca said, and I whipped around, ready with a flip remark, but she was serious.

"You mean that, don't you?"

"Of course." She ceased darning her black stocking and looked up at me, smiling.

"Yes, I thought you did. It must be wonderful to have such faith," and I mumbled something else pious, and joined the other group. Where does she live? Is she really that accepting? Does she have any feeling? No one knew how she felt when her mother died. She just spent more time in chapel. I know; I watched her. Why didn't she put me off, make me suspicious?

Some novices said, "Welcome to the will of God" in jest, especially if their entire day had been battered to dust. Some said it to impress others or themselves; I didn't have trouble spotting that kind. Then, there were people like Rebecca who said it and meant it. Sometimes, I wondered if she were slow. Could she be that dead to her feelings? However, as often as I questioned her judgments, I never doubted her sincerity.

I moved over towards Edna, towards someone I knew. She and I didn't have any darning to do, since our clothes were new, so I cut out Bryand's yoke and sleeves, while Edna held the yarn for Timmy who was rolling a ball of black wool from skeins. From across the room, I appraised Rebecca like an artist. She boasted storybook features: her face, an ideal oval, straight nose, black hair, white skin, high coloring, deep blue eyes, and heavy black eyebrows, which, of course, she couldn't pluck. Just her luck. They added to her startling beauty.

She neither criticized nor complained. The other members of her group tried teasing her, then gave up. She'd never be one of them. They liked her but couldn't offer friendship, only protection. Rebecca's only attachment was to the rules.

As I had moved away, two second-years slid over towards her and began a pleasant conversation. Since her mother's death, members of her set rarely left her alone. Bryand, Timmy and Edna were discussing Thomas Merton and a few second-years sitting near Mother Patricia began harmonizing to an old hymn, *Night folds its Starry Curtains 'round.* Sweet and cloying, but, somehow significant.

> *'Night folds its starry curtains 'round,*
> *As day has faded on the hills.*
> *And in the silence so profound*
> *Calm peace of fragrant balm distills . . .'*

These girls were the same age as my college friends but what a difference! No conversations about clothes and dates and no gossip. The scene exuded a pleasant warmth, gentle, unreal, and quite unlike the wild gatherings Saturday nights had offered me lately. What would I be doing if I were out tonight, I wondered, if I weren't here? A frat party at RPI? What was Jimmy doing? Looking for another girl, I hoped.

What were my college friends up to and my family? Had Mom made Manhattan clam chowder for dinner? Was Katie getting dressed for the Canteen? Could she fit into any of my clothes? Mom promised me she wouldn't give them away for at least a year in case I changed my mind.

I knew I wasn't going to change my mind, whether I understood what was going on here or not. I must belong, I thought. I can think about all this and not be lonely. All the novices who knew the hymn were singing now.

'Not man nor angel can portray,
O Dearest Lord how sweet thou art.
To call us from our cares away
To rest within Thy Sacred Heart.'

CHAPTER THIRTEEN

Rains had washed March away. Stubborn gray hills of sooty snow, framed in soggy leaves, clung to curbs, remnants of a relentless winter. Forsythias budded, willows wore pale chartreuse and maples glowed dull pink. The dirt smelled clean. The air blew fresh. Easter was coming, spring was coming and everything was ready to burst, including me. Despite dreary March, the solemnity of Lent and the pressure of all the silence, I had stumbled upon the meaning of the Mass, and the joy of it.

I laid vestments at night for the priest and lit the candles in the morning, though it was really Bryand's duty, but she ironed and cleaned instead. Lighting candles in front of all the sisters wasn't for her. Too shy. She was funny that way. Getting up and clowning was one thing; on display at any other time rattled her.

On the mornings Father Phelan taught religion classes to the novices, he said Mass, and I watched him vest as I moved inconspicuously around the sacristy. As if in a trance, his lips moved, praying over each piece of linen, kissing it, clothing himself in the amice and alb and cincture I had spread out for him the night before. He picked up the folded amice and wrapped the strings around himself, totally absorbed, like a virtuoso at the piano or a glass blower I had seen one afternoon at the Museum, keenly aware of his purpose and nothing else.

He impressed me so that Mass began to take on another meaning, a far deeper meaning than it had when I was a child because then I went to church because I had to. I didn't mind too much because I liked the comforting feeling during the consecration when the bread and wine became Christ. I went to Mass to think about myself, to let my mind wander over my actions and decide whether or not I was good or bad and could I try for better the next time. Sometimes I thought about my clothes. Did I have nylons without runs to wear to the dance Saturday night? I thought about arguments I had with Katie, or how much I wished I looked like Barbara Stanwyck, I mean that walk and shoulders, and I would strut around in my mind as my thoughts raced away. Then I would be ashamed, rein myself in and try to concentrate on the mystery; but the Mass was personal, a time for private prayer, a time for me.

I was relearning. The Mass, this meeting of God and man, rose above anything personal. The Mass represented not just me and God, not just the sisters in the chapel, or all the sisters in all the chapels, but the whole human race. Man meeting God, every morning, right at this altar and at every altar in the world.

One night after five o'clock prayers as I read Guardini's *The Church, the Catholic and the Spirit of the Liturgy,* I paused and reread certain passages. It struck me. My heart swelled, and I caught my breath and thought...Man, with what he is and what he isn't...and God, with all that He is...meeting at this solemn moment. Whether proclaimed by a single priest and singing bells...or by three priests in unison, enveloped in swirls of incense, and swellings, then whispers of Gregorian chants.

It made no difference.

Man, with what he is and what he isn't and God, with all that He is...meeting at this solemn moment.

So this is what it means, so THIS is what it means! This is what the Mass means! The Covenant!

I was enveloped in the presence of God! I clapped my book shut, startling my neighbors in their stalls and put Guardini away. I wanted to stand up in chapel, right in the middle of spiritual reading, and sing something, anything! A psalm, maybe, and do a dance down the middle aisle, with a tambourine or castanets.

There was a glow on my face in the refectory that night because Edna caught me after dinner and asked, "What's up? You seem so inspired, more than usual. Give me a hand and we can talk."

Most of the sisters had left the dining room by now but Edna was the refectorian in charge of checking the tables for breakfast, putting out cereal and making sure each sister had returned her complete place setting and that the knife blade faced the plate.

"Oh, Edna," and I tried to tell her. "I've been reading about the Mass. Father Phelan is so devout when he prepares for Mass, not like some of the other priests who joke around with the altar boys and the sisters. I've been watching him, thinking I must be missing something. Why is he so intent, so reverent? And I've been reading this book and I'm, I'm, well, I'm seeing some things for the first time."

"Such as…"

"Mainly, God, and what He is, and how He wants us, and chases us down, and never gives up on us. I mean, just think of what He's done!" I was warming up, my hands flailing the air, my tongue speeding over the words as I waved a fork around, gesturing occasionally to make a point. "Like the Last Supper and what it really means. Turning Himself into food so He could become part of us…I mean, how intimate can you get?" I took a breath, and Edna listened. Think about us, the way we are, everyday people with petty complaints and trivial lives, and stabs at grandeur…yet, He doesn't care what we're like. Instead, He says, 'Gather whatever dignity you have, the good and the bad of you, and come celebrate your rituals, your ceremonies, come, dress in your costumes and deal with Me, everyday, come deal with Me at Mass, and I will become part of you.'"

I paused, my arms outstretched, looking like the priest at the 'Dominus vobiscum'. Edna stopped arranging the heavy glasses, stopped loading them onto the tray and was watching me intently, urging me on with her eyes. "At some time during every day, there's a Mass going on, and God is fulfilling His promise, keeping His bargain, no matter what we're like, or how carelessly we lead our lives. Oh! I don't know. I can't say it right."

"I think you said it right. You can't figure out why He bothers with us or why He cares, but He does." Sister Timothy interrupted our discussion. "Well, are you two still solving the world's problems? You'd better hustle yourselves upstairs to recreation before you're late. Because that WOULD be a problem." She laughed at her little joke as she walked out of the room, switching off the lights, leaving us to set down the trays in shadows and find our own way out of the dark.

* * * * *

The next afternoon before our four o'clock class, Edna and I walked down to the statue of Our Lady, then cut over the wet grass to the path along the chain link fence, which bordered the woods.

We compared our lists. Each of us was responsible for half of the novitiate, for ferreting out any ideas each novice might have about religious life. Most said something pious, and we decided the novices were pleasant and kind but accepted religious life the way it was.

We concluded Rebecca did everything because she believed everything she was told. Blind obedience didn't faze her; she would go out and water a stick if told to do so, and not question it. But Rebecca was not of this world.

Bryand obeyed because there it was, and I thought Timmy was that way too. Whether they believed God was interested in blind obedience, I didn't know. They didn't say. But, regardless of who told them what to do they thought God could make anything come out all right. That was the extent of their faith. However, I doubted if they believed Rebecca's stick would bloom.

"I like all the novices, but I don't think they know any more than we do," I told Edna, concluding our discussion. "There's Father Phelan and Sister Bertrand, and Father Phelan isn't a sister and Sister Bertrand is telling us that we religious don't belong where we are. What she doesn't say is where we do belong in this world and how to get there."

"You'd better become more like Helen and me and learn to sit and listen and not ask so many questions. The sisters like to listen to Bertrand. Not everyone wants to hear from you. After all, who are you?" Edna asked.

"What do you mean, who am I? I'm someone becoming a nun." I kicked a small stone in the path, and it skittered out of sight into the weeds. "And it's not easy for me to keep still and not ask questions. How else am I going to learn?" Edna had said what she had to say, and we walked along in silence. The sun was warm, the breeze was cool, but the wind knew it was spring…busy…busy…seeking out each new scent, swirling around the wet earth, wrenching musky odors from soggy marshes beyond the woods, and coaxing tangy perfumes from forest pine…gathering…gathering, then, sated, flowing right through our chain link fence from the woods grabbing our long skirts and short veils, touching our faces with invisible fingers, and playfully lifting our very souls out of the dead of winter.

"Oh, Edna," I whispered, "don't move, don't turn. Look, to the right." A fawn with wobbly legs stood staring at us, unblinking, unafraid. A few feet from it, the doe, head down, nibbled at new shoots. After a few seconds the fawn cocked its head and stretched its neck towards us and the doe, alerted, looked up, and they were off.

Poof!

Gone.

I was still staring when Edna tugged at my shawl. "Come on, we're just going to make it to class. It's time for the bell."

"Edna, did you see the fawn? It had no fear at all."

"Yes, I saw it." She had lifted her skirts as she trod along the slippery path. "And you're like the fawn. You know no danger." She turned around and looked at me, still hoisting her skirts.

"And I'm like the doe. Danger, I can smell it."

We were facing each other, close up.

"What danger? What do you mean?"

"Quit questioning the rules. Your questions are loaded no matter how innocently you couch them. To some of the sisters, the rules are their whole life.

"Finally, stay out of 'Dead Eye's way. You annoy her."

"What did I ever do to her?"

"You don't have to do anything. You just *are*."

"Well, that's great, just great. I don't even know what I'm doing wrong."

"I know, but that's what I'm for. I'm the doe and I know when it's time to bolt, and now's the time or we'll be late for class."

CHAPTER FOURTEEN

It was Holy Thursday, nearly Easter. I was enchanted as the liturgy drew me into its divine mysteries. Psalms burst out of the Old Testament from love-filled hearts, chants moaned with unspeakable sorrow and restrained joy. The incense, the weighty scent of white lilies, memories of darkened churches and lighted candles enticed my imagination. The rituals and trappings coaxed my spirit, tempted my senses to taste the principal celebration of the Church, Holy Week with its profound mystery, the Last Supper, the Crucifixion, the Resurrection of Christ.

The sisters not only cleaned up their souls during Lent but tackled the convent, too: every wall and ceiling dusted, every floor washed and waxed, every window sparkling, each piece of furniture polished. The discreets canceled novitiate classes since all hands were needed to ready the Motherhouse for the bishop's blessing on Holy Saturday. As I finished shining up the brass candelabra, I searched for their place in the bottom of the sacristy press.

"He even blesses the laundry?" I asked Bryand, "and the Catacombs, the kitchen pantry, our cells?"

"That's right." Bryand nodded, stuffing some newly arrived lilies into a huge vase. "Drat! I can't stand Easter lilies. No matter what I do, they look like flocks of quacking geese."

"You need to break the formality. I'll do it. The vinca's in bloom, maybe a couple daffodils. I'll find some greens on the grounds and cut a few sprigs."

"All right. I'll finish dust mopping and leave the flowers for you. Take the scissors and go." Bryand tossed the shedding maidenhair fern into the waste paper basket and washed her hands. She searched vainly for a towel, then yanked up her skirt and dried her hands on her sateen petticoat.

"There's a legend about the first sister in chapel on Easter Sunday," she said, straightening her clothes. "She's like Mary

Magdalene arriving first at the tomb. The first sister in chapel receives a special grace."

"Is this one of Annunciation's old Irish tales?" I asked her suspiciously. "Are you making it up?"

"Cross my heart."

"Bryand, you're beginning to sound like Rebecca," and I pranced out of the sacristy with the scissors, ducking the wet dust cloth that flew after me. I needed that special grace. Edna had jolted me the other day with her warning about 'Dead Eye', and I determined to beat everyone into the chapel on Easter Sunday, even if the whole thing were poppycock.

Slipping out the back door near the sacristy, I picked my way across the boards the contractors had laid out slip-shod over the mud; they led around the new building to the front of the Motherhouse.

Far across New Scotland Avenue, some children were jumping rope. They yelled and waved, pointing to me and to each other and I waved back. Shrieking with delight, they yelled some more but I turned, humming to myself, snipping off greens, choosing the freshest sprigs. Returning to the sacristy, I arranged the flowers and lugged the heavy brass vases out to the altar, barely genuflecting. Rush, rush, rush!

On Holy Thursday, members of the novitiate took turns on adoration at the Dominican monastery next door where the Blessed Sacrament was exposed in the gold monstrance. Edna and I had signed up for five o'clock. Thirty minutes left. I was a mess and wanted time to wash my face and comb my hair before I went on adoration.

"Sister, you shouldn't be humming in the sacristy. The sisters are in the chapel trying to pray."

I turned and stared at Mother Patricia.

"I'm sorry, Mother. I didn't know I was humming."

"That's all right." But she didn't leave. "Did you fix the flowers in chapel?"

"Yes, Mother."

"They're beautiful, so natural, they're like something I'd come across in the woods." She paused. "But I'm afraid they're inappropriate. The solemnity of the ceremonies calls for formal arrangements. Take out the daffodils and vinca and put them in front of St. Anthony. Sister James will be pleased. It won't take too long to rearrange the lilies." She smiled and left.

Well, there goes my clean face, and I lugged the heavy brass containers back into the sacristy and began my task. When I finished and had returned the solemn vases to the altar, I stood back and observed the chapel. What a difference from the makeshift, ill-ventilated old attic, which some of the sisters still treasured. It was cozy, they said, stuffed with memories. They could hear the 'Angelus' peal forth, a ceremony they loved, and their hearts were further distressed when they discovered that the bell would now be rung automatically by electricity.

But the new chapel! There were no pillars, no supports, only pure space. Polished rose marble stretched up to meet the ceiling, interrupted only by white alabaster squares in bas relief, the Stations of the Cross.

Familiar saints, most in habits, holding sheaves of lilies or open books, solemnly observed me from the eight huge stained glass windows that transformed all sharp, intruding light into a bright, soft glow. The pale green terrazzo floor flowed into the solid wooden stalls and pews, which were hewn from white oak, highly polished. Light bounced from window to wall to ceiling to floor to wood, glowing always glowing.

A choir included stalls on three levels and made it convenient to chant the Office. A huge, Byzantine-like mosaic of the Sacred Heart flung His arms across the dome over the altar. I had artistic reservations with that one but I concentrated on the welcomed luminescence and space.

Gone were the dusk, the dim corners that haunt old churches, the stately pillars, the darkened wood. Gone were the gloom, the feeling of hiding, of being swallowed up, of trying to grope ones way to the altar without tripping over something in the dark. Turning back towards the sacristy, I fussed over the last details, then grabbed my shawl and, as fast as propriety would allow, strode towards the front door where Edna stood waiting.

* * * * *

"She actually smiled and told me the flowers were nice, but I have to rearrange them to fit the season," I told Edna, folding up my shawl and tossing it over my hands like a muff. It was twilight and the early spring air blew both warm and chill; some cars had headlights on, a few men on their way home from work wore topcoats and fedoras, the evening paper clamped under their arms. Two young boys riding no-handed on their bikes sped by, yelling at each other as they passed.

"Edna, this is our first time out. I mean we're really OUT."

"Ummmmm."

"I know it's hardly a block from the front entrance of our convent to the front door of the monastery, but we're OUT." I stared up at the maroon buds on the dark maples. "Look, the trees are budded." But she didn't look.

"What's wrong with you, Edna? You don't seem happy. You never did tell me why you were crying the day we entered."

"You wouldn't understand."

"How do you know?"

"All right," she continued, staring straight ahead, "I envy you. You're perpetually happy. Don't you ever get the urge to tell someone to go to hell? Don't you miss your home, your friends? You skip around the convent like Shirley Temple. Do you love it here this much or is it all an act?"

"It's no act," and I began to bristle. "I am happy. I battled my way into this place, Edna. You know how my parents felt." She didn't say anything, just kept walking, so I continued. "I feel chosen to have a vocation, to be called. Things become clear when you fight for what you want. I can't fathom all the rules, so I'm trying to concentrate on the liturgy, important things."

Edna's eyes were cast down; her face entertained no expression at all. "Besides, I'm enthusiastic by nature. No matter what I do, I throw myself into it. It's part of being an artist." That was true, but I was worse lately. Maybe I'd better try to slow down a little. "I knew before I came what I couldn't have, what I was giving up. It was part of it. I mean, what are you going to do?"

"And it doesn't bother you?"

"No. It doesn't bother me. I went through it before I came."

"It bothers me," Edna admitted, shrugging and finally meeting my eyes. "It bothers a lot of people."

"I know. Last Saturday afternoon up in the trunk room, the one behind the old chapel? I found two canonicals sitting, looking at the roofs of their houses. One of them had been crying. Is that why you were crying on Entrance Day, because you miss home?"

"Not exactly."

"Are you going to leave?"

"I hope not."

"You're a puzzle," and as usual, our exchange was aborted as the monastery loomed before us. Would we ever in our whole life have time to finish a conversation?

"Later," Edna sighed, climbing the steps. We entered, blessed ourselves with holy water, walked straight up the middle aisle, our eyes demurely cast down, and relieved the two novices kneeling on the priedieus in front of the Blessed Sacrament. We were on Adoration for an hour.

The Dominican nuns were cloistered, their private chapel separated by a wall to wall screen. Vague outlines of two sisters were visible from our side, which was open to the public. They chanted the Divine Office and the old one had a scratchy voice, but on they went, oblivious to the crowds milling around the back. Voices from nowhere.

Everyone visited the monastery on Holy Thursday. Visiting churches was an old Catholic tradition, and on Palm Sunday, the priests would caution the parishioners not to make comparisons. Some churches were wealthier and more beautifully decorated than others, but the monastery excelled every year and the whole city knew it. There was never any parking. As Edna and I knelt before the altar, I could hear the rustling of feet behind us, admirers of the nuns, secret donors, muted voices of friends meeting unexpectedly. I heard the chapel rhythmically filling and emptying.

What was Edna thinking as she knelt there? What deep hidden yearnings were churning in her soul? What was her vocation like?

How did she pray if she were angry with God for calling her? Was her prayer life personal? Did they banter? Mysterious. Would I ever know her?

Our conversation had stunned me. Envy ME? She appeared to glide through life, but did she? She handled the convent agendas effortlessly but what about that dark Irish cynicism that rose occasionally to the surface? Passionate disdain for things I was trying desperately to accept.

I concentrated on the Blessed Sacrament, exposed in the monstrance, a big gold sunburst on an ornate pedestal, banked by lilies and white chrysanthemums, completely covering the altar and the reredos behind it. Earthen pots and brass vases stood on high tables and wire stands, and finally, flooded the floor, cascading right down to the altar step. The scent was intoxicating. I stared at the Blessed Sacrament. What are You thinking? What do You see in us? Will they keep me and will Edna stay? What will we be like when we're the old sisters at the Motherhouse? Will I be calm and 'look down at the world from a great height' like St. Teresa of Avila? Can I be a mystic like St. John of the Cross?

Blessing myself, I sat down in the seat. We'd been working long hours, and I was tired. I closed my eyes, just to rest them, feeling dizzy from the inebriating scents rising from the blankets of flowers.

I felt myself ascending above the group of adorers, my arms lifted like St. Teresa, blessing the astounded crowds, carrying a sheaf of lilies, smiling serenely, cradling my lilies, my beautiful lilies, with trailing vinca…my, my GEESE…

DEAR GOD!

They're quacking geese… they're flying…

They're flying away…

I'm falling…

I'm…

A hand on my shoulder pressed down and Rebecca's soft voice whispered, "Sister, you're relieved. You may go now." Was I snoring? Oh, dear God! Snoring? In the Dominican chapel?

Edna and I genuflected sedately. I was ready to burst, could barely wait until we were outside, to tell her.

"Edna, you wouldn't believe my dream!" I stopped short, looking into the familiar face of a tall, young man who had taken the steps of the monastery by twos and now stood grinning before me.

"Jimmy? Jimmy O'Neill! I'm not supposed to talk to you," I stammered. A blush crept up my face, a face I hadn't washed since breakfast. O God! I feel like such a fool, standing here in this silly outfit, with white cuffs, and a short limp veil, a cross between Little Orphan Annie and Cinderella. I'd lost my edge. Where was Lady Mary when I needed her? I darted a pleading look at Edna, who seemed amused no end. No help from her. I'll kill her when I get back to the convent.

"Mrs. Donovan saw you and called me at work. I just thought I'd drop by, see how you were doing. How ARE you doing?" That irrepressible grin, those long thin hands, that sandy hair, still with a mind of its own. I recovered whatever dignity my appearance would allow. "Jimmy, you remember Edna McMahon?" She bowed her head a bit towards him.

"Sister." Damn! Look at the two of them! They're in cahoots! Loving every bit of it. I smiled and through clenched teeth, I said, "I'd like to kick you right in the shins, Jimmy O'Neill. They'll probably send me home for this one. Why don't you come on visiting Sunday, with everybody else?" Why did I say that? I had hurt him. Would I ever stop hurting him? His lips kept smiling, even though his eyes didn't.

"The convent doesn't approve of gentlemen callers." He shifted his weight onto his other foot. "I don't want to get you into trouble. Just wanted to know how you were." He took my hand and shook it. "Good luck, Mary." Before I could say a word, he turned, and walked down the stairs as if he had boots on, stamping down the stairs.

"Damn, damn, damn, Edna, damn, damn, damn."

"Hmmmmmmm."

"Oh, Shut up."

She looked at me in mock solemnity, hand over heart, blue eyes dancing, serious expression. "Have I said anything? Answer me that. Have I said anything?"

"Oh, piffle," I huffed, starting to smile. "No."

"Just glad to know at least you're alive." Edna slowed down; we were barely strolling down New Scotland Avenue. "Well," she began, "I know who Jimmy is but what's he to you?" Everybody knew everybody in Albany, and their grandparents and what their father did for a living. I told her about Jimmy, how close we had been as kids, then, as teenagers, too close, and Jimmy's plans and my plans and how I wanted to be friends, just friends, and how I broke up with him in my junior year, knowing I was going into the convent, how he didn't like it, but how I was possessed by my vocation.

* * * * *

After dinner, Bryand and I had set up the chapel and sacristy, preparing the altar for the total devastation of Good Friday. I crept into the visitor's lav and looked at myself in the mirror. I took off the veil and shook my limp brown hair, which waved a bit where I set my pin curls, then fell in tendrils around my face, a heart shaped face. I stared at a pointed chin, thin lips. My green eyes, speckled with gold, alert and probing, stared back at me.

Who are you? I asked the mirror. You're soaring in the clouds one minute, dreaming about mystical experiences, and acting like a teenage jerk the next, stammering and blushing, wishing you had on a Chanel suit and clean makeup. Edna doesn't care how she looks and Rebecca and Bryand could dress in burlap and not care either, but you care. Why? You thought you were doing great, so great. Well you have some work to do, Lady Mary, some real heavy work. So you'd better get cracking and throw yourself into a spiritual life or you're not long for the world you've chosen.

CHAPTER FIFTEEN

There was nothing good about Good Friday. By ten o'clock that morning, Bryand and I stood facing Reverend Mother in her office as she sat behind her huge oak desk, facing Mother Patricia, barely seated in a straight backed chair and 'Dead Eye', looming behind the two of them, glaring at us unrelentingly. It was a long story. Me and my damn light bulb, I thought. Me and my damn light bulb! The light over the altar had burned out, we couldn't find Mr. Shoultz and what was so hard about changing a light bulb anyway? I had begged Bryand, "Let's replace it." It seemed simple enough and I wanted everything perfect for Easter.

We had climbed the ladder buried in the sacristy closet, then walked across the catwalk above the ceiling. Bryand figured she could lean over and unscrew the bulb but it was beyond reach. Jockeying for a better spot, she slipped and her entire leg, right up to her garters, plunged through the flimsy acoustic tiles, splitting two of them and sending another four crashing to the sanctuary floor below.

"Oh, God, Bryand!" A horror swept over me!

But Bryand was nimble. She grabbed the steel girder, yanked her leg back through the ceiling, and rolled over on her back where she now lay, on the wide steel bar, gasping for breath. She did it in one motion, one fluid motion. "I'm all right, I'm all right," she panted. "Saved by my petticoat and skirts. Close, that was close." After those few seconds of frantic scrambling and finally, safety, my knees felt wobbly, so I joined her on the girders, and we lay there on our backs, not moving, breathing heavily, gradually becoming aware of the commotion below. Shouting, running, everyone giving orders. Sister James was wailing something about "The Russians are coming! It's war. It's war."

Oh! God! She was senile already! From our perch on the wide steel beams, we spotted Annunciation through the hole, hurriedly shuffling her way up from the back pew, swooping up James and leading her out the side door, cooing and patting her all the way. With her free hand, she waved us down, mouthing the words, "Careful, careful," until she disappeared out the door with the raving Sister James. One of the novices wheeled out poor Rose right behind her. Edna appeared from nowhere, looked up at us, grimaced, drew her right index finger quickly across her throat, pointed to us and then disappeared, following Annunciation.

"Are you okay?"

"Are you?" Before we descended, we planned our moves. Bryand knew her position in the novitiate so things wouldn't be too bad. "Don't open your mouth. No matter what. Look contrite but *don't* open your mouth."

I don't think our feet were off the ladder and on the sacristy floor before we heard Edna's voice. "The R.M. wants to see you in her office." Was it pity, or sheer wonder in her voice? So here we were, facing the three discreets. We were not dead, we were not maimed, but there was an hysterical old sister downstairs, a huge hole in the ceiling of the new chapel and the bishop was coming tomorrow to bless everything.

Oh, God!

Reverend Mother finally spoke.

"You both could have been killed! From the ceiling to the floor of the chapel is a three-story drop. You could have been killed! Whatever possessed you, especially you, Sister Bryand? Couldn't you have waited for Mr. Shoultz? I never would have expected such poor judgment from YOU." Which didn't say much for me! She was partly exasperated, mostly relieved. We just stood there, silent.

Bryand had warned me, "Keep still and let me handle it. It was *my* leg that went through the ceiling, not yours. Besides, you let people spout, and say nothing. People won't listen until they're finished with what they have to say."

"Do you two realize that Sister James nearly had a heart attack?"

We realized it. I would hear James in my sleep, wailing in the chapel as I frantically lurched at Bryand. The silence lengthened and Bryand must have concluded that Reverend Mother was finished because she began. "Reverend Mother, what we did was inexcusable. We exercised poor judgment. We're sorry we've caused everyone such concern. I'm sure nothing like this will ever happen again." She stared at Reverend Mother matter-of-factly, as if that would do it, and it DID. Reverend Mother mumbled something and told me I was excused, but I lingered outside her door, waiting for Bryand. I could hear them talking. Better not get caught eavesdropping, I thought. I'll wait for Bryand downstairs, and I took the back stairs to the sacristy. I opened and closed drawers, aimlessly. Where was she? I'd better clean up this mess. Where was Edna?

Someone was moving. I stared out of the sacristy towards the altar and then up towards the ceiling. Just look at the ceiling! Four squares were gone and two more, which were hanging by threads suddenly dropped to the floor. I heard Mr. Shoultz and the contractor talking and laughing softly on their way across the catwalk.

"Well, little lady," Mr. Shoultz said after descending the hidden ladder, "that will teach you to change light bulbs without me." He chuckled a bit at my discomfort, then added, "We can have it fixed for the bishop tomorrow."

"You're going to fix it by tomorrow? Oh, thank you," and the two of them ambled off to find some extra acoustic tiles.

Going to noon prayers was a horror. A few titters accompanied my entrance into chapel. I was so embarrassed kneeling under the gazes of the gaping black hole above and those of the sisters below. They could hide behind protruding veils, but my face was totally visible.

In the refectory, since it was Good Friday, all the chairs had been pushed to the wall and the sisters ate their meager meal standing at the long tables. Most sisters performed public penance, lying prostrate on the floor or kneeling with arms extended as Sister Timothy stood at the lectern and read the Passion. I wished I could have prostrated myself, or dug a hole under the linoleum and crawled in. Would the meal ever be over?

* * * * *

I had volunteered to wash the windows on the third floor corridor on Good Friday afternoon and now was I thankful. It was a perfect escape. After the interminable lunch, I filled a galvanized pail with hot water and vinegar and shoved a bundle of newspapers under the other arm. Washing the inside wasn't bad but they didn't look clean. The dirty outside canceled the shiny inside. I opened the window and perched myself on the sill, anchoring my feet under the hot water pipes below. Pinning the top pane tightly across my lap, I washed away. What a gorgeous day! How I loved the spring. I had finished six of them when I felt someone grab my legs and pull open the window. "Get in here, you fool! What *is* the matter with you? Are you bent on getting yourself killed?" Edna hissed.

"I'm perfectly safe," I sputtered indignantly as I climbed back inside. "The window's clamped on me, on my legs. How do you *expect* me to wash windows? I can't reach up that far from in here."

"Reverend Mother took a call from the hospital. The old biddies on the fifth floor have been watching you hanging out the window and they alerted the floor nurse. R.M. sent me to bring you in." She stared at me and sighed.

"Look, go to chapel, will you and pray to St. Jude. It's nearly three o'clock, time for the Stations. I'll put all this away." She folded up the papers, picked up the bucket and stomped down the corridor towards the hopper in the lav.

"Does, does Reverend Mother want to see me?" I called after her.

"No, she's had enough of you for one day, but 'Dead Eye' is on her way over from the hospital. If you move fast enough, you'll be safe. Claim sanctuary."

"Was she the one who called?"

"She was the one. Hurry."

But I wasn't fast enough. Dead Eye was waiting for me outside the last music parlor.

"Sister, step in here, please." Here it comes, I thought. She folded her light shawl, draping it slowly over the mahogany piano bench. Pulling herself up to her full height, she inserted her hands into her big sleeves and stared at me. First disadvantage. I had no big sleeves and nowhere to put my hands. Finally, I cupped them loosely in front of me, assumed a modified position, a la ballet, and raised my eyes to meet hers. Here it comes, Lady Mary. Gather your forces.

"I find your behavior incomprehensible. Although you were not responsible for this morning's mishap, I was not at all surprised that you were present, and most likely influenced Sister Bryand whose demeanor until this incident has been above reproach." I didn't flinch. That's a laugh, I thought. Influencing Bryand.

"I realize that Reverend Mother and Mother Patricia have already spoken to you, but I have my own complaints." She seemed to be puffing up before my very eyes, like some wild animal trying to impress its prey.

"I question your common sense. Sitting outside on a windowsill, washing windows in full view of St. Peter's! You made a public spectacle of yourself!" I said nothing. No questions asked. No answers given. But I'd like to know how I could clean windows without washing the outside.

"You were also seen yesterday afternoon waving to children across the street from the convent. A public street! Aren't there enough gardens in back of the Motherhouse for you?" Rhetorical question. No answer. Does this woman head up the OSS?

Her eyes narrowed. She was getting nowhere and I could sense the final blow. "And I shall ask Mother Patricia to excuse you from further visits outside the convent as talking to young men while dawdling on the steps of the monastery is totally out of order." That did it.

"I beg your pardon, Mother, but it would have been extremely rude of me to ignore an old friend. Mother McAuley said we should above all be ladies. I did not instigate the conversation and I did not prolong it. I can not hold myself responsible because I met 'a young man' on the steps, or for anything else that other people do, either." I didn't mind taking blame for what I had done (and I thought I had handled it well) but I wasn't about to take on responsibility for Jimmy and the whole world. I continued looking right into her eyes. I knew she was furious but I didn't care. If she wanted me out, then she could send me, but I wouldn't be scared off.

"Be careful, young lady," she sniffed, "the rules in this community are for all of us," and she swept out, forgetting her shawl and closing the door behind her.

Whew! I collapsed on the chair and sat for a few minutes. Rules, rules, rules. But where are the rules about changing light bulbs and washing windows and speaking to people who speak to you, especially old friends? The door squeaked open and Bryand stuck her head in, then closed it quickly behind her.

"Are you all right? She's been gunning for you since the day you entered. Oh, no, don't cry."

"I'm just so mad and so nervous," I sniffed into my hanky. "Nothing is going right. Here you are comforting me and you're the one nearly killed."

"Well, don't get your knickers in a knot. I'm fine. You're tired and hungry, but tomorrow's another day. Look, I'll steal a hot cross bun out of the refectory for you and put it on your press tonight. Tomorrow's a busy day. You look tired and pale and you'll faint if you don't eat." I honked, loudly.

Bryand sank down in front of me, sitting on her heels. "How can you blow into that handkerchief with all those beautiful white flowers on it?"

I looked at it. "My Mom embroidered it. Pretty, isn't it?"

"And that's another thing. You haven't seen your family and you're probably lonesome, and you're worried your father won't come, but he'll come. You'll see them all Sunday. Come on, come on." She stood quickly and pulled me to my feet. "I'll lay the vestments and tidy up the sacristy. You don't look too bad but go wash your face and go to chapel. You can make it before the crowd gathers at three o'clock."

"You're a pal."

The entire convent and its occupants were submerged in deep silence during the holy hours. I held up my head, cast down my eyes and hurried into chapel and into my stall. Mr. Shoultz and the contractor had replaced the tiles and the light. Everything finally perfect. But not me. Far from it.

Bryand always spotlighted the practical. "You're hungry, you're tired, you're lonesome." Here's the problem. Let's solve it. If it were only that simple. I usually did what seemed sensible to me, though at times, it might have seemed outrageous to others. I didn't work at it; that's what I was. However, being unpredictable, not fitting into a box, made people nervous. I *used* to think, "Too bad about you. If you don't like it, lump it. What's it to me?" Now, I'd have to learn to move through everyone else's mind. No more spontaneity. I sighed. How could I guess what other people wanted from me? Each person has a different frame of reference. Impossible. But it was becoming clear that if I wanted to stay, I would have to do the impossible. Other sisters *became* nuns. I'd have to settle for *acting* like one. Hello Lady Mary, good-bye Playing- in-the-Fields. I could hear doors slamming, feel my determination rising.

I could do this. I know God wants me here. I can do anything.

* * * * *

That night, true to her word, Bryand left me a fresh hot cross bun on my press, which I ate eagerly. Standing next to the window, I read the note by moonlight.

"Never think at night, In Christ, Sister Bryand." It is a tenet I have tried to practice to this day, but as I mulled it over, I thought, "Never think at all" would have been more like it.

CHAPTER SIXTEEN

Holy Saturday unfolded bright and crisp and promising, and pushed Friday right out of my mind. By noontime, the bishop had finished blessing the sparkling rooms and neat closets; he bestowed benedictions upon the walk-in fridge, the huge black range, the adjoining dining room...downstairs: the tubular wooden washing machines, the mangles, the individual ironing boards, and after returning to chapel and calling upon God's watchful eyes and tender mercies, he sprinkled the sisters with holy water and departed.

A spirit of joy and anticipation filled all the corners of the Motherhouse. On Easter Sunday, we not only celebrated the Resurrection of Christ, the primary feast of the Church, but also the congregating of the community for its annual retreat. The sisters assigned were due in tomorrow night. Some of the novices volunteered for kitchen duty, the same old gang, the ones who always made time for others and odd unexpected jobs: Bryand, Timmy and Rebecca, second year novices in charge; Mercy and her friends; Helen, Edna and I. Mercy's group was on vegetable detail. Helen, Edna and I were cleaning seventy-six chickens and finally had a block of time together.

The light pouring through huge sparkling windows, some opened to the fresh air, brightened the industrial-type kitchen with its high ceilings, white linoleum floors and white tiled walls. Mammoth pots and pans hung from a sturdy rack above the oversized stainless steel worktable in the center. Three sets of deep, double sinks and stainless drain boards hugged the inside walls. Next to the immense mixer, a large wooden block encased the razor sharp knives. All the industrial machines on the tiled counters had directions printed on brass plates tacked to them. DO NOT CLEAN WHILE PLUGGED IN, etc.

Except for the prominent crucifix nailed to the pantry wall, it could have been a kitchen in a good hotel or small hospital.

Timmy had pulled up a four-legged stool next to Lazarus, the huge potato-peeling machine, which groaned away in the corner near the pantry. Someone had forgotten to rinse it out once and after three days, it stank. It wasn't supposed to devour the potatoes, just the skins so Timmy observed it with sporadic interest, checking it now and again between reading a chapter from *The Imitation of Christ.*

Mercy and her crew drew salad detail, and they stood, sniffing and weeping over their onions. Rebecca helped out. Bryand was cutting five-pound blocks of cheese on the slicer, which whirred away, making our private conversation possible.

The chickens were all ours.

Helen cut through the breastbone, and Edna and I scraped them clean, relieving them of their innards, scraping every rib. Someone started a hymn now and then or the group harmonized to a sweet ballad or cracked jokes, but we three, crowded into a corner by the sink under the windows, discussed the nature of the Almighty while we gutted fowl.

Helen, Edna and I had a little community going. All our lights, inspirations, interpretations of Scripture, spiritual reading, group instructions or anything else that caught our fancy we turned over and around and inside out, approaching religious life from every possible angle. Most of the novices found our conversations uninteresting, so the three of us met when we could, and tried not to be exclusive. It was my idea. They were flowing along on their own but the quiet currents that carried them were sandpaper to me. I needed their insights now more than ever in view of yesterday's fiasco. How did they view the Rule and how could they accept parts of it without question? Or did they ignore the implications of it? What was really going on inside their heads and could I make it go on in mine? Today, we weren't going to indulge in personal conversation. We had decided to discuss the Resurrection, and it was my turn.

"I think God has evolved," I ventured, beginning the conversation. Edna closed her eyes, preparing her mind for my onslaught.

"I do, and I think I'm right," I continued. Helen and Edna were too tired to argue or protest because preparation for retreat, cleaning, moving cots and mattresses from the trunk room, making over eighty beds, had left all of us weary.

"Pray, continue," Edna prodded. "This I want to hear."

"I'm serious."

"You're always serious, lately," Helen drawled, rolling her huge brown eyes, clipping off the chicken wings and dropping them into a big stockpot. "I think you're losing your sense of humor."

"Helen, what could be funny about the Resurrection?" I prepared my thoughts and started again. "All right, think about it. First, there was just God, forever and ever, and maybe He was lonely. He had a deep desire to share His Love so He created the angels, spirits like Himself, all the choirs of angels, and it didn't work."

I waited and Edna finally said, "Lucifer and his pals wanted to be God."

"Right. So God turned them out of heaven into hell, fire, and damnation. No forgiveness, no mercy, no nothing." I paused dramatically.

"Watch that cleaver, Helen," Edna commented, "or there'll be more than chicken bones in that pot." She turned back to me. "Go on."

"Okay, get the picture. There were all these spirits. He made them once and that was it. There would never be any more. No angel families, no baby angels. It was static. No more."

"I think I see where you're going with this. Go on." Helen listened and kept whacking away.

"So maybe He was bored, or wanted something else to do. So He thought up another kind of creation, the world and everything in it. I mean, it was a new dimension, things you could feel, and sense." I was excited and talked faster. "The stars, the weather, things that bloomed and grew, things that you held in your hand, animals...crickets, and finally, us," I gestured. "Now this new batch propagated its own. There would be more of them, new ones and God could keep creating souls, over and over, and they would keep doing different things over and over and they had their free will, so God never knew what was going to happen next and it was interesting. Oh! You know what I mean. He'd never be bored again!"

"I think He came at it from a different perspective," Edna commented.

"Whatever, but that's difference number one. And difference number two is that when they fouled up," and I laughed, holding up the chicken, "'fowled' up, get it?" Not a smile from either of them. "When they fouled up," I continued, He didn't dispatch them to hell. Whoosh, away with you. He had tried a second time, and man, like the angels, failed Him. But this time, He didn't damn them to hell. He gave them a second chance."

"So?"

"But don't you see the differences? God's actions changed. Compare the angels to man. He sent the angels to hell! He didn't become an angel and try to redeem them." I was talking louder than I should, and Bryand looked up quickly, and sensing nothing more serious than one of our conversations, returned to her block of cheese. I lowered my voice. "And then there's man and God's dealings with man. Compare the Old Testament to the New! An eye for an eye, a tooth for a tooth. "After Christ's coming, it's mercy, forgiveness. God treats the human race like a bad little boy who He takes on his knee and pets...like a grandfather who says, 'There, there'."

"All this is leading up to the Resurrection, isn't it?"

"Yes."

"What you're saying is that He's getting soft?" Edna laughed.

"What I'm saying is that He has created a being that He loves especially, one He won't give up hope on, I mean, think of the mystery of God becoming man and the Crucifixion! Think about it!" I stopped working and caught their eyes with mine. "We don't make it real enough. Christ's total devastation and betrayal! Suppose some goons came crashing in here now and grabbed one of us. And the other two didn't raise a finger to help, and said, 'Take her, she's nothing to us. We don't even know her.' I know I'd be devastated, hurt to the quick. You are my friends. I rely on you."

"And the pain, the physical pain...those were real nails..." a shiver ran through me and I shuddered. Edna interrupted me.

"The mystical part of the whole thing is beyond my comprehension. God becoming man, becoming a creature that He made, and then, His sacrifice " Helen stopped pounding and the three of us, without any embarrassment at all, attempted to grasp that great mystery. I broke the silence.

"But He *did* and that's it, you see. He did it because we mean that much to Him. It's like the human race has *charmed* Him, that He won't let us go, that He can't keep out of our business. That He has a yearning to be loved and appreciated as much as we do! I, I can't say it any better."

"You're so intense these days. Don't you ever think about things like good mashed potatoes or how to roast a duck or what it's going to be like teaching a class of live first graders?"

"Not lately. I've never had a glimmer of what my religion was about until this Easter, not really, of this involvement of God in our lives. Whether it's the Psalms or daily Mass or the trappings they're so attached to around here, or Father Phelan and his fervor or chanting the Office, I don't know, but I think God has evolved and He wants us and with these few thousand words, I rest my case."

"God is so real to you...the way you talk about Him. I envy you." That was the second time in a few days Edna had said that.

"You know how excited I get about everything," and I tried to make light of it. I couldn't imagine myself knowing more than Edna.

"Are you going to be the first one in the chapel tomorrow? Are you going to be Mary Magdalene?" Edna asked.

"Oh! Don't make fun, it's innocent enough." I attacked the chicken backs with gusto, and then looked up at her. "Don't make fun of me, Edna. I need all the help I can get. Superstitious or no." And I thought of Lady Mary swallowing me up and robbing me of all my good parts. Edna continued, talking to no one in particular.

"Faith. It's your faith. Incomprehensible. Some claim they're born with it, that it costs them nothing. Others say faith insults their intelligence and that believing would cost them everything. And then there are those who *want* to believe, who really want to, but they can't lie to themselves." She was slapping the chicken breasts ferociously, tearing off the fat under the skin, and thrusting the pieces under the cold running water, splashing herself and Helen and me. I sensed her angry mood and as I glanced up, Helen turned off the water and looked straight at Edna.

"Maybe wanting is enough. Just wanting. God understands our weaknesses." She was staring hard at Edna. Then, she changed the subject, and talked about the monastery, wondering what the life was like; our conversation drifted to convent concerns, who would be on retreat, who might ask permission to see us. I let my mind wander, reliving the conversation. Faith? I was the one born with it. I knew I was. I felt this Easter had bestowed on me a glimmer of a light. I felt I was a child who sat on God's lap, in all that safety, with all that nonchalance, leaning back the way a baby will, resting up against a warm body, one pudgy hand resting on a knee. I sat on His lap, staring out at the world as if I owned it, as if it could do me no harm because I knew He protected me.

CHAPTER SEVENTEEN

" *A* *nd in the end of the Sabbath, when it began to dawn towards the first day of the week, came Mary Magdalene and the other Mary, to see the sepulchre.* "

I was going to be the first one in chapel Easter morning if I had to sleep in my clothes. Me and Mary Magdalene.

Rebecca's turn to give the call. Her cell adjoined mine. I counted on hearing her rustling around just before six.

The minute she knocked on my door and announced, "Benedicamus Domino," I chirped back, "Deo Gratias," dressed as quickly as I could and galloped down to the lav. Wouldn't you know I'd forget my comb? I can always refix my hair after breakfast. Slam, bam, bam, bam. Whoops! Should have held on to that door.

"And behold there was a great earthquake. For an angel of the Lord descended from heaven, and coming, rolled back the stone, and sat upon it. And his countenance was as lightning, and his raiment as snow. And for fear of him, the guards were struck with terror, and became as dead men."

I took the back stairs to chapel. Terrific! No lights. Skidding into the sacristy, I flicked the switch, and the overheads came on.

"And the angel answering, said to the women: Fear not you for I know that you seek Jesus who was crucified. He is not here, for HE IS RISEN, as he said. Come, and see the place where the Lord was laid."

Yes! Made it! I barely genuflected and when I turned to climb the step, to my astonishment I saw Edna already kneeling in her stall.

EDNA!!!!????

CHAPTER EIGHTEEN

Visiting Sunday was over. My friends couldn't believe I had lasted. My sisters had looked stunning in their colorful new suits: Pat in fuchsia with a lime print scarf and Katie in gray, rose and navy. Mom held my hand the whole two hours.

Dad really came and brought me a giant Easter basket and a big box of Fannie Farmer candy, which he insisted I open. Two pieces were missing, notes left in the wrappers. "You know how much we love caramels. Enjoy the rest. Love, Pat and Katie." We laughed a lot. I was so glad to see them. It was four o'clock before we knew it.

The retreatants had begun pouring into the Motherhouse in the early part of the afternoon. We couldn't talk to them and I was avoiding trouble at all costs, so Helen and I escaped the bustle by walking down to the statue of Our Lady.

"Helen, I couldn't believe Edna was in chapel this morning. Was she serious? She only laughs when I ask her."

"How well do you know her, her family, her life before here?"

"She doesn't say much about it. I feel I know her, maybe because she knows me."

"Her mother died when she was five. Her father never got over it. In the end, he drank too much." Helen shivered a bit in the cool breeze. The sun was setting and she had left the cloister without her shawl. "You know Monsignor Fenner?"

"Umm, chancellor of the diocese, right?"

"Well," Helen continued, "Monsignor and Edna's father were the terrors of St. Patrick's Grade School when they were young, inseparable, and both sweet on her mother. Her father had to leave school after eighth grade and worked at the roundhouse in North Albany, eventually worked his way into management, and HE got the girl.

"Monsignor Fenner became a priest but the three of them remained close. When Monsignor was stationed in the North end, he ate every Sunday dinner at Edna's, played cards on Saturday nights.

When her mother died of cancer, he practically moved in. Edna's father was devastated, devoured by grief. Monsignor wanted to do something for the family so he sent all the children to private school, hoping someone would pay attention to them there.

"I don't think Edna ever got over her mother's death, but she learned to live with it, the sorrow and loss."

"But, Helen, that was so long ago. Her mother died years ago. How could Edna remember her?"

"Death is no fun ever, but at age five, it's indelible. Children blame God." She hugged herself with her arms, hidden in her big sleeves. "Edna turned wary, always expecting someone to push her down a pair of stairs."

"How do you know all this? Did she tell you?" Why wouldn't she have told me? I tell her everything.

"My mother grew up with them and I made the connection when I heard Edna was entering. The way she feels about her life is my own idea." Helen stopped strolling and looked at me. "Mary, not everyone is like you. Not everyone grew up the way you did, has your outlook. You haven't seen tragedy, poverty, known serious interruptions. Your family loves you. You're smart. Life has gone your way."

I wanted to sputter but stopped. What could I say?

"Did it occur to you that Edna went to chapel early this morning for the same reason you did? She wanted that special grace, even though she barely believes it exists! She's searching. She doesn't know what she's doing here. Her spiritual life isn't clear like yours. You're like a glass of seltzer with sun shining through it. Most of us swim in muddy waters where God is concerned. Wake up! She doesn't have your faith."

"Why do *you* think she's here?"

"Why is anyone here? As many reasons as there are sisters. Some are here because there's no place else to go. Some, because they're children. Most nuns are here because they seek a life of service or they want God involved in their lives in some special way."

"Is she here for God? Are you?"

"Of course." We began walking again.

"It's not fair, Helen, that I can't see things the way you do."

"Don't feel bad. I don't see the way you do, either." As we continued strolling down the muddy path, I thought, well, she's right. Our outlooks are different. I wasn't maimed, marred, or suspicious of happiness but what could I do about it? What did people want from me? Sarcasm, dour, jaded views? I knew through experience that I'd be easier to take that way. How dare I be sunny? Why did everyone resent my being an optimist?

Did I have to see black to join the human race? Even as a child, I felt resentment from adults who had recently crawled out of the Depression. "We'll squash this one. She's too happy." Let the gloomies sit in puddles, I thought, and danced away. But here, in the convent, there was nowhere to dance to except to Helen and Edna. They might laugh at my antics, but they respected the serious conclusions I drew.

"Helen, if we're going to understand everything clearly, let's join forces, become a real community, the three of us. After Edna's and my Reception, we'll have the same Instructions and classes. We'll see more of each other." I paused. "You do think we'll be received, don't you?" Helen didn't pause.

"Yes, and in the new chapel, too." We walked in silence a few steps. "Do you know why it hasn't been formally dedicated yet?" Helen asked. "In deference to Edna. Monsignor Fenner is Chancellor and has the power to dedicate the chapel and bless the altar. He could do it tomorrow if he wanted to. But Edna is his protégé, and he wants the bishop to preside over a big ceremony for her He talked him into it. It will be one big day of celebration." Helen turned and looked at me. "And he told her what he was doing."

"She's never said a word to me!"

"She had no intention of telling me either. It slipped out and she swore me to secrecy."

"Who else knows? R.M.? Mother Patricia? 'Dead Eye'?"

"The three of us. That's all."

"Well, I'll be." We had reached the statue of Our Lady, tucked far back on the grounds near the fence. She smiled down on us, arms outstretched, roses under her feet. We turned and started back on the muddy path towards the Motherhouse.

"Helen, some of the outdated customs smudge the reason we're here. They're dusty, confusing. No wonder Edna can't find help with her spiritual life. But if not here, where?"

"You don't understand. Place means nothing. People search for God everywhere and she chose here. She's learned to live with it. She doesn't like it but that's the way it is. Not everything can be fixed. She's resigned."

"To what?"

"To the way she looks at life."

"She's too young for that."

"Edna hasn't been young in years. I don't know if she were ever young." The professed sisters were standing in groups on the cloister, chatting and laughing, greeting newcomers enthusiastically. Some were strolling around the circle near the cloister, involved in conversation, practically veilboard to veilboard. Helen and I stepped aside as two junior professed we didn't know brushed by us, smiling. What were they talking about, I wondered?

"We'll go in through the kitchen and avoid all that," Helen suggested. I pushed open the door and we stood at the bottom of the stairs in the mudroom, surrounded by a dozen empty wooden milk cases, savoring our last minutes of intimate conversation. She scraped her feet on the hemp mat. "Let's move inside before we catch our death."

I blurted out, "Helen, will dedication to trivia make me holy? Like the Little Flower? Will it work? Even if I don't see how?"

She didn't laugh. "If you don't believe it, it won't work. Right now it's all we have. But, it's not going to last, Mary. It can't." She paused a few minutes. "Our way of life as we live it is already gone. The war swept it away. There's nothing left but the shell and they're presenting it to us the same way it was presented to them. If you want to be a nun, though, this is it. For now, anyway."

"Well, I can think in the future but I can't live there. I'm here. I want to be holy, a saint. In a few months, I'll be a canonical novice and I'll have one year, ONE year to become a saint. After that, it'll be back to studies, then out teaching, into the real world."

"I thought a saint DID deal with the real world, just dealt with it differently from others."

"So did I."

"Well, I'm not escaping into the past. I intend to stay real."

"My staying real gets me into trouble."

"What are you going to do?" Helen squinted her eyes and looked at me hard.

"I don't know."

* * * * *

That evening, the Jesuit opened the retreat with one sentence. "You have only one life to live. Why not live it heroically?" I could buy that. A religious life was a serious life. Heroically was fine but, which way to go? On one hand, we had rules and regulations, silly obediences that took up everybody's time, like getting permission to throw out a pair of stockings that was worn to threads, darned to death and beyond hope.

On the other hand, we had Sister Bertrand scratching beneath the surface of myths about Mother McAuley, uncovering a saintly, practical social worker, a woman far ahead of her time, fettered by the prejudice of customs and the stubbornness and envy of a blind hierarchy. I looked at the altar, at the tabernacle. Elusive, aren't You, I thought.

The priest had finished his first conference and one by one, the sisters were drifting out, headed for bed. The great silence would extend over the whole week. I sat there and flipped through Guardini, to page 70, to a favorite section.

"Each one of us possesses a pattern of his being, the divine idea, in which the Creator contemplated him. It comprises not only the universal idea of human nature, but also everything besides, which constitutes this particular individual. Every individual is unique, and a unique variety of human nature. When this unique quality of a man's individual being is allowed to emerge, and determines all

existence and activities; when he lives from the centre of his own being, not, however, putting an artificial restraint upon himself, but naturally and as a matter of course, he is a free man."

That's it, I thought. That's what I'm after.

"He is free who lives in complete harmony with the divine idea of his personality, and who is what his Creator willed him to be. He has achieved a complete equilibrium, the effect of a tension but a resolved tension, a powerful yet gentle rhythm of life, a life at once rich and concentrated, full yet restrained."

Yes, yes! It didn't make sense to bury myself through obedience, to give someone else the keys to my kingdom. Listening to all those Nazis during the war crimes trials, "I was told to do it. I merely obeyed."

It made me sick.

I put away Guardini and turned to page 500 of Tanquerey, Mother Patricia's bible.

"Beginners apply themselves, first of all, to observe faithfully the Commandments of God and of the Church, and to conform to the orders of lawful superiors with diligence, punctuality, and in a supernatural spirit.

"More advanced souls carefully ponder the examples given by Jesus from the very first moment of His existence, when He pledged Himself to fulfill in all things the will of His Father, until the last instant of His life when He died a victim of obedience."

I wasn't so sure I bought that. I believed that Christ gave Himself up for Crucifixion because He loved us and we were worth something to Him, not just because God told Him to do it. I have doubts here, I thought.

"Perfect souls go even further. They submit their judgment to that of their superior, without even considering the reasons for his command. This is what is termed blind obedience, which places us in the hands of superiors 'after the manner of a staff, after the manner of a corpse.'

"We are to see God Himself, or Jesus Christ in the persons of our superiors, since they have no authority except from Him."

What about 'Dead Eye'? I guess if God wanted to run me around through her, it was His business. I raised my head and stared defiantly at the Blessed Sacrament. I could take it! But did I believe it?

How could I resolve this? My common sense told me that we must examine better ways that the times suggested. Yet, the Church said…

I had to wait until all the sisters had left chapel before I could turn off the lights and lock up. I began to peruse the other notes I had written during spiritual reading, ones scribbled on the back of the senior sisters' old envelopes and Christmas cards. I shuffled them into two piles: the first, the traditional path to holiness; the second, the more current path and the one I liked.

Deep down, I believed Tanquerey and the traditionalists were myopic. Their idea of perfection was self-centered and medieval, historically anchored to other times. The Victorian Era and its corsets and stiff brocades and strict class systems suffocated life and produced narcissists, autocrats and hypocrites.

The new doctors of the Church claimed that time had swallowed up Jesus' message. Gone, its simple luster, caught in the mire of bureaucracy, greed, the sound of hollow voices. I shifted in my seat. The chapel was nearly empty. One of the professed sisters was making the last few Stations of the Cross.

The Church had to face it. The old ways weren't working anymore. Before World War II, European Christians had worn their religion like Sunday clothes that had no further purpose; after Mass they hung their religion and its responsibilities in the closet until the next week. The Holocaust proved it. So-called Christian Europe had collapsed like a makeshift tent in a strong wind.

What the new theologians said made sense to me.

My sanctity, my spiritual life? I had just entered and would be in the novitiate for another two and a half years. And as Helen had said, the old ways were all we had right now. I knew I was a poor fit, but I could work on it. Nothing is impossible to God.

I would devour Tanquerey and tackle myself the way a sculptor attacks a piece of marble. Chip away at this fault, hack away at that one and prepare to end up a beautiful statue. I laughed at myself. A statue. A stiff unbending piece of stone. I'd seen some of them in religious life. Brrrrr.

I shuffled the papers into my notebook and snapped it shut. I had decided. After all, if the old ways got one where one was going, why not give them a try? I would plow through the Purgative Way, skip through the Illuminative Way, fly into the Contemplative Way! I would become selfless. I would destroy my vanity. I would mortify my body, my memory and imagination, my passions. (Passions weren't too much of a problem. Except for my temper, I didn't think I had many bad ones. And the good ones? Well, I'd box them up, that's all.)

I would discipline my mind and train my will. I would stare into the face of temptation and tell it to go to hell.

After Reception, I would kneel at Mother Patricia's feet and let her cut my hair. I would become another Rebecca and float around the convent and live in another world and stick to the rules like honey on bread.

I'd become the model novice, not move unless I found it in the Holy Rule. No more escapades, no second guessing the customs, no more common sense or spontaneity. No more changing light bulbs or washing windows, unless I could find it written somewhere. I would water the stick, recognize the will of God in the voice of my superiors, instead of just doing it because I had to. I would say, "They're right, they're right, even though I didn't believe it."

However, no way would I throw out Guardini. His time would come and I would be ready, even if I were seventy.

The last professed sister had gone to bed and the chapel was empty. I left my stall, genuflected at the altar and then knelt for a minute. "Look, I don't know if this is a good idea or not but if I don't do something, I'll be out on my ear. I want to be a saint, and if I'm on the wrong track, it's up to *You* to let me know."

I turned off all the lights, leaving the chapel in darkness, except for the dim but steady flicker of the sanctuary lamp.

CHAPTER NINETEEN

The novitiate and parts of my life seemed empty. Three weeks after Easter, Bryand, Timmy and Rebecca along with the rest of their set were professed and sent to various branch houses. Even though Helen, Edna and I saw each other, I still missed Bryand and all the others. However, between solving problems in trig and pondering dilemmas in moral theology, we didn't have much free time to pine. Our household chores doubled after the newly professed left, and spring soon flowed into summer. When the school year ended, the junior professed streamed back into the Motherhouse for college classes, and even though we couldn't speak to them, their very presence was exciting and welcome.

I was consumed by the Purgative Way, trying to become a saint. I walked slowly down the corridors and deferred to others at recreation, letting them talk, drawing them out, and threw myself into studying. No one could fault me for that. I sat still long enough to read poetry and wept over Chekov's short stories. My spontaneous self had flown away, and a stiff, dutiful person roosted in its place. The R.M. was grateful, 'Dead Eye' was suspicious and Mother Patricia was thoughtful; dramatic shifts in behavior among the young sisters in the novitiate alarmed her.

"Sister, are you feeling well?"

"Yes, Mother." I smiled brightly.

"Is anything wrong at home?"

"No, Mother." Same smile.

"Your sister Pat called yesterday. She needs a fitting with you for your bridal gown for Reception. How kind of her to make it for you."

"Yes, Mother. She's very generous." Same smile.

"Do all of you sew?" I could tell she was searching for someone she couldn't find.

"No, Mother, just Pat and I." Same smile.

"Yes, well, she'll be here tomorrow evening. You may see her in the first parlor, and please limit your visit to one hour. She should be finished by then."

"Thank you, Mother." I stood demurely, eyes cast down, as she walked away. Oh! boy! Pat, and a whole hour! I mustn't ruin it with any enthusiasm at all. Just keep using Rebecca's smile. Everything was fine, just fine. I walked slowly down the corridor, nearly tiptoeing, into the chapel.

* * * * *

"Mary, look at you! You're a rail! Don't they feed you in here?" I was standing in the first parlor on a ladder-back chair, without my habit; I wore a tee shirt, my black petticoat and no bra. Pat had slipped the dress over my head, and as beautiful as it was, it just hung there as if flung over a coat tree.

"You're a rail, a rail! What are your measurements...16, 16, 16?"

"Oh, c'mon, Pat."

"Don't 'c'mon' me."

"I weighed this much when I entered."

"I *don't* think so."

"Well, can't you take it in?"

"Get down off the chair. Get DOWN." I did.

"You're not going to wear this dress without a bra. I brought one and I padded it and you're going to wear it and don't argue with me. If you think I'm going to put in this kind of time and have you look like a ruler in a ruffle, you're crazy."

"Pat!"

"Pat, my eye! Just do it." I wriggled my arms out of the tee shirt one by one and pulled on the bra, struggling under the underwear.

The gown was exquisite, made of a sheer, printed organdy, lined with taffeta. The fitted bodice was set off by a pointed collar and tight sleeves, pointed at the wrist and decorated with six tiny covered buttons. The bouffant skirt had a slight train but the head piece was special. Pat had made a helmet, covered it with the tulle and added a short net veil. Even with no makeup and black stockings and oxfords poking out of my petticoat, I began to look promising.

"You're not going to look like a frump." Pat bustled about, making me stand on the chair, and then get down and parade around to be certain I could move gracefully. When she was satisfied, I slipped the dress over my head and as she repacked it into the box, I pulled on my habit.

"I gave Jimmy a ticket to your Reception. I'm sure they wouldn't let you send him one. It was extra. Dad isn't coming."

"Dad isn't coming?" I tried to hide my disappointment.

"He couldn't handle it. I wanted you to know." Oh, Dad, I thought. It's that bad, is it? My entering has caused such pain.

"What do you want me to say, Pat?"

"I want you to tell me you're happy here, that this is what you want." She was gesturing with her free hand.

"Pat, this is where I belong. You know how I feel about my vocation. I *belong* here."

"Are you happy here? Look at your fingernails. You'd better let them grow before Mom sees them. You have one month until Reception."

"How is she?"

"You know she'd never stop you from doing what you wanted, but she misses you. She mourns the years you'll never have together. She's resigned, Mary, but she doesn't have to like it."

"Pat, you're wounding me."

"Dad expects you to walk in the door any day."

"And Katie?"

"She cried all night the day you left, and kept the whole house awake."

"You're not making this any easier."

"Why should I? I'm your older sister. You've done crackpot things all your life. I want to make sure this isn't another one of your larks."

"Pat, these are pretty high stakes for a lark."

"Maybe so, but it never deterred you before."

"Well, I'll settle it for you, then. This is the life for me. I don't understand all of it or how it works, but I'm trying. I've made wonderful friends here and I feel inspired." How was I going to phrase this? "You were the devotional one, Pat. Mass and Communion everyday during Lent and Advent, Benediction every Friday night, the Rosary. I was never that way, and I'm still not. Whatever it is with me is different. God intrigues me and nothing else matters."

"Not even Jimmy and that big white house you two loved near Norman's Kill, and your thirteen children you named that night after you saw *Gone With The Wind*?"

"Nothing else matters."

"All right, I'll never bring it up again. But I had to know. Mom will rest easier. And if you don't want her to drag you out of here on your Reception Day, you'd better wear a touch of this lipstick." Pat dug through her purse and handed me a new tube of blush pink rose. "A touch on your cheeks, too. Don't look aghast. Just do it."

"All right." Pat and I hugged and then she left. She had such a great hug. I thought about Jimmy as I returned the parlor chairs to their resting places, drew up the heavy shades, straightened the antimacassars on the uninviting armchairs and rescued a stray pin that had eluded Pat.

You'll get over me, Jimmy, I thought. But in my heart, I didn't believe it. Jimmy and I went deeper than casual, because he was a romantic. He'd had a rotten life, dominated by a heartless, cruel father, and a silent, faceless mother who had given up on herself years ago. He loved my parents, my home, my disposition, the upbeat, the fun, our zany friends, but he grew old too soon. There was sorrow behind those kind, sensitive eyes, that subtle self-mockery.

I was his sunshine, and I loved him deeply in a way, but I didn't need him. And that made the difference.

I heard an "Uh-hum" behind me and Sister Bryand, looking so important in her black veil, gave me a small wave and a big wink. No talking. I grinned back, and she continued on her way to the chapel.

I must be crazy, I thought. Giving up all the people who love me to join ranks with friends I can't talk to and not-so friends who want to make me over.

This 'lark' had better be worth it.

CHAPTER TWENTY

On September 9, Monsignor Fenner delivered a celebration to end all celebrations. Our Reception day began early with the consecration of the altar and dedication of the new chapel. Finally! Every sister physically able to be there was there, along with the bishop, the monsignori and the brass of the diocese. The major superiors of neighboring religious orders, both male and female were invited, along with Reverend Mother's friends, the Brooklyn major superiors. The remainder of the chapel was filled with donors, civic bigwigs and relatives.

Festive food was the order of the day. The bishop and his group were served in the priest's dining room, the sisters ate in our refectory and all others were invited to a lavish luncheon at the hospital. Those who wished could return at three for Edna's and my Reception ceremony.

I've never seen anyone throw feasts the way the sisters did in those days. The artists met a month before to plan a theme, then descended upon the Motherhouse with baskets, and flowers and whatnots, in hours transforming the refectory into a fairyland. If it were fall, leaves, and cones and dried grasses did the trick. In winter? Boughs of green, shiny holly, and cascades of ribbons. For this celebration, the novices combed adjoining fields for Queen Anne's lace, plunked the stems in pails of water laced with blue food dye, coloring the blooms to a faint blue in honor of Our Lady. Every place setting held a white linen napkin, folded like a swan boat, carrying a fresh bouquet tied with silver ribbon.

Sister Consolata, the wild chef in charge, planned menus according to season using bits of leeks and shallots or celery roots, vegetables most of us had neither seen nor heard of. 'Connie', raised by two French aunts, simmered her sauces for hours with the correct wines she procured from some generous donor or wheedled out of a sympathetic superior.

Using special wooden paddles, the novices rolled butterballs and placed them in crushed ice for the hot fresh breads and rolls. Three of the senior professed sisters molded individual lemon gelatin salads flavored with juice and a touch of white wine vinegar, and spiced them with minced onion, diced celery leaves and shredded carrots. Served on a lettuce leaf and decorated with one tiny raw vegetable, and a stem of fresh parsley, each one was a work of art.

Dinners were usually simple but delicious...roasts lavishly garnished with oven-browned vegetables and steaming dark gravy. Lazarus grumbled day and night because there could never be enough mashed potatoes. Colorful side dishes of fruit preserves and yellow, orange and green vegetables enlivened both the table and the palate and made that bit of difference, gave the whole feast that special zing.

The 'fancy cooks' Connie summoned from various branch houses, prepared desserts. Cakes and cookies served with sherbet and drizzled with raspberry sauce were easiest. Each sister was in charge of something. We might not have money but we did have panache *and* Monsignor Fenner who contributed whatever resources the R.M. would allow. Before the lavish feast, we toasted God, the world and each other with cranberry juice and ginger ale served in stem glasses, topped with a dollop of sherbet, and a sprig of mint one of the novices had gathered, washed, sorted, flattened between layers of linen towels and chilled. In the end, it was a symphony, with Sister Consolata waving the baton.

Waldorf Astoria, eat your heart out.

The refectory was crowded so the novices make-shifted with stools and sat on inverted large pots in the kitchen. Tired, relieved and pretty dirty by then, all of us had to spruce up for our ceremony at three so we ate fast. At least we could leave the mess today. Monsignor had hired a clean-up crew from the hospital.

"How did he ever prevail?" I asked Edna. Monsignor had pressured the R.M. to hold both ceremonies the same day.

"He convinced her it made sense. Why disturb the bishop twice in one week? He presented it as the bishop's request." Edna nibbled languidly on a buttered roll. "But on one point, the R.M. wouldn't budge. She insisted the sisters, and not the clergy, eat in the refectory.

The party was for them; they were the ones who slaved to build the chapel, not the guests." She pointed her roll at me. "That's character." Out of nowhere, Sister Leonore, one of the sisters serving the bishop and his entourage, interrupted us, beckoning Edna and me into the storeroom, and then she shut the door.

"Compliments of the Monsignor," she said, and produced two glasses of red wine. "The clergy is drinking it with dinner, but Monsignor feels you two are the brides of the day." She disappeared, leaving Edna and me opened mouthed.

"Hey, this is great!"

"To us," and Edna lifted her glass.

"To us."

* * * * *

Our Reception ceremony was magnificent! Edna and I glowed: the excitement, the wine, the tube of blush pink rose. The sisters attending, despite the unseasonable September heat, donned their heavy white wool church cloaks, and formed the long procession wending its way into the chapel, which overflowed with flowers and light wafts of incense left from the morning's dedication. The novices preceded them in their long cloaks and bright white veils. We two brides walked directly in front of Reverend Mother and Mother Patricia, who along with the other two discreets, brought up the rear. The bishop, in an expansive mood after his food and drink, yielded the short sermon to Monsignor, who was prepared, delighted and kept it short.

After his talk, we approached the altar, Edna and I, escorted by Reverend Mother and Mother Patricia, our glowing candles in hand; we knelt at the feet of the bishop, while Sister Rita Mary softly played Schubert's 'Ave Maria'.

"My children, what do you request?"

"The blessing of God and the holy habit of religion."

"Do you do this of your own free will?"

"Yes, your Eminence."

"Reverend Mother, are these candidates acceptable?"

"Yes, your Eminence. They have met the obligations of the Holy Rule."

"As the elected Superior of this community, do you accept these candidates into the Religious Sisters of Mercy?"

"I do."

"Accept the holy habit of religion," the bishop intoned. By now I was so excited, I thought I would burst. He continued in Latin as Monsignor Fenner took the habits, folded in neat bundles and handed each one to a novice who approached, received them and then stood next to us. Edna and I exited out the side door towards the parlors, followed by the two novices and discreets. Voices from the choir swelled. 'Magnificat, anima mea Dominum'.

The six of us turned into the first music room, shut the door and off came the wedding dresses and on went our habits, the novices grabbing veils, dresses and silk stockings as fast as we could peel them off. The linens, fitted and pinned days before, hung like empty rag dolls on mop handles. I slipped mine on, sliding my hands up under my veil and tied the coif strings and Oh! God!

I'm a nun, a nun, with linens and big sleeves and everything. I'm a nun! It's worth it all.

We were ready, Edna and I, sneaking smiles at each other and kneeling at Reverend Mother's feet, the six of us barely able to squeeze into this position in the small parlor. Reverend Mother lay her hands on my shoulders she said, "You shall be known in religion as Sister Mary Irene," and to Edna, she said, "You shall be known in religion as Sister Mary Edna, as you have requested to take your mother's name."

Reverend Mother stared into my inquiring face. Irene? I had asked for Winifred, Thomas, Patricia Mary, Kathleen. Why Irene?

"I have named you, Irene," she said, simply, "because it means peace. Your patron saint will be St. Irenaeus, an early doctor of the Church, whose ideas are considered forever new."

That was it.

The rest of the ceremony floated by, dreamy sensations of the choir's inspired hymns, the Gregorian chant, and 'Veni, Sponsa

Christi'. As we reentered the back door of the chapel, I saw Pat's and Katie's elated faces, and my mother, ashen and weak, supported by her two daughters.

And Jimmy?

Jimmy looked worse than my mother.

I beamed and beamed and beamed. I couldn't do anything else! My insides were my outsides. We prostrated ourselves on the chapel floor, promising to love God above all others, and my heart swelled with the thought of it. "Magnificat, anima mea Dominum."

My soul doth magnify the Lord.

If I were to die at this moment, I thought I would float off in a bliss unknown to man.

We had an hour with our family and friends after the Reception and before we began our canonical year. I managed to shift emotional gears, and Lady Mary appeared, calm, correct, gracious, basically missing in action. Mom could see me drifting away from her and was resigned. Pat and Katie were concerned for Mom, Jimmy remained devastated, while my friends were still dumb struck.

"Go away with all your demands," I thought. "I can't do two things at once. Don't tear me apart. I'm here. I'm happy I made it. I'm going to stay." They all went home and the day came to an end.

* * * * *

I couldn't sleep. I looked at my new pocket watch, Dad's gift, by the moonlight. Twelve-thirty. I had to see Edna.

"I'll obey every rule starting tomorrow," I thought, as I tiptoed down the corridor and tapped at Edna's door.

"Who is it?" She whispered.

"Me." She opened the door and pulled me in. The room reeked with smoke.

"Lucky Strikes, Edna? Where do you get them?"

"Don't look the gift horse in the mouth. Want one?"

"No, thanks."

Edna's cell, across from the elevator, faced New Scotland Avenue so her shade was drawn. Gold ribbons from the street light below streamed through the tiny cracks and fell in cockeyed patterns across her wall and crucifix.

She sat there on her bed, in her nightgown, smoking. We didn't speak. We didn't need to. After a bit, I asked, "How did it go for you today? Monsignor seemed ecstatic." No answer. "Your father looked good."

"He's not good but it went all right. How about you?"

"My family will never be ecstatic and I doubt if I'll see my college friends again. I can't visit with them during canonical year and they'll soon be on to other things. To be expected."

"I suppose." Pause. "And Jimmy?"

"I hope Jimmy will get over me even though he is a romantic. I'm sure his new life will push me out."

"Au contraire. Romance lasts forever because it needs nothing to feed upon except itself."

"Nobody's that romantic, Edna! Not today."

"Hmmm." We sat there awhile, in comfortable silence. "What do you think of your name, Irene? Do you like it?"

"I didn't expect it. R.M. said she gave it to me because it meant peace."

"Insightful."

"I know you're glad yours wasn't changed, its being your mother's name and all," I said, thoughtfully. "It must be hard on you not having her here today."

"It is." Our cozy mood was suddenly cracked by a disturbance below. Some rowdies were strolling down the street, slurring their songs.

"What's going on?"

"Drunks, probably," Edna commented.

"In front of a convent?"

I pulled the shade over a hair, and peeked out. Sure enough. Four young college kids were sauntering along, singing the Notre Dame fight song, or trying to. Drunk as skunks, barely able to walk. One of them propped himself up against the lamppost in front of Edna's room. She cautiously edged the other side of the shade over, and I wondered how many shades were being cautiously edged over downstairs where the discreets slept.

"It's Jimmy," I gasped. "Edna, it's Jimmy and Jake and I don't know the other two, but I recognize Jimmy."

"So I see." At that precise moment, he broke into an off key rendition of 'Good Night, Irene', a popular new song, and was soon joined by the others who weren't bad.

"Oh, my God, Edna, Oh, my God." "I hope Dead Eye went back to the hospital. I'll never keep a straight face if I see her tomorrow."

"Relax and enjoy. They can't blame you for this one." The voices rose, waxing stronger and sounding better.

"Irene, goodni-i-ight,
Irene, goodnight.
Goodnight, Irene, goodnight, Irene,
I'll see you in my dreams."

"Oh, God, Edna," I gasped as the tears ran down my face, "wait until Dead Eye hears." By now, it was striking the boys as funny as it was us, and they hooted and clowned and shushed each other, and with hands over their hearts, standing facing the windows, they continued.

"Sometimes I live in the country,
Sometimes I live in the town,
Sometimes I have a great notion,
To jump into the river and drown."

They began moving off, singing their way down the street.

"Irene, goodni-i-ght,
Irene, goodnight . . .

Goodnight, Jimmy. Goodnight, Jake. And I raised the shade and waved to their backs retreating into shadows.

CHAPTER TWENTY-ONE

Nearly two years had passed. Edna, Helen and I were sauntering down beyond the statue of Our Lady and across the grounds to where I had spotted the fawn two springs ago. Helen would be professed in a month. Where had our time in the novitiate gone?

"You can't keep this up," Edna began.

"You can't, Mary." Helen walked backwards in front of us, trying to reinforce Edna's observations and keep her balance on the uneven ground. "You're not yourself." She turned as she spoke, graceful despite her girth, carefully watching her feet, and continued down the dirt path, cracked with frost heaves. We walked towards the far end of the grounds near the monastery wall. March remained its bleak and dire self, but hints of spring flooded the air. The skinny, bare trees in the distance stood proudly against the slate gray sky. The crab apples, deciding to test the freezing gales, had sacrificed a few rose colored blooms.

We were leaning up against the fence now, our view of the hospital blocked by the back end of the Motherhouse, frugally unadorned, and landscaped by nothing more than a black tarred road. From where we stood, clutching our wool shawls around us, the redbuds across the street near the hospital were pink spun sugar, the large willows, misty green clouds. Although few leaves and no flowers were out, the bark itself shone with color, ready to burst with its promise of new life.

"You have me cornered, don't you, the two of you?" I laughed. Helen spoke slowly, deliberately, picking her words, the same way her feet picked sound places to step.

"You're not yourself," she repeated. "You look like the perfect novice, yet inside, I don't believe you've changed a bit."

Edna propped herself up against the chain links. She pushed her veil board way back on her head, revealing her childlike profile. "I've watched Sister Karl on your case in the laundry," she began. "She sees right through all that 'nice' and she's dying to get at you, to find a crack. Karl's a mean and bitter person and you, the cheerful martyr, let her push you around. She'd never dare pull that malarkey with Helen or me because we'd tell her where to go and she knows it. But you take it, all her miserable taunts and criticisms. All her digs. I swear she stays up nights skulking around, trying to discover your weak points because her aim is uncanny."

Edna was as deceptive as those bare gray trees, teeming with life inside, I thought. Calm demeanor, fathomless blue eyes and a mind filled with whirling razor blades, slicing and snipping and trimming the truth. "You're leading two lives," she continued.

"What do you mean?" I countered. "I'm into this life whole hog. I'm trying to be obedient, humble. If I don't act like this, they'll send me home."

"Why don't you act the way you feel? You've brought Karl on yourself. Into the novitiate you waltz, dripping self confidence. You feel sorry for her and she resents it. Then, you become a novice, turn syrupy and she attacks. On the surface, you're the martyr and she's the wretch. You use her and lap up the ridicule she sends your way, but underneath, you know you're smarter than she is and that you control the situation. Don't you think that's an act?"

"That's not fair!"

"Why not? That's what you're doing. You're supposed to work from the inside out. So tell her to drop dead. That's how you feel. It'd probably do her some good."

"How can I do that?"

"Why can't you? I'm talking about Karl. She's not your superior, she's the laundress and she's making your life and herself miserable and you're letting her. I'm telling you, if she treated me that way, I'd dye her underwear blue."

Helen jumped in. "If you're not truthful and you allow people their destructive behavior, that's not charity, Mary, that's manipulation."

"Helen's right. Tell her off. You told Mother Patricia off the day she sent Helen to bed."

"That was different."

"Why? Do you believe Helen's worth defending and you're not?" I dodged that question because I didn't know the answer. I used to think I was but now I wasn't sure I was supposed to be. I was supposed to be the 'Little Flower', who sat next to people at recreation whom she didn't like so she could constantly suffer.

"I can't tell Karl off!"

"You can! Look her in the eye and say, 'Sister, I think your attitude is uncalled for,' and if she asks you why, have a specific list ready, or she'll deny everything. Stare her down. Bullies collapse easily. And while you're at it, why don't you admit to yourself you're proud that you can stomach all her nonsense. That in itself should make you humble! What you're doing does-not-humble make."

"But I'm supposed to *act* humble."

Helen moved in. "You just said 'act humble'. 'Act' is the key word here. Do you think that's right, or holy? Do you think that *acting* like the Little Flower is going to *make* you the Little Flower?"

Mother Patricia went on and on about the Little Flower, a young Carmelite saint who died at twenty-four. She praised her 'Little Way' of offering every tiny moment and action to God, of welcoming humiliation and embarrassment.

"The reason the Little Flower made it work being the Little Flower," Edna explained, "is that she *was* the Little Flower. Get it? She *was* the Little Flower."

"And I'm not."

"Hardly." She stared at her hands for a while, giving me time to absorb what she had said. "What a fake! You make people nervous, always so sweet and compliant. Get on track. You're not a cloistered Carmelite nun like Therese, and you're never going to be. You're preparing to be a religious teacher. It's your duty to form strong opinions about education, children and how they grow, history, and why things happen. Your middle name is strong opinions. I know we have to be trained but this is an active order, not a cloistered one. Our life isn't going to be like this when we leave here.

"I'm trying so hard to fit in," I answered, fighting back tears.

"How true, Mary," Helen drawled sympathetically.

"And I'm not you, Helen, and I'm not you either, Edna. I've always had to work to keep a lid on. Nothing bothers you two."

"Of course things bother us but that's exactly our point. We say so quietly or we let it go. No, you're not me and you're not Helen but you're not Rebecca either. The Little Flower's way fits Rebecca because she has the same nature. Your nature's different from all of ours." Edna, trying to clothe her thoughts in words, looked up at the dreary, bleak sky, gray concrete unbroken by cloud patterns.

"What did you expect it to be like here?" Edna finally asked.

"I didn't think it would be this taxing, where I'd have to sit and think about everything I did and how I did it. It's like putting my life before a jury when I don't know what I'm being accused of. I guess I thought I would just do what I had to do." I turned my hands palm up and shrugged.

"And you don't think you can do that?"

"No, I don't think I can do that."

"Why not?"

"Even when I try, it doesn't work. Take Karl. Why me? I run into flak when no one else does."

"All right, now we're getting somewhere," Edna said, rubbing her hands together.

"Ummmm. What kind of flak?" Helen asked.

"Okay. Suspicion. Everyone accuses me of the worst scenario, guilty or not! And that's the problem. I feel the superiors are sure I'm always up to something, or that I'm not humble enough when I ask for permission..." I was nearly in tears.

"You see yourself as the problem," Edna mused.

"Yes, don't you? Karl didn't land on you, did she?"

"What do you think, Helen?" Edna asked. Helen tried to trace a line in the soil with her toe.

"I think she's right. But I don't think you'll have these problems in a branch house, Irene. The novitiate is different. More contrived. It's a crash course in accepting our life as a penance."

She paused again. "They want us all to end up the same." She stopped making circles with her toe and looked up. "That's where I think your problem is, trying to be the same. You're not." She looked at me to make her point. "And you can't hide it. You are the person you are and no matter what you do, you'll never be able to hide it, and why should you?

"That doesn't hold water, Helen. Nobody in this place is the same. Everybody's different."

"There's different and there's *different*. If anyone were to look at Edna and me, they'd say we were not different from each other, and they'd say you were not like us at all, and they'd be wrong on both counts. Superiors have to judge the exterior and when the novices' exteriors appear the same, they're satisfied."

"That's exactly what I've been trying to do, make the exterior the same."

"Mary, some of us can pretend but you can't! You can't hide yourself and you're stuck with it. You are not meek; you are not mild. Your physical energy exhausts me. But some superior in some branch house is going to appreciate you and put you to work. When you have a chance to perform your duties, you'll be fine."

"What am I going to do now? I'm desperate."

"You have only five months left. Do the best you can, but keep in mind it is your love that God wants, not your ability to follow rules. One can teach animals to follow rules." Helen lazed against the fence but chose her speech carefully, as if rehearsed. "If you think the rules are crazy, then you think the rules are crazy. God knows you think they're crazy and it can be your little secret. You can't play games with God."

"Helen is right," Edna added. "Only five months left. Concentrate on our summer classes. We'll take Methods and Materials this summer, all practical, and they've tapped our best teachers. Cheer up," and she leaned over and gave me a motherly pat.

Helen shifted her position. "You're always going to have trouble following the rules, Mary, because you don't believe in most of them and you never have and you find it hard to let things go. Remember eighth grade and your antics when you wanted to be in Sister Grace's room? You thought the rules were unfair, and nothing stopped you from challenging them."

"Well, what can I do?

"Face up to Karl, then stick your nose in a book and keep it there until you're wearing the black veil. Our set will be professed next month, and you'll be overwhelmed by extra duties. Summer classes begin after the 4th of July. Before you know it, it will be September and you'll be out of here. Five months."

"Five months. I hope I last."

"Of course you'll last." Hope, hope, blessed hope.

* * * * *

At nine o'clock that night, I was still sitting in my stall, staring at the Blessed Sacrament. Most of the sisters had left chapel but I could stay until nine o'clock without attracting attention. Maybe I had become too keyed-up, too strict, too humorless, too Pollyanna. Edna said I was no Little Flower. True, but I was *something*. I had to be *something*, but what? I still didn't know.

Regardless of the price I paid trying to make myself over, I didn't regret the intensity one penny. During the hours I spent in chapel, I bargained with God and argued with Tanquerey and Thomas Merton who both assured me that busy souls had little chance of becoming contemplatives. Not so. I had concentrated on the litanies, chanted the Office, let the Sacraments transport me. I was positive that God appreciated my good will and hoped an inner glow might mean I stood in God's presence. The sheer intoxication of the Mass, interior transformations, silent insights! Maybe I wasn't a contemplative, but I had managed to develop a strong spiritual life because I wasn't the same girl who had waltzed in here two years ago. I held a different view. I had put myself into God's presence, and He was always with me.

I began one of my interminable conversations with the Blessed Sacrament. "I'm giving up this idea of perfection. What is it anyway? I don't understand it. I've become self centered, concentrating on my every move. I don't like myself and nobody else likes me either. This can't be the way. "If I put myself into Your presence and stay there, what wrong can come to me and what can I do wrong? Everything I do should be perfect in your eyes no matter what it looks like to everybody else. That's got to be it, God, that's got to be it."

I felt bone tired, but I felt chosen, promising, on the edge. The novice who was locking up poked her head in, looked at me and then at her watch meaningfully. "A few months from now," I told God on the way up the stairs to my cell, "I'll be out of here and into where? Whatever you have in store for me, I'm game, but please put me someplace where I don't have to drive with my brakes on."

PART TWO

"... people confess to the priests if they want God's forgiveness...they go to the nuns when they want something done."

CHAPTER TWENTY-TWO

It was the day after my temporary Profession. My parents were taking me to my first mission in Dad's new Dodge. Since he hadn't seen me in my black veil, I was bubbling over. "Well, they have you for the next three years, anyway," he teased. The trees were teasing too, spreading dabs of brilliant color among their dull green leaves, promising a marvelous show of things to come in October. The visual splendor fall delivered in the Northeast was unrivaled, and I wallowed in the treat.

I had been assigned as the new kindergarten teacher to Sacred Heart School in Van Olstaad, an early Dutch trading post located twenty miles south of Albany off Route 9W. The town meandered away from the shore of the Hudson River across a splattering of working farms, wandered through fields and eventually petered out near the granite quarry to the north, and the old Dutch cemetery on the east near a new posh development.

An imposing red brick Catholic Church, distinguished by a tall, skinny steeple, dominated Main Street and the whole southern section of town. The complex included a rectory hidden by overgrown shrubs, and a box-like school floating in a sea of tar. A new addition sprawled across the back, diminishing but not devouring the playground. Across the way, a huge covered porch wrapped itself around the prominent Victorian convent, which was painted white and trimmed with forest green and gingerbread; contractors were adding a new addition in the rear to meet the needs of the expanding faculty.

Van Olstaad was aesthetically laid out, not like the ticky-tacky ranch house developments springing up in the suburbs of Albany. The town did not look crowded because the lots weren't. Huge elms and oaks shaded the neat, modest houses, built in the twenties on half acres or acres of land. Around the turn of the century, the affluent had fled the city to escape the summer's heat. When the era waned in the thirties, the Italians who had settled by the upper river near the quarry, filtered into town and bought the old homes. They had money because they didn't believe in banks. The first thing they did was build the Sacred Heart Church. The school came later.

I knew about Van Olstaad. Sacred Heart Parish was famous throughout the Albany area for its early autumn spaghetti supper and our family had never missed it. The celebration began in order to support the parish building fund, and the reputation of the extraordinary food spread. People marked their calendars and made reservations early. By popular demand the event expanded to include four nights on two successive weekends, two sittings each night, but if someone forgot to make reservations by the first week of September, too bad for him.

Parishioners came out in force. If a person could walk, he could help do something. The women even dragged out the old men, whom they'd relegate to small offices off the large hall, and they'd fold flyers and tell raunchy jokes in Italian and smoke up a storm, loving every minute, even though they'd grumble at the world and swear they came only to maintain peace in the household. The congregation sighed and moaned and complained constantly about the work entailed but no one would miss helping out. It was the social event of the year, with all the petty politics involved in small town doings, and of course, the intrigue lay right there.

Who would be in charge of what? What recipe would they use? A strictly rhetorical question. Who would dare tell an Italian woman how to make tomato sauce? One graduated to sauce maker, a place of honor, climbing the ladder from table setter, dessert-disher-outer, salad fixer, server, to finally, a cook!

Of course her recipe was the best, time honored, orally transmitted by grandmothers, aunts and mother, learned at their elbows, or so they claimed, and could those ladies cook! There were northern Italian, Sicilian and sauces from Tuscany but no matter whose recipe they promised each other they would use, they did exactly as they pleased, with mouth-watering results.

Everything possible was home grown: the tomatoes, the Italian parsley and herbs, the garlic, the onions, the peppers, the carrots (for the stubborn ones who insisted on using them to sweeten the sauce), everything. They used to bake fresh rolls but that was impossible now. Too many people.

"This is wonderful," I said, breaking the comfortable silence. "It's like all those Sunday drives we took when we were young. Remember? Remember how the three of us used to carry on in the back seats?" No one answered. Mom was sitting in the front, smiling at nothing, probably delighted to have her little girl to herself again, even for a few hours. Dad concentrated on Route 9W.

"I didn't know until last week where I was going. They couldn't decide whether to send Edna or me to Van Olstaad."

"Where is Sister Edna teaching?"

"She's stationed at de Paul...going to teach Kindergarten, too." And take college classes on Saturdays, I thought, but I kept that information to myself. My father would not take kindly to anyone studying if I were not. Dead Eye had been appointed the superior of de Paul, so my assignment suited me fine.

"How long will they keep you teaching Kindergarten?" I had been waiting for this.

"Now, Dad, listen. I've finished only two years of normal school. The superiors try to ease in the new sisters slowly, let them wet their feet in the school system without being swallowed up. Besides, I love little children."

"Ummmm." Dad was unconvinced. We had pulled up to the convent and I grabbed my small bag out of the car as Dad stood there, after slamming the door and examining the place, as he was to do to every convent in which I ever lived. He wasn't an engineer for nothing, and he noticed everything: the granite cellar, "Mice," the large double hung windows, "Drafts," and the stained glass decorating the panels flanking the solid oak door, "Quality."

"We're not buying the house, Tom," Mother commented on her way up the porch steps. She stood, admiring the vine that claimed the north side of the porch. "Look at that honeysuckle. You'll have hummingbirds, Mary."

We hadn't even rung the bell when the door flew open and two youngish nuns stuck out their heads, grabbed my bag, gushed over my parents and led us all into a comfortable parlor. "Mr. and Mrs.

Bergan, we're so glad to meet you! I'm Sister Lukas," the tall one said, "and this is Sister Willamena. Sister Irene, welcome." Then ensued hugs all around, my father included, and before any of us could speak, we were seated and served steaming hot coffee in good china and homemade goodies on plates with doilies and entertained by two delightful sisters who never let the other finish a sentence because she must have felt that she could do it better herself. No one cared. This was information time.

"Sister Matilda isn't home," Sister Lukas ventured.

"She's the superior, you know."

"She and Sister Regina are out on visitation. She'll be distressed that she missed you."

"Mr. Gabriell...just home from the hospital." Sister Willamena offered this tidbit to Mom confidentially.

"But I know she'll be here when you come next week for the spaghetti supper. Sister Matilda, that is."

"He had a series of shocks, unexpected." Willamena had caught my mother's attention.

"Next Sunday, we'll be finished cooking and the convent won't smell of garlic. The spaghetti supper begins next weekend and everybody helps out. Sister Irene, do you cook? I hear your mother is a wonderful cook."

"Mrs. Gabrielli's in charge of the sauces. We're concerned about her husband and all, and how she'll manage the supper," Sister Willamena clucked to herself. My father's face had split into a wide grin, and I read his mind. Real people in a real room with real good coffee and real food. Maybe it's not so bad after all.

Sister Willamena then took my mother through the convent, stopped in the chapel, let her visit the Blessed Sacrament a moment, while Sister Lukas engaged Dad in a conversation about the two by six construction of the new wing.

Who were these two? Fairy godmothers?

After spirited good-byes to my father and promises of recipes from my mother, Sister Lukas pushed back her veil board, blew through the parlor, collecting any remnants of our snack and corralled Willamena and me into the kitchen while she cleaned up.

"Are you hungry?"

"Something substantial?"

"A sandwich?"

"More dessert?"

I felt as if I were watching a tennis game. "No, no, I'm fine. Such a welcome. My parents really appreciated it."

"We know they weren't too thrilled about your entering," Lukas offered, drying the last cup and denuding the tray, as Willamena shelved the clean dishes. In a small community, there were no secrets, and I wondered what else they knew.

"The Motherhouse is sooo dreary and cold and formal. Branch houses are friendlier."

"Some."

"Not de Paul."

"Bad as the Motherhouse." They looked knowingly at each other, and then at me. "We're glad you're here." By now, the kitchen was quite spotless. "Shall we show her her cell?"

Lukas looked at me. "Do you have a sense of humor?"

"It's not quite ready," Willamena explained.

"It never will be. It's temporary, anyway. Grab your bag." They shooed me up the back stairs, past the second floor and up to the attic. "Don't be upset," they said. "You'll have your own cell soon." The 'room' was a space, marked off by a sheet, containing a cot, a dresser and a crucifix hung by a nail from the bare two by sixes.

"Watch your head." Willamena wrung her hands. "The bathroom is downstairs. It's the best we could do. I told Matilda I'd be glad to move up here but you are the junior," she clucked again, "and protocol and all."

"Willamena sewed new curtains." The bright chintz fabric decorating the small window valiantly attempted to cheer up the dismal scene.

"Don't be discouraged. They'll finish the new wing in a few months and you'll have a brand new place."

"It's fine, it's fine," I said. Anywhere was fine.

"All right, drop your suitcase. When your trunk comes, there's room for it near the top of the stairs." We dodged the bare bulb hanging from a wire.

"Watch your head."

"And your feet. Everything creaks." We were back in the kitchen. "Have a cookie?" Two cookies and a glass of milk appeared in front of me. Willamena handed me the glass and Lukas absently dropped a paper napkin in my lap. I wondered if she'd wipe my chin, but I listened intently because I sensed my fate was in their hands.

"We should go out."

"Give her time to finish her milk." They both turned and looked at me as if I weren't even there. Lukas, the tall one with the straight nose and wire rimmed glasses, habitually stood like a totem pole, arms clasped in big sleeves and mouth nearly hidden in her long, serious face.

Willamena, the one with the warm Renoir figure, cocked her head a bit to the left and leaned forward at all times, like a perky bird, instantly ready to offer compassion whether one needed it or not. Although constantly occupied with their own conversation, which they took seriously, between them, at the right moment, their smiles could light up a room. This is going to be fun, I told myself, curious as to what they were cooking up presently.

"Shall we take her to the cemetery?"

"Too far."

"The school?"

"Too late."

"The church?"

"Father Kearney?"

"Perfect!"

"We can escape in fifteen minutes." They turned and Willamena asked, kindly, "Would you like to meet the pastor now? Sister Matilda will bless us if we bring you over. She'll hate to do it. She's so shy. Do you want to meet him?" As if I had a choice.

"Let's leave supper for Sister Matilda and Regina." The two of them bustled around the kitchen, prepared and wrapped sandwiches, giving me the time to look around. The back stairs or morning stairs, led into this large, cheerful room; airy, ruffled dotted Swiss curtains filtered the bright sunlight which I was sure poured through the eastern exposure in the morning. An aloe plant and small plaster statue of Our Lady of Lourdes stood on the windowsill over the huge enamel sinks. Shiny white paint, layers of it, covered the woodwork, doors, and all the cabinets. Neat rows of plain white dishes peeked out of glass cupboards, neighbors of decorated orange juice glasses that once held jelly. The old gas oven had a hood, a devil to clean, I thought to myself, as I observed the shiny copper bottom of the teakettle. A seriously neat group. In the center of the room, the sturdy utility table proved the sisters not only cleaned in this kitchen but they cooked too.

From the cozy breakfast nook where I was sitting, watching, I thought I could be in any woman's home. They rinsed the dishes, chatted with each other gaily, warned me not to forget my big sleeves and ushered me out of the convent and across the street with a warning. Father Kearney was talkative and all that was required of me was a sweet smile and maybe my name if he asked me, and not to worry. Our exit was planned.

The pastor was a huge man, his face distinguished by kind eyes, a red bulbous nose and a sprinkle of auburn hair combed across his pate to conceal a receding hairline. His voice matched his bulk and his meaty hand swallowed mine as he shook it soundly, while the four of us stood in the vestibule of the rectory.

"Sister, let me apologize for your accommodations. The workmen are running behind schedule but I'm sure they'll be finished by the end of next month, if your patience will only persevere. I could not afford to postpone opening the kindergarten until the convent was complete, because some other pastor would have you by then." He laughed boisterously at his own humor which triggered them both who simultaneously began explaining that we must return to the convent *immediately* since Sister Matilda and Regina were expected home *immediately* and they would be expecting to see me *immediately*, and he understood *immediately* and it was done.

Step one. Meet the pastor. On to step two, the superior. Both Sister Matilda and Regina were in the kitchen when we arrived, eating the sandwiches that they had left for them, neatly wrapped in waxed paper. I smiled nicely as they looked me over and told them how welcome I felt. I sensed at once that Lukas, who I learned later was only twenty-eight, was in charge of this house; she shared none of the glamour but all of the responsibility, just the way she seemed to like it.

Matilda, on the other hand, acted as if she wanted neither, only to be left alone as a librarian somewhere, tucked away on some quiet college campus. But we had no college and the R.M. needed a superior who would teach third and fourth grades at Sacred Heart. She appointed Matilda. A rather large and awkward woman in her mid-fifties, she never made eye contact; her beaten expression broke occasionally into a grateful smile, usually aimed at Lukas. I remained in the background, nodding, observing, noticed by no one. I'll fit in here fine, I thought.

After a casual sandwich supper and a relaxed evening of recreation, the bell rang and off we all went to bed. I made a few awkward moves unpacking, took my shower, said my prayers and fell, exhausted on my back and stared up at the rafters. I could hear stage whispers at the foot of the stairs.

"Is she all right?" (Sister Regina)

"We don't want her crying on her first night here. Did you feed her enough?" (Sister Matilda)

"Matilda, I told you to let Sister Willamena sleep up there." (Sister Regina)

"Willie, go up and see if she's all right." (Sister Lukas)

The stairs creaked as Sister Willamena tiptoed up them and finally stared into my face. "Are you warm enough?" It was seventy in the attic.

"I'm fine, Sister, thank you. Just fine."

"You won't be up here for long. The extension will be finished in a week or two," she said. "Good night." The creaks ceased creaking, the stage whispers died out and I turned over on the cot, muffling my giggles. Well, I'm one up on Edna. I'll bet Dead Eye didn't tuck her in!

CHAPTER TWENTY-THREE

We were up at five-thirty the next morning for prayers and meditation in our chapel. Father said Mass in church across the street, so we traipsed over, preceded by Sister Regina who walked with difficulty. Seven or eight old ladies, members of the parish I guessed, shuffled around inside saying their stations, dusting the statues, chatting in hushed voices, their shiny white hair gleaming in the candle light. After Mass, no matter how old or infirm they appeared, they managed to cluster quickly in the dark vestibule like a fluttering flock of crows to jury the newcomer.

The crones wore black: black kerchiefs, black dresses that rose in the back and sagged in the front, black coats, black cotton stockings, black oxfords. Several of them kissed my hand when Sister Matilda introduced me, and like Lukas and Willamena, they talked about me as if I weren't even there.

"So young."

"What's 'er Mahmah think?"

"So thin."

"How will she manage the children?"

"Very well, thank you," I answered, smiling at them and immediately, they broke into Italian, nodding their heads and eyeing me shrewdly. Whatever the test, I hoped I had passed. I wanted to be nice but still keep the upper hand, because I'd faced this problem before. People equated being young and enthusiastic with being witless, and I didn't put myself in that last category. After the introductions, Lukas and I left. Streaks of red split the eastern sky.

"Who are these people?" I asked as we hurried down the steps in the dawn towards the convent.

"We call them 'churchers'…all widows except for Old Lady Marino."

"Why is she in black if she's not in mourning?"

"I didn't say she wasn't in mourning. Did you notice the beautiful statue of Our Lady over the side altar?"

"It's outstanding. Hand carved, isn't it?"

"Yes, imported from Italy. She donated it to the church."

"I'm confused. In memory of someone who died?"

"No. In thanksgiving that she wasn't killed when her husband threw her down the cellar stairs."

"My God!"

"Her sons came to the house the same day, packed their father up and moved him to a small place down by the river. He was a drunk. They told him they'd take care of him as long as he lived, but if he ever went near their mother again, they'd kill him. Old lady Marino is in mourning because they're separated. Watch out for that car." A blue sedan rounded the corner at top speed, barely missing us in the dusk. "Angelo Vascucci," Lukas commented, looking after him. "There'll be a coffee cake at the front door."

"Why?"

"Angelo's probably had a fight with his wife. It happens often. When they argue, she gets up at four in the morning and bakes up a storm. Since she's mad at him, he gets none so she leaves it all on our doorstep. Wait until you taste her cakes. You'll secretly pray they battle forever." Lukas was right. It was delicious, warm and sticky with honey and caramel and loaded with pecans. This place is going to be interesting, I thought, definitely interesting.

At exactly eight o'clock, several third graders arrived to escort Sister Regina to school. She was built like a basketball on little short legs and had trouble moving, but her helplessness invited the attention the children were only too eager to give. Prodded by parents who revered the nuns, the third grade boys and girls fluttered around her. A regal quality emanated from her; she never requested, simply expected. Willamena clucked over her constantly but Willamena clucked over everybody. I sensed, like most people taken with themselves, that Regina thought she would have been a more proper superior than poor Matilda would and I instantly took issue. I sided with Matilda on the spot; it wasn't her fault her appointment ill-suited her, and I decided to defer to Matilda whenever I could without being obvious. Fair was fair.

I watched the parade exit. Regina bowed towards her book bag and one of the boys picked it up. Some stringy little girl took one arm and an eager boy took the other. A gallant pudgy cherub opened the heavy oak door and away they went, supporting Regina down the stairs. They gossiped about their weekend, each one snapping for her attention. What could these children do on weekends? What innocent pastimes were possible in such a small town? Go to Albany, take a Sunday drive? There were no movies.

I thought I was in another world.

* * * * *

The old school had four huge classrooms on the second floor; the kitchen, offices and auditorium (which last year housed the kindergarten) were on the first floor. Each of the sisters, except me, taught double grades, and I had double sessions, which I would teach in the only room finished in the new annex, the kindergarten, equipped with its own little bathroom. I found out later that they had offered the room to Regina, but since she relied heavily on the help of the older children, she had refused. Except for the stairs, she enjoyed the convenience and camaraderie the second floor offered.

The parish, like all parishes after the war, was expanding; people were relocating outside the cities, families were growing, schools were becoming dreadfully overcrowded. We would begin splitting the grades next year, enlarging the faculty and classes one by one. Sister Regina taught first and second. Her darting eyes, no-nonsense voice and imposing manner compensated for her infirmities. She surveyed three to four groups of children working on their own. The bright, older children tutored the younger ones while she labored with the slower students in the front of the room. Constant movement but total order reigned in her classroom; she did excellent work, and knew it.

Poor Matilda commanded no order at all but managed with threats. Usually, the superior-principal taught the seventh and eighth grades but Lukas and Willamena had strongly suggested she leave them to Lukas who ruled the young teens like a czar. So-so teaching in third and fourth grades supposedly did the least harm so Matilda labored away the best she could and struck terror into hearts by threatening to tattle to parents if her charges stepped on her rules. It worked. In the main, they were good, and she read them *Charlotte's Web* as a reward.

Willamena loved her students who were all in love with her. They pranced about and made her laugh, and that morning I watched the hugs and good-natured ribbing on the playground. Most children flew, screaming around the new blacktop during recess, but Willie's kids trailed after her, arms around her and each other, begging for attention. It didn't take long for me to size up my new mission.

They had set up a neat little life, uninterrupted and unobserved because of their distance from the Motherhouse. Expediency and kindness to the parishioners had overcome protocol and the faculty was more bent on being accepted by me than I had anticipated. Could I go with the flow? Did I carry tales? Would I rock the boat? Or would I fit in?

You bet I'd fit in! If it killed me, I'd fit in and I began my first morning, making it my business to introduce myself to the janitor, the lunch ladies, the milkman, anyone connected to the school. Lukas' students had hung colored pictures of bunnies and bears all over my spacious room. Clusters of construction paper leaves and framed autumn scenes cut from *Ideals* were sprinkled everywhere and they had done their best to clean up after the workmen. I spent the first day unpacking boxes, straightening the cabinets, setting up easels, begging clothes for the dress-up corner, and filing the registration slips. Antonucci, Victor Bellini, Joseph Boggia, Vincent Carlino, John Chicorrelli Robert Amodeo, Maria and Kathleen Fitzpatrick. Kathleen Fitzpatrick? Where did she come from? Hmmmm, her mother was Angelina Temperino.

I wondered what they would look like? Would they come in the first day dressed in dark knickers and smocked dresses and big bows, the way we did when we went to school nearly twenty years ago? I had finished a twelve-hour course in August in Early Childhood Methods and Materials, during which time I had culled my memory and picked out my favorite kindergarten experiences. With the bravery and naiveté of the uninitiated, I typed out a letter to the parents and explained that the children would be involved in messy projects, such as finger painting, floor games, gluing, water play, climbing and outdoor recess, and I suggested that after the first day, they come to school in washable play clothes. Since no notice could leave the school without the principal's permission, I brought it to Sister Matilda who read it and sent me to Lukas for final approval. Her entire class stood the minute I tapped on the door: the boy's feet apart, hands behind their backs, the girls, making an ever-so-slight curtsy, and in one voice, they chorused, "Good morning, Sister."

This will take some getting used to, I thought, after Lukas introduced me. She looked at the note and then at me awhile with her face screwed up in thought. She finally spoke. "The parents have spent a small fortune outfitting their little darlings and want to show them off the first days of school. Wait a week, then send it home."

"What, what will I do with them the first three days?" I groaned, thinking of the hours spent on my lesson plans.

"Anything that won't get them dirty. Teach them how to walk with partners, how to use the bathroom, flush the toilet, wash their hands, how to remember each other's names, how to open milk cartons, how to put their toys away, where to park the toy trucks. Some of them will cry all day and some won't be talking. Most of them will be terrified, probably more than you will be."

"I won't be terrified," I lied, remembering that every single minute in my plan book involved smiling, happy, capable children moving smoothly from one enticing spot to another.

"Teach them to say grace, even one sentence, and a song. Their mothers will love a song, and make sure they have something to bring home, something simple. I'll have my girls cut out leaves. Don't let them glue yet. Too messy. You could staple them together. You'll need help opening the milk cartons. Maybe I'll send a few girls, ummmm, they can spend the day..." and she reentered her classroom and shut the door, leaving me standing, horror struck and overwhelmed by what lay ahead.

Before I could move, the door opened and she stuck out her head again. "And make certain you parade them around the school, into every classroom, through the kitchen. They'll be cooking next week for the spaghetti supper. Make sure everyone sees them. Give them a tour. It will keep them busy, off guard, as you walk them around… give them something to say when they get home. I'll see you after school. We'll talk about it."

She shut the door and I noticed the class was still standing, motionless, at attention and had been throughout our entire conversation. Shades of the past, I thought, remembering my days at St. Teresa's. I wonder if they'll play John Philip Soussa when they march out at lunch time.

They did.

CHAPTER TWENTY-FOUR

Wednesday was my first day with a real live class. I met parents and reluctant children on the playground and when some realized that Mommy wasn't going into the room with them, there were a few sniffles. Nothing drastic. Lukas was right. I was terrified. She had Willamena keep an eye on her class while she assisted me and sweetly explained that no mothers were allowed in the classroom and that meant grandmothers too, because, after all, we wouldn't want our babies to cry, now, would we? She glided between groups, inquiring about relatives, commenting about the children, their clothes, hair, growth, tans. What poise!

I told myself I knew what I was doing, that I always had self-confidence, but why did I have to prove it in front of this audience? Every mother, grandmother and father took off the morning to launch his baby into the sea of education.

I herded my charges into a long line, extracting a few from clinging parents and we slapped our feet on the ground and marched into the room without incident, clapping to our own beat. A few mothers cried but Lukas was there to comfort them. I followed her directions, changing tasks every fifteen minutes. In the kitchen, preparations for the spaghetti supper bordered on the chaotic; the school was drenched in unspeakably luscious smells and all the relatives oohed and aahed as I paraded the children, dressed in their new Sunday best, past the more important town members, giving everyone his chance to show off. The old men shuffled out of their caves, still smoking their cigars, waving and smiling at their progeny. I was too nervous to eat lunch but figured, if I could persevere through this day, the rest would have to be better.

Everything did get better, until Friday afternoon. We had been practicing for the fire drill all week and the children knew how to put their index finger up to their mouth and walk out on tiptoe through our private door and onto their special place on the black top. Why in the name of God do they have to have fire drills the first week of school when any deviation frightened the poor things out of their wits? But it was law that a quota of drills be filled by the end of September.

I had exhausted my bag of tricks. My class needed to run and jump and be messy and be four and five-year-olds. The rhythm band! That's it! I hauled out all the instruments, the tambourines, triangles, drums, maracas, the sticks, shakers and for the best behaved in the room, the cymbals. It's fun time! And it was grand. The noise deafened us all and we began laughing and banging as I crashed out little tunes on the piano. Then I saw a few of the children waving at people outside the huge picture windows. Mothers! Drat! In an instant I realized they weren't mothers, but the entire school lined up by grade outside.

At that moment the door opened and in strolled the fire chief, two firemen in full regalia, yellow slickers, black boots, axes and all, and Sister Matilda looking more woebegone than ever. Now what? Am I ever going to get through this day? The fire chief was greatly amused. "Sister, didn't you hear the alarm?"

"What alarm?" How could I hear anything? The other two firemen ignored me and as I explained the fracas of the rhythm band to Sister Matilda and the fire chief, they began pointing to the ceiling. "What about flashing lights?" I heard the big one say.

"Yep," and he stroked his chin.

"Like for the deaf. Red ones. The kids'll see 'em."

"Yep. Or the jumbo bell. I'd go for the jumbo bell."

Now that some of the din had subsided, I could hear the dull clanging of the fire bell, and turned instinctively to my class. The children didn't want to stop playing just because I wasn't, so some still banged and clanged. They read the situation well.

Sister was busy.

Rule number one. Never take your eyes off thirty-six four and five year olds in the midst of an activity. Richard had wanted the cymbals and bored by the sticks, decided to play on the head of the boy in front of him, who responded with a huge howl. A few more, tired and frightened by the appearance of strange uniformed men and the loss of their teacher's attention, began wailing, which triggered them all and mayhem broke loose.

"Go, go," and I ordered all the adults out. As the men tried hiding their smiles and Sister Matilda her dismay, I showed them the door and attempted to restore order, which wasn't easy since the entire student body was staring into the windows from the playground, enjoying the show. I solved that problem by drawing the shades and made the children lay their instruments on the floor and put their heads down on the desks. As I tiptoed around the room patting backs and collecting the rhythm band instruments, quietly returning each piece to its place in a cardboard carton, I asked myself, would this day never end?

* * * * *

One wonderful thing about our branch house was that after litanies at five o'clock, the sisters were free to say the rest of their prayers outside the convent chapel strolling in the back yard. At five-fifteen, I left the chapel to say my Office while I strolled around our backyard. Old man Valastro who I had met Monday was next door feeding his exotic birds, the peacocks and Chinese pheasants. Some were white, some a brilliant blue with emerald green spots. The ugly one with a bad disposition was orange and brown.

The old man looked like his birds, with his hawk nose and thin neck. His head bobbed like a chicken pecking at the ground, but his eyes were kind and humorous, unlike the birds. Mr. Valastro was tall and courtly and in his day, must have been handsome. I could hear his voice cajoling them, seducing them in soft Italian to eat a bit as he scattered the seed.

I'd been out of the novitiate less than a week but I loved the place. Everyone was real and readable and did human things. I felt eyes upon me and stopped to chat. "Good evening, Mr. Valastro. How are Caesar and Cicero?" Exotic birds deserved exotic names.

"Ah!" he clucked sympathetically, "Ah, okay. Okay for them and okay for me. But bad day, Sis, for you."

"It hasn't been an easy one, Mr. Valastro." How had he heard about how I botched the fire drill? News travels.

"Ah, and all alone, you sit and read," and he walked away, clicking his teeth and shaking his head, repeating, "All alone." I finished reading my Office and sat on the bench, my imagination captured by an article about the priest-worker movement in Europe I had found in *The New Catholic*. I read Father McCarren whenever I could.

"*. . . During the war, a few priests volunteered to be sent incognito into the concentration camps, to share in the prisoners' hardships, offer them succor, comfort them. For the priests' safety, no one knew who they were.*

"*When they had bread, interested Christians would gather in secret and say the words of consecration together, hoping in their hearts that a priest was among them. At times, he was.*

"*After the war, other priest-workers joined factories and did manual work in order to be with the people on their own level, to be poor with them, to be a laborer among laborers, like Christ.*

The instigators of this movement believe that some of the clergy belong with suffering victims, belong with the alienated poor and the working class, not inside safe rectories and monasteries.

"*The theory, as usual, has met with mixed reviews from Rome. Cardinal Suhard holds that the movement is necessary to revitalize the Church, but others see only danger.*

"*The men who volunteer as priest-workers are not seventeen or eighteen-year-old zealots, and are not asking others to join their ranks. Hopefully, they are dedicated but experienced. Now their movement is in jeopardy because all those walled in by comfort, leisure and safety are afraid. They believe that the priests who have squirmed out from under their thumbs will come to no good end . . .*

170

or perhaps reveal by comparison the excessive love of some clergy for luxury.

"Of course there will be casualties! Human nature is human nature. But what is the alternative? Allow the Church to separate itself from the very poor and unwanted that Christ Himself came to save? Are we to sit on our hands and do nothing?"

I folded back a tiny corner of the page, closed the magazine and concentrated on the brilliant trees, the muted voices of children playing down the street, the beautiful fall day. From all my reading that Father Phelan had suggested, I realized that the Church had done just that for years. Before I entered the convent, I had believed the Church simply had to BE, just sit there and emanate truth, because it had the key to eternal life. The Church must have believed it too, or why would I? Now, European theologians espoused that much more than passivity was necessary. When the Church sat on its hands, look what happened. The miserable war and the Holocaust!

I lay the magazine on the slats of the green bench and thought, here I am, safely cocooned, with 'dinner on the table at six o'clock'. I'm warm and fed and have time to read and philosophize with my friends. What would I have done if I were in Germany or France during the war? Would I have had the guts to risk my life and smuggle Jews in and out of my cellar and lie to the Gestapo?

I was uncertain about that but sure of one thing. Giving witness as a priest-worker intrigued me. Although the idea was a new and exhilarating one to me, it was as old as the life of Christ. To be part of a group, a carpenter or fisherman with carpenters and fishermen, to be yeast in the dough, to do the same thing, to live at the same economic level, but, to shine, because the reasons for doing the same things were different and came directly from a devoted Christian life. "So let your light shine before men..."

I was inspired, truly inspired. I could smell change, and I was going to be part of it! When people see me, they will know I am doing things for God, that I'm trying to let Christ shine through me, and my light will shine before men.

But let's get real. I'm a pretty obvious witness, sitting here in an obvious habit, in the backyard of a convent. True, I *am* working for people and living poorly. Sleeping in an attic with nun's wet laundry drying on clotheslines over my cot isn't luxury. But I'm still separate from the people. What kind of witness do I offer? The people here look at us as if we're saints or already holy, so different from them…protected from all human problems and interruptions.

Mr. Valastro was cutting his Concord grapes and I observed him carefully clipping each bunch, cradling them in his hand. That generation is of the Old World, I thought, as he sorted the fruit and puttered among his tools and boxes and pieces of chicken wire strewn across the back lawn. The old women kiss my hand and he bows when he sees me and it's as if, somehow, I'm better than they are. But I don't think so. Their lives have been more difficult than mine will ever be.

Am I a witness to the old women at Church who have seen poverty and sorrow, who cling to the faith without question, whose lives have been nothing but hard work? And to Mr. Valastro? He sees me here, I thought, praying and doing my spiritual reading and maybe I *am* an inspiration. Maybe he knows I'm praying for him and the whole world and am trying to bring Christ to Van Olstaad. I sat up a little straighter, and looked serene, like the picture of Mother McAuley in the front entrance of the Motherhouse. I heard Mr. Valastro's cluck and saw him beckoning to me.

Approaching the fence, I looked into his big soulful eyes. "Poor Sis," he said, as he handed me a brown paper bag over the fence. "You sit all alone and read-a dah book. You have-a no hub. You have-a no kids. Here, take-a dah grapes."

CHAPTER TWENTY-FIVE

It was Thursday, the second week of school. The electricians were installing larger bells in the new addition, plus several flashing lights. During music time, instead of playing the rhythm band, we marched around the room and clapped and stamped our feet to the record player. The parents had responded generously to my request for kitchen corner paraphernalia and it became a favorite hangout. Only the well- behaved could play there which made things easier for me. Nothing like a reward.

We finger painted and slopped ourselves with flour and water and salt. Masterpieces lay on sheets of oilcloth, drying on the new linoleum floor, or hung from makeshift clotheslines strung across the room. I became deft at anchoring my veil board back as I tied up my skirts and covered my habit with a big man's shirt I filched from the dress-up corner.

My approach was different from that of the preceding teacher. I insisted they use the jumbo crayons when they colored, moving their whole arms. No ditto pictures. No stay inside the lines. They crawled on the floor every day so I could note gross motor skill development. Every extra minute, we were out on the playground running, swinging, jumping and letting off steam.

Art and music were favorites of mine and I was young and had wells of energy and I loved children. Last summer, I had absorbed the works of professors at Yale University, Gesell and Ames, who had written volumes about young children and it paid off. I had a class of bright-eyed cherubs who would fall into line for me, sit when I asked them to and put their heads down on the desk during naptime. Teaching wasn't so terrifying after all.

Story time was my favorite, and Sister Martina, our children's literature teacher, would have been proud. The children gathered and sat cross-legged on the floor and I would let them tell the story from the pictures. Some of them rubbed my veil between their fingers, resting against my legs or played with the shiny ebony cross that hung from my oversized rosary. The habit fascinated them and so did I. I'm sure their older brothers and sisters had warned them that I was an ogre who would eat them up if they weren't good. Getting this close physically was an adventure and by the time I had finished a book, they had inched their way up and several were standing, leaning against me and I would good-naturedly shake them off as if they were crumbs in my lap.

I felt accomplished when I walked my class out at the end of the day and they stood placidly in line until a mother or older brother picked them up. Yesterday, the children made the sign of the cross and blessed themselves and everyone was so proud, especially me since I had had to learn to face them and do it backwards with my left hand.

* * * * *

The spaghetti supper was scheduled for the next two weekends, and my stomach rumbled all week. The odors, the tastes! The cooks came by daily to each teacher with a small cup of sauce and a meatball and insisted she taste it and give an okay. Sister Matilda told me that under these circumstances, it was permissible for me to eat in front of seculars. "Never before have I tasted better," I'd say and I meant it.

Late Friday afternoon of my second week, during snack, Antonio Amodeo spilled milk all over his pants. He was crying, ashamed and soaked with chocolate goo. I sifted through the play clothes and came up with a pair of jeans three sizes too big and used pink cotton rope from the art supplies as a belt. "There, there, you look fine, honey," I said, trying to console him, but the others were laughing and pointing at him until a bigger boy moved next to him and said, "I'll play with you, Antonio. Don't cry."

His name was Johnny Chicorrelli.

"All right, you two play in the housekeeping corner while I clean up the mess." Johnny had been so quiet and unruffled by school that I hardly noticed him, but I was thankful for him now. Then I scolded the rest of the class for laughing and making fun of someone's mistake.

At this moment, the door opened and in walked the spaghetti lady of the day, Antonio's grandmother, along with a helper who kept her eyes on the children while we tasted and talked. When Antonio spotted her, tears ran down his face and he waddled up to the front of the room, a slight little boy, stumbling in his huge trousers, arms outstretched, sobbing, "Nana, Nana." Here we go, I thought, and immediately, most of the class were out of their seats and swallowed up in the two pairs of wide arms, sobbing and wailing, and loving the comfort of soft pats and "There, there," and big warm breasts. They clung to legs and skirt hems if they couldn't find an empty body part. A few stayed in their seats and watched, hoping for my praise. I noticed Johnny cleaning up the housekeeping corner.

It was nearly three o'clock, the situation was hopeless so I sat down and laughed. "I'm going to get sick on Friday afternoons and you can sub for me."

"No problem, Sister." The two older women shooed the children back to their seats, except Antonio, who clung, sniffling, to his grandmother. Speaking in rapid Italian, Mama dispensed the other woman while the two of us drew the shades.

In a few minutes, she returned with three friends and little paper plates and wooden spoons that came with Dixie cups and dished out some hot cut-up spaghetti for each child. Yummy, why not? The women clucked and mothered the group and the children lapped it up, including the spaghetti, while Mrs. Amodeo and I talked.

"They're so young," I commented, as I chased the sauce around my plate with the wooden spoon.

She nudged me. "Use the bread, the bread."

I gladly took her advice. "They get upset. Poor Antonio spilled his milk and Johnny Cicorrelli was so nice to him, I let the two of them play in the housekeeping corner together." Antonio, plopped in his grandmother's lap, leaned against her shoulder, and looked at me gravely.

Her eyes narrowed. "Johnny? Where is he?" She motioned to him and he came up and stood before her, grinning. "My other grandson," she said as she hugged him with her free arm. "They're cousins, Antonio and Johnny."

"How's your Mama? And your brother, Robert?"

"Fine," Johnny said, and stood there grinning, his hands behind his back, his feet apart, like the seventh grade boys.

Johnny sat down again, smiling at nothing and I noticed Mrs. Amodeo's tears. "What's wrong?" I asked. But she patted my hand, and blew her nose loudly.

"My daughter. I don't see her. We fought. I don't see the grandchildren often. And my daughter, I don't see her at all." Antonio clung closer to his grandmother, but his tears were shed. Hers fell down her cheeks, and she dabbed at them, unashamed.

How do I comfort her? What do I say? Lukas would know. I sat there, patting her big hand. I had to say something, anything. "Johnny seems so old for his age."

"Of course. Maria, she's raised him right. He's a good boy." She stood and dispatched Antonio with pats and smiles and he wobbled back to his seat, next to Johnny. She straightened out her printed housedress and voluminous apron. "See her for me. I want you to see her."

"Who?"

"Maria, my daughter, Maria. Go visit Maria. You tell me how things are." I looked at her, stunned.

"Don't worry. I'll take care of it. I'll tell Sister Matilda. It's things you do. Visit the sick."

"Is she sick?" I managed.

"In some ways, she's sick. Don't worry. Call her. Tell her you're coming. Just go. This Sunday, just go." She was nearly at the door, and she turned. "I'll tell Sister Matilda it's about Johnny, too. She'll send you."

* * * * *

She did and that's where I was headed right now. I had mixed feelings as I trudged down Main Street towards the river. I'm scared to death. What do I know about social work? Friday night, I had whipped through the Book of Customs of Mother McAuley but that was 1842 not 1952. Drat! I was set afloat with no oars. I didn't even have a companion. Nuns always traveled with a companion. But the other four had made plans to go to Albany Sunday and it was too late to alter them.

Matilda did not like the idea of my going down to the river alone but Lukas convinced her I was no baby and that all the eyes in the town would follow me. "It will be the topic of conversation in every house in the parish Sunday night. And it will do them good. If they're talking about Irene, they wouldn't be talking about anyone else. Besides, she's visiting old lady Amodeo's daughter, and Mama Amodeo is a pillar of the our church. Who would dare question?" It eased Matilda's mind but not mine. I recalled over and over all the things that Lukas had told me when I cornered her in the kitchen Saturday afternoon. She was making apple pies for the spaghetti supper.

"Bring something," she said. "But don't eat anything. You can have a cup of coffee or tea. No soft drinks."

"Why not?"

"Someone might think you have liquor."

"You're fooling!"

"No." She sifted a light coating of flour onto the waxed paper and pushed the dough down with the palm of her hand. "Don't laugh too loudly. Don't watch the television. Don't listen to gossip. Don't ever stay in a room by yourself with a man even if he's eighty and don't stay longer than an hour. Don't let the children kiss you and don't let the woman's husband drive you home unless she goes with you, and you sit in the back seat.

"You can't let people become familiar and you can't give them reason to talk." She wiped her hands on her apron and attacked the pie dough with the marble rolling pin.

"What shall I talk about? I'm no good at this, Lukas. This is no ordinary social visit. It's conducting business in someone's home. I'm my mother's daughter. 'A home is a home,' she'd say, 'not a place of business.' It's been drilled into my head."

"Stop worrying. I've yet to see you at a loss for words. Tell her the story about Johnny and the spilled milk, and how capable he is and how much you like him and how he took care of Antonio. Tell her that's why you came. She'll take it from there. The time will fly. You'll see." She flipped the piecrust off the waxed paper and into the pie tin, fluting the edges as she talked. The flour stuck to her hands, barely spilled. "Robert's only three. He'll be cute and entertaining. And tell her you saw her mother who inquired after the children, and then don't say anything. She'll talk about her children. You'll want to bring home some good news, some stories for Mama Amodeo, no?"

"I suppose." By now, I was peeling, coring, and slicing the apples, sprinkling them with a mixture of cinnamon, sugar, and nutmeg, chopping the cold butter into small pieces. "The parishioners rely on us a great deal, don't they?"

"Ummm?"

"Lukas, do you think people respect us or admire us or pity us?" and before she could answer, I added, "Mr. Valastro pities me." I told her the story about the grapes. "I didn't know how to feel, but I know I don't like pity."

After a quick laugh, Lukas scrunched up her mouth and rolled the crusts with more vigor. "How do you expect an old man to understand why you would give up a family and a husband of your own to take care of someone else's children? And what difference does it make whether they admire us or pity us? They *need* us. Who did Mama Amodeo turn to when she wanted someone trustworthy to visit her daughter? Her sons? Her friends? Old man Valastro?"

I had thought about it last night and I thought about it now as I headed towards Maria's. She was right; people did turn to us for help. So I was needed. We'll see. I walked with my eyes cast down, but not down so far that I would miss my street. Willamena had told me the local bar was so wild that there were bullet holes in the ceiling left over from the thirties but still visible, like the wild west. An old rooming house of ill repute occupied the upper floors, filled with retirees and men out of work and drunks who weren't rowdy. I was glad I didn't have to walk past there.

This part of town was grubby, like a scene from a B movie. I could imagine men inside, their suspenders pulled over their underwear, drinking beer, and peering out cracks in shades at deserted streets, searching for G-men in gray suits and fedoras. You don't want to be here and it's all in your imagination, I told myself as I approached the house, checked the number and climbed the stairs. Your first visitation and you're not even trying to enjoy it. Look happy and tell yourself you're bringing God into this house; you're performing a work of mercy; you're doing your job as a nun.

But my hands were wet and my mouth, dry, and I couldn't remember one warning Lukas had given me. At least I had wrapped up three big oranges and hidden the festive basket in my big sleeves. At best, I'll have a good story to tell Edna at our junior professed meeting at the Motherhouse next Saturday.

CHAPTER TWENTY-SIX

"Edna, it's been wild and exciting and the people I live with are so funny and so many nutty things have happened, I don't know where to start."

Being a junior professed or a J.P. in a branch house was tricky. The superior must protect the young sister from such evils as Saturday night TV, and maintain a semi-novitiate, while initiating her into branch house living. However, she couldn't punish the rest of the nuns by discontinuing adult recreation. Thankfully, rules regarding J.P.'s were nebulous, and most superiors continued their regimen and relied on the young sister's discretion when she visited the Motherhouse. However, Lukas and Willie warned me about being circumspect repeating anecdotes. Little said was good. Nothing said was better. I saved my stories for Edna.

"Leaving here and living there agrees with you. You've gained weight and you have fingernails," she quipped. "Any bad days?"

"Not in Van Olstaad, but you and Helen and Bryand are the only ones I'd tell if I did," and I told her about Lukas being the real one in charge and how much she'd helped me. "Lukas treats me as if I were finally professed. They all do."

"I might as well be back here," Edna sighed after we broke away from the group and took the familiar path past the statue of Our Lady to the monastery fence. As we walked, we hiked up our skirts to protect our best habit from the clawing weeds and brambles bordering the path. I fumbled for the largest safety pin from the cache woven into my yoke and asked Edna, "Need a pin?"

She shook her head, no.

"De Paul is a miniature Motherhouse, and the sisters treat us like novices. Thank God for Timmy and Bryand or I'd have no friends at all. You know Dead Eye. She runs the place like a prison. Fortunately, I'm busy with college work. Did you know most of the nuns at St. Rose have their doctorates? None of us do."

"Most of us don't even have a master's degree. Probably because they have a college and we don't." Helen and Edna and I had discussed the advantages to a religious order of having its own college: the proximity of a good library, frequent conferences, new ideas, free education for community members- all were available to the nuns at St. Rose. Besides that, a large centralized community could exchange sisters and educate them in various areas of the country, a broadening experience. "You know how we are. We don't have much money, and if we can get away with what we have, we will."

"You're so right. They've got Timmy teaching the trombone," and Edna laughed.

"The trombone? She can't play the trombone," I exclaimed.

"She can now. They transferred Clotilde and Timmy got stuck. She's one step ahead of the pupil."

"Leave it to her. How does she make out with her classes?"

"Terrible. She should never be in a classroom. Maybe graduate level. Even then, I'm not so sure. No discipline. Rumor has it they're going to send her to Catholic Central in Cohoes to teach the honor classes. Chemistry and biology. Sister Judith needs an operation. Timmy'll take her place."

"And you'll end up teaching the trombone." We laughed again and cut over to the far corner of the fence so we could lean against it and survey our little world. The catalpa tree near the refectory wing had turned dull yellow-brown, but the barberry bushes, peppered with red dots, wore deep crimson and maroon. Brilliant orange and gold leaves saturated the stand of sugar maples between the monastery and the service driveway.

I quoted, *"September glitters orange and gold against the hard blue sky "* I'll never take fall for granted. Beautiful, isn't it?" We fell into a companionable silence. Edna threw her veil board back, closed her eyes and tipped her face to the warm sun. "Well, what's up? You've been bursting to tell me something."

"Oh, I am," and I went on about Maria Chicorrelli and my visitation. It had turned out so well that Mama Amodeo and Matilda had made plans for me to see her every other Sunday.

"I can't believe parishioners are that clubby with the superior. Does Mama have the upper hand?"

"Not exactly. Matilda is a soft touch but she knows her mind. If she's stuck, Lukas handles it and she is so smooth. Talks people into seeing things her way. She's something like Bryand, tense, competent, unruffled and shy. The parishioners respect Matilda and never go over her head, yet they know Lukas makes most of the decisions." Edna encouraged me on.

"Willie loves everybody, exudes this motherly warmth. Most of the parish confide in her. Her class swarms around like ants on spilled honey. And I hand it to Regina, acts like the queen she thinks she is. A little pompous at times but witty and good humored, a thorough teacher. She's really handicapped, Edna. If she weren't at Van Olstaad with us, she'd be at the Motherhouse, or retired and it would kill her." Edna was listening, eyes closed, absorbing both words and sun.

"Regina teaches her class and that's it. She has no other duties. Some houses would be too shorthanded to absorb her, but the three of us are young and cover for her so she's in a perfect spot. Each sister has her own little sphere of influence and we're involved completely in the parish."

"What do they want from you?"

"Acceptance and a pair of willing hands. Religious instructions begin this Saturday and the three of us will drive down to Catskill in Father's car. If I weren't there, Matilda or Regina would have to go. They're thrilled to have a younger sister aboard." The sun was warm and I unhooked my big sleeves and tucked them into the back of my cincture.

"It could be an explosive situation," I continued, "if a troublemaker were assigned there, but everyone seems happy and it works well."

"No one knows anyone in our parish," Edna mused. "Nobody visits, no one sends in food or anything else, for that matter. No one volunteers transportation for the sisters. No communication with the parish at all."

"Well, my place is hopping," and I related stories about the spaghetti supper, the old crones at church and the coffee cake, then paused for breath.

"I know you're bursting to tell me something. What's really on your mind?"

"An article I read about priest-workers in Europe. Perrin wrote a book but it's not in our library. Try the St. Rose library, will you? We'll meet here in another month. Can you get it for me?"

"Give me a precis and its exact name." I did and she opened her eyes and sighed. "You love the intrigue, don't you? You traipse down to a questionable neighborhood to mend rends in a family's fabric, all alone, but that's not enough. Now you want to work in factories. Will you ever be satisfied?"

I waited awhile before I answered. "I don't want to work in factories, Edna, because I don't think I'd be good at it, but they have a point."

"You're fascinating but you tire me out. Shakespeare and his tragedies are beginning to look good."

"Speaking of looking good, you look rotten. Is your schedule too tight? Are you going to bed nights?"

"Yes."

"What about school?" Why they ever put Edna in a kindergarten, I'd never know. High school religion or English, that was where she belonged. "I'll bring my lesson plans next time, and art ideas and Beatrice Landeck songs. And my schedule. Lukas helped me with it. Okay?"

"Thanks, but I don't need anything. I'm team-teaching with Mrs. Condon, and she's like a mother hen. Plans most of the activities and is so glad I'm not a prima donna. I figure I'm her aide. Suits us fine."

"We both lucked out."

"We did, but we'd better get back to the group before someone misses us." Edna pushed her veil board forward and unhooked her sleeves from her cincture.

"How is Bryand doing? Do you ever see her?" I asked.

"She's thriving. Business is her strong suit and she's young and vibrant; the girls appreciate her and she teaches the boys typing and

183

loves it. It's been a long time since there's been young blood on the de Paul faculty. But this is the best Bryand story," and Edna opened her eyes, lowered her head staring over imaginary half-glasses. "She's a poet."

"Puh-leese!"

"And a good one! Romantic. Why are you so surprised? Think about the ditties she'd compose during recreation; she's clever, and believe it or not, deep."

"I never thought she was a dope, but where did you come across her poetry?"

"In class. Rose Cecilia assigned sonnets and read hers aloud. Beautiful. The girl's a true romantic."

We started our trek back through the weeds to the Motherhouse, and I strained to hear Edna who was walking behind me. I dodged the burrs and ragweed until we were on the grass, and shook out my good habit, allowing it to fall gracefully to the ground. Edna did likewise, and we observed the J.P.'s standing in groups on the cloister and those strolling along the path; their young voices and hushed laughter rolled gently down the slopes towards us, a gentle, dreamlike scene.

Out of the blue, I faced Edna and asked, "Are you happy?"

"Surprisingly, yes. More than I've ever been." I didn't know what to expect but I hadn't expected that.

"Surprised you, didn't I?" And she laughed.

"I'm not you, seeking the unknown and the activity surrounding it. I'm neither a crusader nor a fencer. I'm the fisherman, remember?" Her eyes didn't meet mine but rested upon the statue of Our Lady, the cold marble statue with the outstretched arms and beckoning hands. "I think my vocation is to learn, to study, to approach God with my intellect, to fish for the truth, whatever it is."

She turned and faced me, her blue eyes flat and steady, not half-shut and cynical as I'd seen so many times. "I'll never have your faith, Mary, your personal relationship with God. I'm in awe. I can't understand the way He works, or why and I can't accept…many things. The answer for me is religious studies at St. Rose. The answer for you is Maria Chicorrelli, but don't let me hear you're living in that broken-down hotel and working in the mushroom plant." Before I could respond, the other J.P.'s gathered us up in their laughter and conversation, surrounding us.

"Too bad Helen missed the meeting," Sister Mercy commented. "Couldn't get a ride down from Ilion. She's in the boonies for sure." And everyone began talking at once.

"Later," Edna whispered to me, "later."

* * * * *

Lukas and Willamena chatted vivaciously in the front seat as we cut into 9W traffic and headed south for home in Father Kearney's black Cadillac. Lukas, the only one in our branch house who drove, riveted her eyes on the road as Willie related convent gossip. Fortunately, no one expected conversation from me, so I stared out the window and sorted out the day. Edna was right. She was the scholar and as much as I loved pursuing intriguing conversations, my forte was action. Our assignments suited us better than those of most of the J.P.'s. We were doing what we wanted.

"How did things go for you today, Irene?" Willamena, twisting around in her seat seemed really interested.

"Wonderful. We all have such different assignments."

"Bet you're glad you're in Van Olstaad and not in de Paul with Mother St. Michael."

"Am I ever." I couldn't imagine Dead Eye as my superior," but Willie had already turned back and began talking to Lukas in earnest.

"Sister Judith has to go into St. Peter's Hospital. She's seeing Dr. Phelan. It doesn't sound good, his being the cancer specialist and all." She lowered her voice. I usually resented being treated like a child but today, I had my own thoughts.

Sacred Heart and de Paul parishes were plunked in two different worlds. The nuns were part of the life of Van Olstaad. Despite the Old World respect for our cloistered and consecrated state, we were honestly involved with real life, all going on underneath...like Clarissa hiding the old men in the hospital attic.

185

How important were the nuns to the people in de Paul parish? I had gone to high school there and who cared about the sisters? Most of the girls called them 'the Miseries' and when they sat smoking up clouds at the 'Greeks', their after-school hangout, whining to their boyfriends. Sitting in crowded booths, drenched in late afternoon sophistication, they ridiculed them. The girls were at a perfect loss to explain why anyone would give up a perfectly good life to teach them.

The parents respected the sisters' sacrifice to a degree, deciding that the nunnery was a way of life just like any other. Sometimes they acknowledged their teaching ability, but still, most were never personable. The nuns' lives were mysterious and their own business.

Not the people in Van Olstaad. They owned you; you were their nun, and they'd track down your past, your cousins, your mother's hairdresser. Mystery posed a challenge to Van Olstaad. After one week teaching there, Danny Carlino, father of one of my students, cornered me outside school. "My cousin, Vito, he's a chauffeur, drives the state cars. Picks up your father and brings him to Sing Sing and Auburn. Nice house, he said. Drove him to Great Meadows last week. Says he's a big deal and runs the prisons." His smile displayed gorgeous white teeth. "Says you like it here."

"He just runs the business part, Mr. Carlino, and Vito's right, I do like it here." I couldn't resist. I poked him with one finger in the chest.

We both laughed, and he walked away, whistling.

Sacred Heart suited me fine, I decided as we sped by the open country, and I reveled in the bright fall colors nearing their peak. "We should be home in twenty minutes or so," I offered.

"Oh, home is it now? That's how you feel." Willamena turned around in the front seat and smiled at me.

"Yes, yes I do."

CHAPTER TWENTY-SEVEN

The weekdays flew by but Sundays went on forever. Sometimes people visited. More often, not. In other branch houses, the nuns would spend Sunday planning lessons for the coming week. But in our house, the sisters completed their school duties on Saturday, leaving the next day for leisure. This Sunday, we had no access to a car, maybe because of the Columbus Day weekend. Lukas and Willie suggested we pack a lunch and have a picnic in the old cemetery.

"The cemetery? Creepy!" I exclaimed.

"It's beautiful. We don't picnic in it, next to it. There's a meadow."

"You'll see," and Willie went hunting for the wicker basket. We cut over the back way on a wide dirt road euphemistically called Valastro Boulevard, and passed a new development that proved Van Olstaad was not as glued to the past as it appeared.

The war had changed everything, even this town. The old timers who had little to no formal education would always consider themselves quarry workers and farmers, but the GI bill had wiped out other subtle class distinctions, giving equal opportunities to all ex-service men. Three of the Valastro boys enrolled in college in Albany after VJ Day; the youngest was still in law school. Last June, the other two finished Siena, the new college the Franciscans had opened in Loudonville.

Their parents looked ahead in the forties, and sent them by bus to de Paul High School in Albany, "to the Brothers. They'll learn Latin, learn to shut their mouths, learn respect." Victor and Antonio had gone to school with my sister, Pat. On weekends those two were rebuilding a run-down summer home near the bluff overlooking the Hudson. We stood above it now, admiring their view.

"The old man used to farm this land."

"Bought all he could when the quarry closed. Shrewd."

"Set up the boys in construction."

"Half of the land is theirs. Gave it to them as graduation presents. They had to finish college or else. Generous." Lukas turned and headed toward a small hill rising gently in the distance.

"Their houses are selling as fast as they can put them up. It's much cheaper to buy in the small towns and drive to Albany," Willie sighed. "Business is booming, and the world is moving to Van Olstaad."

As we turned the bend, I thought, no wonder the old cemetery was such a favorite spot! The Hudson River sparkled beneath the quarry as the rocky chasm sharply bent southward and drew the river out of sight. The cool clear day wore shining blue October skies and deep autumn colors: ochres, siennas, olives and full rich golds. The maples and crimson sumac had waned; the vibrant, dancing oranges had waltzed away and left the oaks and their dark hues to prepare the world for winter. In the distance the crows, gleaning the corn harvest, cawed their satisfaction. The clean scent of rotted manure wafted across the fields, and I turned to Willie and said, "I feel as if I'm in Iowa. Look at the old bluebird boxes, there, perched on the short poles."

"In the spring, they're all over. Nearly tame," Lukas commented.

"If you sit still, they'll build their nests in spite of you. No cats," Willie added, "no cats. That's the secret." Willie and Lukas picked their favorite spot, spread the tarpaulin and covered it with a blanket. We unpacked the good glasses and plates wrapped in towels, the fat ham sandwiches (the lettuce chilled and fresh in its own waxed paper) the last of the tomatoes dressed in olive oil, wine vinegar and fresh herbs, and iced tea and homemade double chocolate cake with fudge frosting. I rubbed my hands together in anticipation.

"This is great, just great."

Willie looked at me compassionately, and between bites, asked, "Are you lonesome?"

"No, how could I be with you two? But I've gained six pounds, and I'm going to have to let out my habit." They laughed.

"How are things going at the Chicorrelli's?"

Bum question. I felt obligated to include them, but couldn't because I'd promised Maria our conversations were private. So I went for my old faithful ploy: Talk a lot about nothing and people will think you either said something or missed their point entirely.

"Robert's a doll. He sits on my lap now and lets me pet him. Johnny doesn't quite know what to think about his teacher being at his house. He's embarrassed, so he plays with his tinker toys. Work is original," I mused and took a big bite of cake, then munched away.

"How is Maria?"

I nodded, "Good."

They must have been satisfied I could keep a confidence, because Lukas said, "There's something we want to tell you but it's a serious secret, like the seal of confession."

I was going to clown and say, "Cross my heart and hope to die," until I saw their faces, humorless, white, judicious.

Willie stood, and shook out her habit. "You tell her. I don't see any sense in my hearing it again," and she ambled over to the old flat gravestones that rose crooked and cracked out of the lumpy ground. Lukas looked at me; her wire-rimmed glasses sat straight on her nose.

"The only way I know how to tell you is to tell you. Don't interrupt me. When I'm finished, you can ask me anything. Old man Valastro is Maria and Robert Amodeo's father. Mama Amodeo's husband was sterile, couldn't have children. He kept pushing her and pushing her, so she saw a doctor and discovered there was nothing wrong with her. In desperation, she turned to old man V. They were good friends and distant cousins. Her husband suspected nothing .He was thrilled with his babies, and happy, and who was to know?"

My God! She took a breath while I bit my tongue. Did Maria and Robert know? Did Mr. Amodeo know? Or was he dead? Didn't Maria tell me he was dead? But why should I know? Why was she telling me this?

"About ten years ago," Lukas continued, not letting go of my eyes, "old man Amodeo came down with a rare blood disease and they took him to Leahey Clinic near Boston for tests. He found out he had a virus as a teenager and the doctor commented that it was too bad he couldn't have had children."

"The old man was dumbstruck. All Mama said to him was, 'You wanted children. You have children.' " Lukas began putting food away, neatly wiping off the plates and wrapping the silver in paper napkins, screwing on the mustard lid. I never said a word.

"His whole attitude changed. He was dying of cancer anyway, and one night, he drank too much and told Maria everything. She fought with her mother, and they've never made up. She adored her father. Too young to understand, I guess." Lukas stopped fussing and asked, "Does this shock you?"

"I don't know. Should it? But I don't know why you're telling me. It's none of my business, and what good will it do? For me to know, I mean?" All I could think of was my mother and detraction and we have no right to know people's secret sins. Was this a sin? I'm sure I should think it was a sin. All I knew was that it was none of my business, and I couldn't understand what was going on because Lukas didn't gossip.

"Years ago, old man Valastro bought the land we just walked by which is now worth a great deal. He has principles and wants to leave something to his other children. If Maria and Mama make up, Mama's a widow and they're distant cousins, it would work and no one need know anything. If they don't make up, people might suspect. Why would he leave anything to Maria, estranged from her mother?"

"Does Robert know?"

"No. Only that they're relatives, and that the old man has been nice to them since their father died."

"Tricky, tricky, tricky."

"Yes."

"Why me?"

"Mama Amodeo thinks you're like Maria, that you both have a 'fire streak'. Her words, a 'fire streak'."

"Who else knows?"

"Matilda, Willie and I know. And now, you."

"Father Kearney?"

"No. She went to confession to the Franciscans in Albany. Besides, people confess to the priests if they want God's forgiveness They go to the nuns when they want something done." I would remember that line all my life, but now, I was internally frantic. What a responsibility! How can I get these two together?

"What can I do, Lukas?"

"Do you judge them? Any of them?"

"No, I'm not God. And I'm not old enough and I don't know enough. I can't get into that." Judge them? By what rules?

"Then you'll be fine. It'll come naturally. Maria is keen and she must know by now we're up to something. Besides, I see her at church. She's looking for an excuse to make up." After I anchored the blanket with the basket, I turned to Lukas.

"Why don't people suspect? This is a small town."

"They think Mama's angry because she disapproved of her marriage. Possible. Most mothers disapprove of their children's marriages."

Willie who had been wandering among the old graves called to us. "Listen to this," and she read from a thin, crooked tombstone. 'Here enveloped in the cold embraces of death lies my Amelia'. She was only four years old." I could hear tears in her voice .Look at these two, I thought, as I helped Lukas fold the tarpaulin. They look as innocent as young puppies, bland as bread pudding, yet nothing escapes them. I wonder what other 'Amelias' lie buried within them.

The walk home was slow and easy. We didn't talk much. I trimmed the honeysuckle on the front porch and before I knew it, it was time for prayers. In the middle of the litanies, the doorbell chimed but when I answered it, no one was there. Under the mailbox lay a large flat package in a brown paper bag, with the word, Sisters, scrawled on it.

By this time prayers were over and Lukas, who was on her way to the kitchen to prepare supper, gestured for me to follow. "What's that?"

"I don't know. No one was there."

"Open it and see."

"Shouldn't I bring it to Sister Matilda?"

"Heaven's, no. In chapel? Open it." I did and let out an audible gasp. Two dead left eyes stared up at me, belonging to a pair of freshly skinned and carefully gutted rabbits."

"Eeeyukkk!" and I dropped the package on the table. "Heads and all!"

"Shhh, shhh." Lukas laughingly tried to comfort me. "Bring them over here quickly by the sink. If Regina sees them, I'll have to throw them out."

"You're going to cook them? And eat them?"

"Of course. Delicious," and she set to work cutting up the rabbits, rinsing the meat and placing the pieces in a glass bowl. "Old man Valastro raises them and sends them over once in awhile. We refer to the dish as the casserole and Regina thinks it's chicken. A tiny bit stronger but with buttermilk biscuits and peas floating in gravy, it's her favorite. Remember, the *casserole*. If she asks, tell her we're having the casserole tomorrow night."

"What about these six pounds I'm sporting? What have you been feeding me? Was that flank steak we had last night or did someone kill a horse? I noticed you marinated the meat for twenty-four hours." But Lukas didn't say anything, just laughed.

That night, lying on my cot, staring at the rafters, my arms folded behind my head, I reexamined my situation. Sub-life was a word I'd discovered in *The New Catholic* and did it ever describe this situation!

Regina was exactly what she appeared to be, but the rest were someone else. Matilda, apparently addled and inept, was wise and compassionate, quietly working undercover. Lukas enjoyed second place, working her magic in peace. But what if she were transferred to de Paul to teach sixth grade, with the stairs, a parlor, and Thursday night supper for duties? What would she do?

How many other Lukases were there, stationed at places like de Paul or at the Motherhouse, who had adjusted to their fate and withered up, lost their spunk, imagination and sense of humor? How many swallowed their gifts in obedience and humility, laying them at the feet of Christ, certain it was an appropriate response. Did He think it was appropriate, I wondered? I was beginning to doubt that.

And what did God think about Mama Amodeo and old man Valastro? If I told my sister Katie the story, she would have been shocked, horrified; Pat would have shrugged. Mom would have kept her thoughts to herself, telling only what she wanted me to hear. If I cornered Dad, he wouldn't have judged.

I felt the same way.

Peoples' stories had always fascinated me. I had watched, listened to and examined adult behavior for years, within ear range, but inconspicuously by acting the innocent who never understood anything. People talked as if I weren't there, and I listened: to my sister Pat's boyfriends, my friends' grandfathers, my mother's bridge club, Dad's cronies, the legislative correspondents who gathered around our dining room table on Saturday nights and talked politics. During the summer, when I was eight or nine, I'd skip down the street and help the neighbors garden or clean house or bake and I learned early that everyone wanted company and someone innocent to talk to.

However, I couldn't always act the innocent, observing, judging and storing tales in my mind forever. But this Mama Amodeo thing? I wasn't ready. I was playing the part of the sweet young kindergarten teacher and trying to get my bearings. I hadn't had the opportunity to mature enough to deal with this situation. Up until a few months ago, I had to brush my teeth and wash my face at appointed times.

I'd talk to Lukas tomorrow.

Tiptoeing out of bed, I pushed aside the chintz curtains and enjoyed the crisp, starry night. I found Cassiopeia, clearly visible, and located part of what I hoped was Pegasus. Would Sister Matilda allow Mom and Dad to give me a pair of binoculars for Christmas, I wondered? I'll bet the fifth and sixth graders would love to go stargazing on Friday night. The cemetery would be terrific. A far-flung idea but Lukas and Willie could swing it. Maybe a hot dog roast and marshmallows afterwards. The heavens twinkled their approval.

I was so happy and believed divine providence had sent me to Van Olstaad…one more assurance that God loved me, tended to me personally and shaped my life. He would help me deal with this new apostolate that I so desired but felt so unprepared for. I went to bed and dreamed I floated on a huge hand, through planets and stars, through unending paths and expanses.

* * * * *

Cornering Lukas the next afternoon in the kitchen, I began my prepared recitation. "I told you before I was no social worker. I don't have those kinds of skills yet. I need some time. What am I going to say to this woman? If I'm not comfortable, I'm stiff. Lukas, why don't you do it?"

"You underestimate yourself. You're articulate. You like people. God will give you the grace. You'll find the words."

"Why don't you do it?" I persisted.

"Because I'm good at *things*. I can arrange things. And Maria is not a thing."

"But Mama Amodeo talked to *you*."

"She told Matilda she wanted you to take care of it, Irene." The complications. It was hopeless arguing with her, though. When her mind was set, it was set.

"What should I say?"

She wiped off her hands on her calico apron, never meeting my eyes. "We are considering a mother and daughter. I know how you feel about your mother. Tell her about your mother, and go from there."

And I did. The next Sunday when I saw Maria, I told her how Mom felt when I entered the convent, about her loss. I told her that when I was little, I had always wanted a music box, but that Mom thought they were frivolous. I told her that on my first Christmas in the convent, Mom had given me a beautiful ebony music box, inset with mother of pearl, the inside lined with deep red velvet and that I never asked permission to keep it. I just kept it. And we both ended up crying, and I told her she only had one mother and I asked her, "Was all this foolishness worth it?" And I never had to say one thing about old Man Valastro.

The reconciliation took place outside the church on the first Sunday in Advent. Mama and Maria were both at the ten o'clock Mass, and Johnny sauntered over and said hello to his grandmother. Then, Robert, spotting Johnny, twisted in his mother's arms and began reaching for her too. Maria and her mother looked at each other over his head and they both began to cry and they embraced and hugged, the children squished between them. Most of the parishioners were there, and I think some of them clapped.

"No wonder operas are written by Italians," I sniffed later at Willie and Lukas. "They're the only ones who get it." The incident flew over Regina's head but Matilda walked around the house smiling at nothing, and the rest of us felt pretty smug, too. Small victories.

A week before Christmas, a long, thin awkwardly wrapped package arrived unceremoniously on the front porch with my name on it, covered with a scrawl which read, 'Don't open till Xmas'. Though suspiciously familiar, I knew it couldn't be a rabbit because it would rot and smell by then.

"Are you going to open it?" We were all curious. What had old man Valastro come up with?

I was a little embarrassed and tore at the brown paper. "Peacock feathers! Cicero. It's Cicero." He had died in November and it broke the old man's heart. "Oh," and my eyes filled up, "what a beautiful gesture." Could I ever be happier than I was now in Van Olstaad?

CHAPTER TWENTY-EIGHT

The year galloped along and I mean galloped. In early spring, I received a lovely letter from the president of my class at the College of St. Rose, Joanne Casey, a good friend. Vocation Day would be in April. Since I, a class member, had entered religious life, would I be kind enough to give a short address? This was an unusual request because our sisters were not allowed to make public appearances. Sister Matilda weaseled out of the decision by sending me up to the Motherhouse the next day to Mother Patricia, who studied my face and asked, "How do you feel about this?"

"Public speaking has never bothered me, Mother," I answered. But since I envisioned delivering a casual chat in a small classroom to the interested few, I felt I'd be fine.

"They have limited the talk to ten minutes," she murmured, staring at the clock over my head. "I see no harm in it if you're willing, but it would be best if you didn't mention it to anyone except your superior, Sister Matilda. It's a school day and Sister can't spare a companion, so you have our permission to travel alone. Someone will have to watch your class in the afternoon. If anyone asks, tell her you have an appointment."

Why the mystery and why did she seem so uncomfortable?

"You're young" she added, "and some people resent others being made much of. Keep it to yourself."

Easy for you, I thought, as I attempted polite conversation from the back seat of the car on the way home to Van Olstaad. I verbally dodged Lukas' and Willie's curiosity. "It's nothing important. I just have an appointment." They probably thought I was sick or my mother was dying or they're sending me home, but they dropped it.

I respected these two so much.

The only transportation Sister Matilda could arrange would leave me stranded at the college for two hours, so she decided to have me dropped off at de Paul Grade School. What luck! I could visit with Edna and then walk across the street to St. Rose. Bryand and Edna were fortunate to be stationed so close to the college and I envied their poetry class, but I wouldn't trade my assignment for a romp through romantic writing. In Van Olstaad, the sisters encouraged me and restored my confidence in my judgment. De Paul was a different scene altogether. In Dead Eye's mind, the only one endowed with proper judgment was Dead Eye.

She was also principal of the grade school but I couldn't find her when I reported in. It was a strict rule to report to the superior or principal when one visited another convent or school. I talked to the next senior, Sister Abigail, who smiled at me absentmindedly as I hurried off to the kindergarten rooms at the far end of the building. Edna was eating her lunch and studying from a battered gold-edged copy of *The Sonnets from the Portuguese* while she devoured a bologna sandwich.

"Where did you come from?" she gasped as I pulled up a tiny kindergarten chair. I teased her curiosity by taking my time before I explained.

"Don't you mind giving a speech? In front of all those people?"

"There won't be many, Edna. I just don't want to laugh. The last time I saw Joanne Casey, I was dancing the conga at one o'clock in the morning at a frat party at R.P.I. I don't know how I'll feel seeing all the girls, but what they're doing holds no interest for me anymore. I thought about it last night and I love where I am. I feel so useful." I toyed with her book. "It will be interesting."

"What are you going to say?"

"Well, the topic is 'Why I Entered the Convent.' I'm going to try to explain a vocation, what it's like to feel that you want to give yourself to God without being corny."

"Good luck."

"Thanks."

We both heard the rap on the glass door and turned to see Dead Eye tapping her ring, then crooking her finger in my direction. I rolled my eyes at Edna and answered the door, thinking, now what? I did everything according to Hoyle.

"Good morning, Mother."

"I am surprised to find you here," she droned, obviously expecting an explanation. "Is Sister Willamena your companion?"

"I have no companion, Mother. Sister Matilda couldn't spare anyone. I have an appointment at one-thirty. I thought I might visit with Sister Edna during her lunch period." I always ended up explaining or apologizing, even though I hadn't done anything wrong.

"You weren't in your office when I reported in so I left word with Sister Abigail," I added and smiled.

"An appointment?"

"Yes, Mother." No soap. I've rehearsed. 'Don't tell anyone' means don't tell anyone. Except Edna, of course.

"Well," she bustled, "Sister Edna's class will resume in a few minutes and I don't want her children disturbed. You may wait in the office until your *appointment.*" She sniffed and turned on her heel and left.

"She can't stand you."

"I did everything right."

"In her eyes, you'll never do anything right."

"I don't need to wrangle with her now and get myself all distracted and nervous. I'll head for the college. Even though there will only be a few at the meeting, I want to be good. How do I look?"

"You look great. Your best habit. No wonder Dead Eye is curious. Stay calm and I'll see you tomorrow at the Motherhouse. You can tell me all."

My sister Katie who was now a sophomore at St. Rose, was waiting for me, pacing around the campus gardens. I soon found out I had not been fully informed about the scope of this Vocation Day. Besides myself, three other speakers, including two Ph.D's who had taught me as a freshman, were to address the entire student body in the auditorium. The principal of Catholic Central would also speak; Monsignor Glavin would deliver the opening remarks.

"Someone should have told you." Katie's face was as white as her knuckles.

"Right, but don't look so apprehensive. You make me nervous."

She smiled tightly. "Mom's coming, but Dad's working." I examined her. The perfect lipstick, the perfect hairdo, the perfect waistline. The perfect college student. What is she thinking? And what will she think when I speak? What will they all think about what I am now?

At least my clothes didn't embarrass me anymore. I looked scrubbed, shiny and neat in my good habit, and I was flushed and excited to see my friends. I silently cursed the fact that I glowed with inner light, washed by brilliant innocence, like the seventh grader who dressed up like a nun for Halloween. So much for sophistication.

"Promise me you won't cry, or I'll take off my shoe and throw it at you." Katie was already teary, as she was every time she saw me for the past three years.

"Mary, Mary! I can't make myself call you Sister," cried Joanne Casey, hurrying towards us down the path. "Someone told me you were out here!" and I was rushed past the yellow gold daffodils and perky white and purple crocuses like a true celebrity. After we entered St. Joseph's Hall, she introduced me to the other speakers who regarded my youth with a mixture of enthusiasm and wry humor.

One amazing thing about a religious habit is that it lends dignity and grace to anyone in it, so I took the advantage. Moving slowly, I nodded my head and smiled a lot, winked at old friends who stood out of earshot and observed me uncomprehendingly and talked to each other behind their hands. Finally, Joanne led the entourage to the stage and seated us all before the entire faculty and student body.

I arranged myself carefully, crossed my ankles and laid both hands, one atop of the other on my left thigh. Hands were a pain. Where should they go? Looking as regal as I could, I surveyed the audience. Ever since I took a course in public speaking, these types of gatherings didn't faze me. It was a game with simple rules. Look relaxed; if you are, the assembly is. Take your time, speak slowly and distinctly and engage the audience. If your hands shake, grab the podium; if your voice quivers, speak louder.

Lady Mary, I thought, it doesn't make sense. You're completely comfortable sitting here, a young upstart, without a snippet of false humility. Monsignor Glavin's presence doesn't dent you; your teachers don't rattle you; your classmates don't embarrass you. You're perfectly confident delivering your message, even though the competition is killing and the college has wheeled out its big guns. Why doesn't this attitude permeate all parts of my life, like when I run into Dead Eye?

I half listened to the other speakers, mentally deleting the sections of my talk they had exhausted, questioning the pro's and con's of Joanne Casey's decision to save me until last. Dramatic, yes, but would there be anything left to say? Fortunately, no one stole my theme. Her introduction was respectful but playful and as I stood behind the podium, arranging the notes I wouldn't use, I surveyed the audience, caught my mother's eye and began, "I entered the convent because I fell in love with God. There was nothing for me after that."

CHAPTER TWENTY-NINE

Ａnd of course they were the lines *The Times Union* reporter quoted in the paper the next day under my picture with Monsignor Glavin, Joanne Casey and the president of the college.

They should have named me Sister Mess.

Arranging a ride home for me Friday afternoon had proved impossible. Mother Patricia had called St. Rose and left a message. I must stay at de Paul that night and walk to the Motherhouse with the other junior professed sisters Saturday. Sister Lukas would pick me up there. If I had been Cardinal Spellman, I couldn't have been more conspicuous. Junior professed *never* visited other convents. But there I was, and Edna and I savored every moment over our tuna casserole, trading stories at the side table with Bryand and Timmy, awaiting the time we could make our break and really talk. Surprisingly, Timmy joined us.

After evening prayers, we climbed the stairs to the flat asphalt roof, sitting on two overturned pails and two dilapidated chaise lounges in need of reupholstering. It was like old times. "How is college coming? Any good? Your poetry class sounds fascinating." I kidded Bryand about being Sister Rose Cecilia's star and our conversation floated out of romantic poetry and funneled into a discussion of dealing with sexual urges and chastity in the convent.

I told them about my college friends at St. Rose, their lives and yearnings. Some were to be married this June. "I knew what they were thinking. We used to joke about the 'quiver in the liver' when we talked about sex in the smoker, and wondered how we were supposed to be pure and deal with overpowering physical impulses at the same time." I studied my nails for a moment. "I wonder what passed through their minds when they saw me as a nun." Without stopping for comments, I continued. "You know, I dissolve reading beautiful poetry and I can swim in romance and passionate love but I feel like an onlooker, like it's something I could do and enjoy, but I'm not driven. I look at Joanne Casey and she's a ripe peach for the picking. She's getting married in September. Some women exude sexual attractiveness and she's one of them.

"And so's Willamena," I added, shifting my weight on the tottering pail. "She drips sexuality. I thought it must be so difficult for her, perpetual chastity, I mean. So I asked her."

"What did she say?"

"That I was wrong. It wasn't that she couldn't love one man, it was that she loved them all. How could she choose? The convent was the place for her, and she laughed as if it were nothing. But you should see the way men look at her in church. I'll never grow into that sexiness no matter how old I get. I'll always be girlish."

"Do you think that's good or bad?"

"Being who I am, I think it's good. I have enough trouble with obedience."

"Were you ever in love, Irene?" Edna's face was hidden in the shadows.

"I don't know. Probably not the way Joanne Casey is. I had strong feelings for Jimmy, but I wasn't in love with him so I guess not."

I looked over the high concrete railing and noticed the pastel sunset. Daylight savings time had unleashed a bevy of fraught children, pent up, yearning for after supper activities. They played in the streets below us, their excited voices bounced around the two-story houses like the balls they threw on the tarred roads, sounds I savored, a reminder of children and home and what we were talking about right now. A radio played softly in the background and little girls chanted as they jumped rope. "Teddy bear, teddy bear, turn around…"

Mothers were issuing ten-minute warnings to the younger ones, their pleasant voices dissolving into quiet conversations with neighbors they hadn't seen all winter. But night air is a famous gossip; it listened to each sound, and carried its tales through the newly blossomed trees. "I'm so sorry, Thelma, about your father. I didn't hear until last week." A slight breeze rustling new leaves drowned the voices out.

Sister Lourdes' gardens were about to explode as we sat on the roof above it all and smelled and heard the fresh spring unfold.

Timmy began bustling, ready to make an escape, but Edna was too quick. "What about you, Timmy? Ever in love?" Join us now or be forever friendless, I thought.

Timmy was not a beautiful woman but she was attractive, like a rosy-faced maiden hurling herself across Bruegel's painting of a wedding dance. Her freckled face had an open quality, pleasant and unaffected, that overpowered her intelligent sensitive eyes. Softly plump and not especially graceful, she had accepted being under-estimated early on and had adopted an easy, self-deprecating attitude. Would Timmy reveal herself? She was, after all, ten years older and educated to the hilt. Why did she have to tell us anything? But she did.

"I can't say I've ever been in love." Surprisingly, Timmy didn't seem perplexed. Had anyone ever asked her about her feelings, I wondered. "There was a chemistry professor at Northwestern who interested me, interested me very much. But he was married. That's the closest I came. Time went on and I felt that if I were going to do something with my life, I should get started. That's why I'm here."

No one moved or spoke.

"The second floor lav calls. I have to clean it tonight. Too many papers to correct tomorrow." She stood up and shook her habit, staring out into the twilight. "However," as she moved to the door, she added, "if marriage had been my calling, I'm sure God would have provided the man."

We hooted and clapped. "Great exit line, Timmy." She responded with a brief curtsy and disappeared down the stairs.

"What about you, Edna?" Bryand inquired.

"Yes, what about you?" I might have been too reserved to confront Timmy, but not Edna, and was somewhat surprised we hadn't covered this ground before. Edna knew so much about my past and I knew so little about her. Since Helen and I had spoken a few Easters ago, I had never pried into Edna's life because I thought it would be too painful. It was different tonight.

We were on a roll.

"Yes," she finally answered. We waited.

Bryand sat up straight and looked at her. "That's it?"

"Yes."

"Unfair!" I said, missing the import and ready to spout, until Bryand pushed her hand in my direction to shush me and leaned forward on her makeshift seat.

"Do you still love him?" she asked.

"Yes."

Oh, brother, I thought. When am I ever going to learn to shut up? Bryand was still for a moment. "Do you want us to stop?"

"No, I'm all right. It might do me some good to air things out. Why should my story be so unique?" And she laughed a tinny laugh.

"I knew him all my life. We grew up together. He practically lived at our house since my brothers and he were fast friends. He was older, two years ahead of me, and we talked about everything. His ambitions, books, my brothers, movies, everything. I materialized out of nowhere when he dropped by. "We discussed his girlfriends at length. He said no matter how beautiful a woman was, beauty wasn't everything. There had to be a quality about her, a softness, to make her a real woman, and he was dating the prettiest girl in his class. Personality of a glacier, he said."

Edna's voice smiled through her memories. "I was astounded at him and asked why he'd bother with a dope? And he said I had a lot to learn about men. Men might date and marry beauty and lust after it, but most men fall in love with compassionate women. He told me that night that I was sure to have men love me because I had 'it'."

Her voice had softened and she paused for a moment. "I never knew if he were telling the truth or trying to buoy up my confidence, for obviously, I'm no great beauty." Bryand and I sat silent and motionless. "He never knew I loved him," she added almost to herself. My mind filled with questions as fast as a sieve plunged into water. Who was he? Where is he? What happened? She must have read my mind.

"He became a brother, a Christian Brother. That's it."

"Is that why you entered?" I asked.

"I'm not dying of a broken heart, if that's what you mean. But he gave me pause." She met my eyes. "He started me thinking that there was another kind of life."

Edna was saved by the bell. "Later," she whispered, as the three of us stacked up the pails and collapsed the chairs. 'They shall obey the sound of the bell as the voice of God,' and I marveled that we did, although I wasn't sure if it were God or 'Dead Eye' I didn't want to offend.

* * * * *

De Paul Convent stood in the midst of a solid middle class neighborhood, proclaiming to all that this imposing building was a dominant force in the area and it had forty nuns tucked inside its brick structure (that was bulging at the seams) to prove it. But in the early fifties, the whole Church was bursting, every building, overcrowded, and de Paul was no exception. The parish had been forced to buy two houses adjoining the back and front of the convent for sleeping quarters.

In the twenties, a well-meaning, generous pastor had built de Paul like a small Motherhouse, and the chapel was purely monastic: the walls and sisters' stalls, carved from solid mahogany...the stained glass windows, tiny jewels...the altar, a modest but ornately carved piece of white marble, set into an apse constructed of matching stone. Eighteen extra oak priedieus crowded into the choir space between the stalls, to accommodate all the sisters who taught at the grade school and high school.

The remainder of the building, though architecturally promising, was deadened by misdirected decorators who believed that anything connected to religious life should be joyless and drab. Large strips of dark natural wood molding separated the high ceilings and walls, which were painted a beige cream. The solid cement walls resisted both sounds and nails and what few decorative prints there were, such as a black and white etching of 'The Angelus', hung from moldings by heavy wire. Floors of inlaid cork had been installed throughout the convent, further silencing any warm traces of human life. Except for the chapel, it was a dismal place, and I was so glad I wasn't stationed there.

Mass was at seven on Saturday mornings. I slept on a cot in the infirmary, which long ago had been converted into a dormitory. The four of us were a bit crowded getting ready for meditation and morning prayers. Of course, we dressed inside our nightgowns, a convent unwritten law, and it was comical to consider us four young women, our backs turned to each other, deftly pulling articles of clothing up under our nightwear and emerging from voluminous white tents minus only our habits and veils.

We bustled around the large room in silent good humor. Today was Sister Abigail's feast, the senior sister in the house, and we looked forward to talking at breakfast. (Normally, breakfast was a time of silence.) Father would also give Benediction after Mass since he was unable to return in the evening.

The old pipe organ that the young sisters had taken turns pumping had been replaced recently by a fancy new electric one and Sister Anne Marie, the organist, approached it with caution. She was tall but bent and humble by design, not nature. Her eternal obsequious smile left Bryand cold. But Anne Marie considered herself at least the organ's master.

However, before Benediction, just as she began the opening bars of 'Veni Creator', the ham radio operator next door decided to contact a Mr. Bugbee in St. Louis. By some electrical quirk, his message bellowed out into the chapel through some part of the organ. "Bugbee, Bugbee in St. Louis, are you there?"

Anne Marie leapt up, astounded, and shouted, "There's a man in my organ. There's a man in my organ," to which Bryand in her inimitable stage whisper, hissed in my ear, "You WISH!"

I had to leave chapel.

At breakfast, the young sisters who served seemed especially merry, which pleased Sister Abigail no end. At our table, we junior professed were downright hilarious.

"Bryand, I'm going to kill you," I gulped between sips of hot coffee. "I'm sure Dead Eye saw me slip out the door. I'll have to tell her I had a coughing fit."

As was 'Dead Eye's' custom, she left the refectory early to get a head start on her daily business and peruse the morning paper before she left it for the other sisters on the community room table. She returned waving *The Times Union* in her hand and silenced the revelry. With a steely-eyed smile, she proclaimed to all that we had a celebrity in our midst. There I stood, on the first page of section two between the bigwigs. Joanne Casey had set up that picture, ignoring the faculty members on the dais with me, determined I was going to emerge the queen of the day. "Perhaps, you'd like to continue your speech for us, since I know the sisters would enjoy it."

"I'll bet," Bryand cussed under her breath, and she leapt to my rescue. "But Mother, it's Sister Abigail's feast. Sister, why don't you tell us why *you* entered the convent?" And as she spoke, she deftly moved behind Sister Abigail and began clapping. We all joined in. Abigail was a sweet and simple woman and she stood and recounted in a few sentences her gratitude to God for calling her into His holy service. I marveled at the obedient spirit. It didn't matter who told Abigail to rise and speak, something she would never ordinarily do. Someone told her, so she did it.

"Pray for me, Abigail," I whispered under my breath. "Pray for me."

* * * * *

The junior professed meeting at the Motherhouse was scheduled for three o'clock. Bryand, Edna and I had walked over from de Paul early, and the minute we pushed back the heavy front door, Bryand had disappeared to find members of her set. Helen had arrived before lunch and the three of us had an hour to chat.

March thaw and April rain drenched the grounds behind the Motherhouse so our soggy old haunts near the monastery wall were off limits. We chose the last music room near the chapel, sat with our veil boards thrown back, and compared branch house stories.

"Helen, can you watch any TV at night besides the news?"

"I'm watching the McCarthy hearings in the afternoon," Edna said and we discussed our friends in other convents and their privileges.

"How are they treating you at de Paul, Edna?" For all her nonchalance, Helen watched over Edna like a mother, even from as far away as Ilion.

But I didn't let her answer. "Ooh," I moaned, "that place is sooo dreary next to Sacred Heart. I thought I'd freeze to death last night in de Paul and the night air wasn't even that cold. Penitential dreariness! Everyone is polite, POLITE, not friendly." The three of us sat, listening to the metronome I had set off inadvertently, tick away the moments.

I sat down on the piano stool and played a section of 'Chopsticks'. "I don't know how you stand it, Edna, living at de Paul."

"It suits me. Your kind of activity exhausts me. I don't want to run around a parish solving family problems. You thrive on it. And I couldn't give speeches at St. Rose, either. I'd die of fright. I love the chapel," Edna continued, "the beauty of the ceremonies there. I love the fact that I have a little time to study and time for a spiritual life that's ordered. I like peace and quiet, Mary. You like activity."

I was stung. "Well, I think God belongs out in the streets, that's all, besides holing up in the chapel. And what you imply is unfair! I sang Tenebrae with the Franciscans this Holy Week. It was beautiful, heavenly. It's not fair to attack my spiritual life. I love Holy Week, and the liturgy, and I"

"Hold it. Hold it," Helen interjected, "You've missed her point."

"I don't think so."

"I do." She paused, fingering the shiny beads of the large rosary that hung from her cincture. "You're hunting for a life of action fueled by prayer and the sacraments. But we're looking for a dedicated spiritual life, engulfed in silence, resulting in good works and good friends, community. I think that life will always have merit. It's what I'm after, anyway. What about you, Edna?"

"Yes, I'm inclined to agee with you, Helen. I enjoy teaching, but not the way you do. I never wanted to opt for a cloistered order, yet I cherish the spiritual aspects of this one. Time to study and pray. The mystery of faith, and what it takes to believe in God...in this vale of tears."

She met my eyes. "Helen has drawn up the two sides pretty clearly. Not incompatible ideas."

"Eventually, Mary, silly customs will die from old age, wearing big sleeves all the time, or asking permission to use the phone or make home visits. Superiors like Dead Eye remain sticklers for conformity, but some branch houses are becoming more human."

"Those aren't the kind of changes I'm talking about, Helen."

"You'll have to be patient, Irene. Remember how you loved Sister Bertrand's explanation of the community, that the sisters who are products of their age determine the spirit of the community? Well, eventually, we'll determine that spirit."

"I guess my problem is that we can't pick the convent where our life will suit the superior's style," I said. "Van Olstaad would be too taxing for you, and de Paul with Dead Eye would smother me." I listened to the regulator clock tick away our precious seconds, and shifted my position on the hardwood stool.

Helen broke the silence. "You're a born reformer, Irene. I've known you since fifth grade, watched you in high school battling all the rules, but be forewarned. Reformers never have a decent life because they're unsettled living in the present. They see the future, what can be. They live on the cutting edge, and it's not a comfortable place. If you want to go that way, Mary, your life won't be easy." She picked up her big sleeves and put them on.

"If you believe things should change, then figure out how you can change them. You've been trying to change yourself since the day you walked in here, and it never worked. I'm glad you've given that up. Why should you remake yourself? Yourself is your *gift*, what you have to offer."

As the bell rang, calling us to our meeting, I had the last word. "And just what do you think Dead Eye would tell me to do with my gift if I were transferred to de Paul?"

CHAPTER THIRTY

School would close in six weeks. I threw myself into my beloved activity and decided to put on a version of *The Three Bears* for the Kindergarten Graduation. NO graduation gown and hats! I wouldn't make clowns out of the children to please the parents.

"I don't know." Lukas peered down at me over her wire rimmed glasses, chewing on the side of her lip. "The parents expect a graduation."

"I can't help what the last teacher did. They should be used to me by now. It's stupid, fake. The mortarboards fall off and everyone laughs. I won't make fools out of children." She looked perturbed. "Besides, Lukas, most people would rather put money into their children's clothes." Lukas did not look convinced. "The play and songs will do the trick," I continued. "Don't worry. It will work."

I called a meeting and told the adults that each child could shine by singing, dancing or reciting, not simply sitting uncomfortably, unable to move around, looking silly, and finally collecting a diploma.

Afterwards, Mama Amodeo sidled up to me. "You've got nerve, 'Fire Streak'. People like to do what they did before." I smiled. It was great fun! If a little girl were speechless with fright or a boy turned to hardwood in front of an audience, straight to the chorus with them. But there was no back row. They clapped to music or waved leaves, visible to everyone, while enjoying the safety and comfort of numbers.

Unfortunately, there was one glitch. Every boy showed up in a suit coat except the only Negro boy I had in my class. Charles looked spanking neat; he wore a white starched shirt and little tie in a perfect knot. His grin and excitement were like warm puppies. I felt a terrible foreboding. All I had asked for were girls in dresses and boys in shirts and ties, but all the boys wore jackets. "Charles, do you have a jacket in the car?"

"Mommy got me new pants, Sister." He smiled all over, elated by his good looks, and the razor sharp creases in the pants. Lukas who was assisting me, fussing and fussing, saw the entire picture in a flash.

"What are you going to do?"

I caught my breath and thought, taking my time. "What can I do, Lukas? He doesn't have a jacket. He'd stand out like a sore thumb." I paused. "No one wears a jacket."

"I knew you'd say that. There'll be hell to pay. Every mother bought her boy a new jacket."

"Why didn't someone call Charles' mother and tell her they were wearing jackets?" I snapped. "I'm sorry, Lukas. I'm not mad at you. It's not your fault. I'll make up an excuse." I thought fast.

"It's hot. It must be 90 degrees on that stage." I was searching, stretching. "Someone might faint, or worse, get sick." Her stony expression never budged. She knew I was hedging. "Lukas, suppose he were yours. Suppose he were *your* son. His parents did the best they could, bought him what they could afford." No response. "I can't send him out there without a jacket." She rolled her eyes heavenward and shrugged. I grabbed her arm. "Please support me."

Turning to my class, I began, "Children, it's soooo hot tonight, we don't need our jackets. I don't want anyone to faint or feel sick. Aren't you hot and sweaty? Look, I'm a roasting goose," and I wiped my brow, panted and flapped my arms. "No one wants to be a roasting goose." The children squealed with delight at my antics, the boys quickly shed their jackets and Lukas and I prayed silently we could face the onslaught after the play. Of course the mothers couldn't let the jackets go by. They talked among themselves, not to us, and finally elected Mama Amodeo chief complainer.

"They spent money, lots of money."

"They're still wearable. It was hot and at least no one fainted or was sick." I continued pushing the chairs back under the tables in the classroom, avoiding her eyes. "Everyone saw the boys parade around before and after the performance, all those who were comparing price tags, anyway."

"I'm delivering a message."

I turned to face her. "Mama, one of the boys didn't have a jacket. What could I *do*?"

"Charles?" There was never any love lost between Italians and Negroes and I'm sure everyone noticed him when he came into the classroom.

"Mama, were you always well off? Charles' parents aren't slobs. They're hard workers. They have five children and the father has two jobs. No one called his mother; she could have borrowed a jacket." She still stood her ground.

"All right. Suppose it were Johnny? Suppose he didn't have a grandmother who could afford to buy him beautiful new clothes? Do you think I'd let him go out on that stage and be the only boy in the class who didn't have a jacket?"

Mama put her arm around me, and tears fell from her eyes. "Ah, 'Fire streak, you're in for a hard life."

* * * * *

Later that evening, I slowly climbed the stairs to the attic where I still lived. As I reached the top, I sighed. Phew, was it hot! This summer had slid in early, and the night was steamy everywhere. During the play, oppressive humidity was especially brutal. The heavy linens around my face were drenched and both the blotters in my coif front were soaked. As I stood in my room, I changed them by moonlight, adding an extra blotter. Looking out my window, refreshed by night breezes, I thought about Mama Amodeo, and Charles and his family.

Was Mama Amodeo right? A hard life? Helen and Edna thought so too. Why? Because I believed peoples' needs were more important than conventions? Wasn't I supposed to? Take poverty, for instance. What did I know about poverty? I looked around me. Despite the carpenter's best efforts, I still lived in the attic. Big deal. I chose to live in an attic. But, as a child, I had never seen a bad day. With Charles, however, there were more coming. Victor Bellini came in last week dressed in a darling silk Yankee's jacket and new baseball cap. "So, you're a Yankee fan," I was sitting on my haunches, fiddling with his stubborn zipper. "I'm for the Dodgers, myself."

"My Daddy doesn't like the Dodgers. They got niggers on their team." I felt slapped in the face.

"Don't ever say that word again!" I grabbed him by the arms, my eyes dark with anger, and he began to cry. I quickly hugged him. "Honey, I'm sorry, but that's a bad word and you don't know what it means. Don't cry. I'm sorry I scared you." He and Charles were great friends and constantly played in the block corner together. I looked at Charles standing nearby, and I hoped he didn't know what a mean word nigger was. I couldn't be sure. But, as I stood by my window, enjoying the night, I realized I was a fragile finger in a dike.

I knew something about prejudice. Mom's experience growing up Irish in Brooklyn was miserable and she never forgot it. Her father died young of blood poisoning. Her mother, despite an excellent education, being Irish, could not find work as a teacher, so she opened a boarding house instead.

Mom excelled in grammar school and won the English prize, but couldn't graduate or appear on stage because she couldn't afford a white dress.

"She's a poor dirty Irish Catholic. What would she do with the English prize? Buy a pint for her step-father?" And the teachers laughed, not caring if she heard them or not.

But she did.

Prejudice was stupid but despite all my efforts, an empty space hung between Charles and some of the other children. I turned, dropped my linens and habit on the bed, and moved again to the window, trying to cool off a bit. Sister Matilda had suggested that I pour some of Old Man Valestro's wine over ice before I came upstairs, and as I downed the last sip, I toasted the night.

"The jacket was for you, Mom, and Charles…and for all the Charleses in the world."

* * * * *

Over the next two years, the atmosphere in Van Olstaad did change, but not for the worse. Lukas retained her position as vice-superior without interference from our new second grade teacher, Sister Laetare, who was in her sixties. A jolly soul, she taught me to make stock from meat and vegetable scraps, and how to use little spice bags when we canned chili sauce. The sisters weren't close, intimate friends, but we knew the meaning of community, of bearing each other's burdens, of reaching out.

Time cruised along, and since Sister Matilda held moderate views about the TV, world problems drifted into our recreation room. One Monday in the spring of 1954, the Supreme Court had finally tackled a century old problem. *Brown Vs. the Topeka Board of Education* declared that the "doctrine of separate but equal" had no place in American life. Separate facilities were inherently unequal, so segregated schools were unconstitutional. It was a unanimous decision, and the backlash was slowly splitting the country

Van Olstaad wasn't in the deep South, and none of us was familiar with either its subtle or blatant practices. We were not on intimate terms with the one Negro family in our parish; we knew nothing about their problems, so the sisters discussed the situation as if Negroes were people living in a foreign country. I was coming up for Profession, trying to play it safe and keep my mouth shut, but one night at recreation, my feelings leaked out. "I don't know why there's such a stir," Sister Regina commented. "Negroes can find jobs. Mrs. McGuire's always looking for an honest maid and someone to mind the children and she can't find anyone!"

"Really, Sister?" I asked, innocently, laying down my mending, and gazing at her across the table. "Why doesn't she ask some of the girls around town, like Dr. Pascucci's girls?"

"Well, they wouldn't want to be maids!"

"Of course they wouldn't. But that's about all a Negro girl can aspire to." Lukas quickly changed the subject. Tough! We're going to have to look at this sometime and soon! I had never forgotten the day my mother stood up on the bus for the cleaning lady, treating her like a person, like everybody else. And wasn't she? Was this nonsense ever going to end? When I was in de Paul High School as a student, one of the brightest girls in the business department, a Negro, couldn't find decent work with the state or any big company after graduation and I remember overhearing Sister Edmund lamenting about her ending up behind a counter in Woolworth's or the White Tower.

"With all her talent." Wasn't it our job to do something about it besides sit in the chapel and pray?

CHAPTER THIRTY-ONE

Edna's and my final Profession date was September 5, 1955. When a sister came up for either Reception or Profession, the decision to admit her into the community was left to the Chapter, which consisted of professed sisters who knew the applicant. They met with the discreets formally and discussed her virtues and failings. The key question, decided in secret using white and black balls, was this. Is this candidate suitable?

The Chapter was a simple but solemn formality; any sister called to appear was already accepted and knew she would be professed. If the community wished to delay receiving or professing a candidate (a rare occurrence), the discreets informed her beforehand in private, explaining the situation in detail.

Our Chapter was held on a Friday evening in early June. Edna and I, in turn, knelt before the small group gathered in the senior sisters' community room, asked for permission to take final vows and left. Since there were only the two of us, we expected the Chapter to last about fifteen minutes.

We strolled back and forth on the cloister, oblivious of time, watching the sun set, smelling the cool, damp breezes rise, feeling the warm evening mellow.

Despite the difficulties with obedience I experienced and the doubts that plagued Edna, our willingness to take final vows said everything and we had never discussed our upcoming commitment. Instead, we gossiped awhile about Sister Paul, a junior professed in Helen's set who had wanted to leave even as a postulant and did so the night before her final Profession.

"Edna, you knew her better than I. Was she ashamed to leave? I wouldn't be surprised. There's an onus on sisters who leave the convent, as if they should be shunned or stoned or excommunicated instead of praised for their piece of generosity." I turned and faced her. "I must admit I feel I'm pretty hot stuff sometimes, pretty special. Down in Van Olstaad, the old ladies kiss my hand and Mr. Valastro bows to me. I feel smug and superior that I've persevered when other novices have left. I guess I'm not above arrogance myself."

"That's the message we get, that we're above it all. Anyway, they wouldn't let her go. The Mistress of Novices said, 'Consider your indecision a temptation. If the Chapter receives you into the community, you must have a vocation.' She kept going through the motions, afraid of betraying God. "The night she left, when her parents came to pick her up, instead of driving to the Motherhouse, she went home with them. The superior found her temporary vows on her bed. She had stayed three days longer than she had to."

"Poor Paul."

"She was tired out." We settled ourselves into the huge white wicker chairs and looked out at the statue of Our Lady. After a while, Edna continued. "They hang guilt on you. You are the 'Bride of Christ' and leaving is practically divorce. It's not fair, and worse, it's not accurate."

"I was ecstatic about being the 'Bride of Christ' when I was received," I mused, and smiled, remembering the year I floated around the Motherhouse like one of those pastel saints pictured on holy cards. "It was romantic."

"What we've learned *is* romantic. Nuns aren't taught religion in depth. We don't learn the same theology and Church history the seminarians do." She sighed as she went on.

"You know Sister Emily Joseph? My Latin teacher at St. Rose? She's translated books about the early doctors of the Church. Like Bertrand, a real scholar. She's the best teacher I ever had. Keeps referring us to primary sources. She's specific about our homework but doesn't care *what* we practice translating as long as we practice."

"Don't tell me you're translating the doctors of the Church?"

"I'm getting pretty good." (That meant she was a straight A student.) She leaned towards me, and into a subject that grabbed her at last.

"The origin of religious life is fascinating. Remember, the Church is Roman and the early practices that became entrenched in the first few centuries of Christianity were basically lifted from their current thinking and law. "The ideas about consecrated virgins came from the vestal virgins, girls who tended the sacred fires of a pagan goddess. Roman, not Jewish tradition. The Jews were earthy, believed in marriage, never made much of perpetual virginity. Most prophets were married. "They drew a line. People were people and God was God. Being married couldn't interfere with one's spiritual life. Ever hear of a Jewish convent or monastery?"

"Only from comedians. Milton Berle, maybe."

"Right. Well, after the Resurrection, times were complicated. Early Christians thought the coming of Christ heralded the end of the world and they embraced their new religion with tremendous fervor, especially the downtrodden and powerless and that included women. Besides the poor, who had nothing to lose, wealthy women flocked into the Church and began ministering to the poor. Many widows, who were expected to remarry whether they wanted to or not, became consecrated virgins through sheer expediency.

"They kept their large houses, gathered others of like mind around them, performed baptisms, gave Communion. Rumors had it that some were priests." She looked at me meaningfully over her glasses, and continued.

"Virginity had many meanings: physical virginity, abstinence within marriage, and virgin widows who did not remarry. Practicing virginity freed one of gender, gave one the male spirit. Many women took to the desert, away from the world and became hermits, mystics, prophets. A fringe became militant, dressed like men and sat in the men's section in church, wouldn't wear veils and declared that if they practiced chastity, they had no gender. They had the spirit of men and demanded their power, to preach in church, to become priests. I'm making this really simple because there were all kinds of heresies afloat, many I haven't even looked at yet, and we'd never finish going through them all even if I did know what they were."

I loved it when Edna got going. She was usually so difficult to stir. I motioned for her to go on. This was a new wrinkle.

"Men have always been afraid of women. Eve and her seduction and all. The only safe woman was one who was veiled and tucked away. And now they wanted to preach! St. Paul didn't help the situation any. By the third century, Tertulian came up with an answer.

You are the 'Brides of Christ'. Veil yourselves like married women, sit where you belong in church and keep quiet! And there it has remained. To this day, the nuns in the Vatican dust, do laundry and cook and that's all they do."

Edna, nestled in the chair, had touched her chord. "What rankles me the most is that women were the early leaders of the Church. When the Church become the state religion, enter politics and enter the men. Before that, it was mostly women who ran it and they were fearless. Whenever the Romans wanted to degrade and squelch Christianity, they grabbed young girls or the virgin widows, skinned them alive, threw them into pits, set them on fire, cut off their heads, raped them or threw them to beasts.

"The Roman emperors feared them, knew their worth and determination, their power over spirits and minds, and couldn't squelch them. Women followed Christ on His way to the cross, stood with Him while He died, buried Him. After His Resurrection, He appeared to Mary Magdalene and women, not men. Think about it. The first one Jesus asked to proclaim that He was the Messiah was a loose woman He met at the well, a Samaritan prostitute!" Edna sat, lost in her mysteries, but I was loath to lose the moment.

"'Bride of Christ'," I continued, "has irked me for different reasons. Where does it leave everyone else? What about men? My mother or sisters? Because they're married, do they mean less to God? You know, Edna, no matter how they pump up our vows with ceremonies, they're promises, not a sacrament. Marriage is a sacrament. It involves other people. My mother and Pat have received a sacrament."

"I think religious life is a matter of degree, not essence," Edna said. "It's a choice of what you're going to do, of how you can best serve. Some serve more than others but I'm not so sure it matters where."

"This is important, Edna. We're taking vows and nobody tells us anything. Why do we have to hunt for the truth by ourselves, with no real help from anyone?"

"I don't know."

"Well, I'm not diminishing the value of our lives, but I still don't believe I love God more, or that married people are less. Just different."

"What's wrong with that?" Edna asked, studying her nails. Unlike me, she rarely became excited during conversation. She made statements she had thoughtfully weighed in private, whereas I leapt at good conversation like an invitation to a fast dance.

"The Church acts like married people have someone standing between them and God," I continued. "I love my mother and father, my sisters, my friends. Does that take away from my love of God?"

"Devotion to God is mystical," Edna added, "on its own plane. No matter how many people we love, that can't diminish our love for God. Look at Christ and all His friends, yet, there are still sisters who feel that, if they love no one, they must love God."

"Dad will never accept my not getting married. He's still having a fit about my taking my final vows. He came to see me last Thursday and was on a tear. 'No family, no children. I'll find you a job. There's still time.' I am going to miss not having children, but I didn't tell him that."

"Chastity doesn't bother you that much, does it?"

"No, with me, it's obedience. But life is changing, coming into focus, like facing the evils of segregation and social justice. So must the Church. I know our thrust is going to change. I have great hope."

"You and your priest-workmen. You still cherish that idea, don't you, of being unrecognized and in the thick of things."

"It's where this community began." We both sat quietly and thought about that one for awhile.

"I found you a copy of *Cry, the Beloved Country*," she continued, "by Alan Paton, about apartheid in South Africa. I was going to save it for Profession but I think I'll give it to you now."

Sister Mary Celestine slammed out the side door near the refectory, and strode across the cloister, using it as a short cut to chapel. "Come inside. You'll catch cold," she warned us, so we followed her into the front corridor. "Aren't they finished with you two yet? What's taking them so long? Are you sure they're going to profess you?" Our laughter followed her as she disappeared down the front corridor.

But she wasn't far off. Ten minutes later, Willie and Lukas stepped out of the Chapter room, stone-faced and livid. I know trouble when I see it. I stood there, as Lukas took my arm and guided me into a small music parlor.

"What does Mother St. Michael have against you?" she wanted to know. "What did you do at de Paul? She said something about the books you were reading."

"Did I pass Chapter?"

"Barely." Not 'Dead Eye' again! Books, books. I scrambled through my mind, searching through each incident. Books, books. Books! The only time I stayed at de Paul was the night I gave the talk to my college class. I did have Guardini and *The Priestworkmen* in chapel because I wanted Edna to read them. But how could 'Dead Eye' know unless she searched my stall? "You mean she'd blackball me because of books!"

"I shouldn't tell you this but when Willie finally asked her what you had done, she turned on her and said, 'It isn't what she's done, it's what I'm afraid she's going to do.' She couldn't pin-point one transgression of the rules, but she thinks you're a threat, a rebellious person."

"Do you?"

"Of course not." Rebellious! I wasn't rebellious. Rebellious was always swimming upstream to shock, or for laughs. I didn't always do the expected but being obedient and being predictable were not synonymous.

"You're high spirited, that's all, and enthusiastic." She sat back and regarded me thoughtfully. "And you have some good friends," she added, "some very good friends."

So, 'Dead Eye' had shown her hand at last. How dare she jeopardize my future by claiming to read my mind? She couldn't produce one incident where I had been truly out of line. Too bad for her. The community had accepted my good will and me and I'd be finally professed in a month. She'd be out of my hair, thank God.

I wasn't as angry as I was relieved.

Being finally professed would be better. It had to be.

* * * * *

In 1955, our world was held together by gauze. Society, which believed itself sprung from solid rock, was changing, imperceptibly, above and below an elusive line. The war had unearthed nagging problems no longer willing to remain buried and ignored. And, although most barely sensed it, that line was weakening, bulging, and about to crack. However, convinced I was so inspired by God, I had decided to throw in my lot with a group of nuns whose sub-life, I hoped, was also about to explode through layers and layers, and reemerge, struggling to become the healthy community first envisioned by Mother McAuley.

Our Profession day, the first Saturday in September, was beautiful, cool and comfortable. For years I had waited for this moment. In one way, the whole ritual was superfluous. I knew what I was about. As the Latin hymns swirled around my ears, the marble walls and polished wood echoed my pronouncement of the vows of poverty, chastity, obedience and the service of the poor, sick and ignorant. Trance-like, Edna and I received our rings and prostrated ourselves on the cold terrazzo floor before the Blessed Sacrament. As the choir sang, 'Veni, Sponsa Christi', I recited in my heart, with neither joy nor glee, but with grim satisfaction. "I shall belong to you all the days of my life."

CHAPTER THIRTY-TWO

The sisters dreaded being assigned to convents where they had to put up with tyrannical superiors, but where they were sent was considered the will of God. After three years at Sacred Heart, because St. Jerome's in Cohoes needed a sixth grade teacher, I was transferred away from my Shangri La.

At St. Jerome's, my superior, a second Dead Eye, took an instant dislike to me and decided to squash me under her thumb (not an uncommon situation for many sisters). Something was always wrong. She'd tear my bed apart after I made it, redust the parlor furniture I had just dusted, especially if she had an audience, contradict everything I said at the table, criticize the meals I cooked. I mean, a gourmet I wasn't, but I *could* cook.

However, one day, determined and wild-eyed, she made the mistake of calling me down in front of my class. About a piece of convent business! I cut that short by stalking out of the room after her and turning on her like a fury. My rage rose up through my veins like boiling ice. I saw white! "Not in front of my class, Sister," I hissed between thin lips. "Never! This is between us." I breathed with difficulty. My body ached and I grabbed my folded arms and clung to myself for fear I'd completely lose control. I had kept my temper in check since I was twelve and I wasn't about to lose it on the likes of her. "I'm warning you, don't ever deal with me in front of my class again! I won't be responsible!" My unexpected anger frightened her and she turned on her heels and fled.

No one interfered with my class! It was the only area of my life that was mine. When I was across the street in the convent, I'd indulge her, but none of that nonsense in school. Being the 'Little Flower' during my canonical year had left its mark, and I still honored suffering fools gladly, considered it part of a nun's sacrifice, 'offered it up', but not in school. I followed all directives and rules of the diocese and state, but my classroom was my territory and I wouldn't tolerate any obedience exercises and jumping through hoops when I was dealing with my children.

"She's crazy!" I told Perpetua. "I've done nothing to her, nothing to annoy her. What's her problem?"

"She's jealous. The pastor likes you, enjoys your choir, and doesn't fuss over her." True on all counts. Monsignor loved music and did not get on with the superior. He would never step into the convent, no matter how I urged him. When we discussed Sunday's liturgy, we stood in the vestibule planning the Mass, shivering in the cold. She would be furious and blame me. I 'chalked it up' but her unrelenting pursuit gave me a migraine headache that lasted two years. I thought I had a brain tumor. Lines ran up and down my eyes and fish swam across them, leaving my head with a dull throb that wouldn't go away.

Helen had dropped in one afternoon on her way to Troy and we grabbed a few minutes to talk as we stood outside her car. "She's the 'Wicked Witch of the North', Helen. Why do they make crazies superiors? The woman is doing serious damage. I can take it, but others in our house can't."

"Can you, now?"

I ignored her. "Last week, she nabbed Sister Bernard for sending out a postcard to *Scholastic Magazines*. She had given it to a student to mail and the 'Wicked Witch' caught her and accused her of disobedience. Bernard's a silver jubilerian, for Pete's sake, and she hit the ceiling.

"'If I am going to dispatch a clandestine letter, believe me it will not be to *Scholastic Magazines*!' Her exact words. I suppose in a way it's funny."

"Nothing about this situation is funny, Irene," Helen commented, dryly. "Did you see a doctor?"

"Ummm. Our family doctor. He asked about headaches, my mother and grandmother, concluded it was migraine agitated by stress, and then asked had I ever considered leaving the convent. Too much constraint for my nature, he said. I've been in for years, now. Taken my final vows!

I think Dad's been talking to him."

Helen stood there silently, still as a poised cat.

"He was kind...told me everyone is not suited for everything. But I'll have none of it." I straightened up and stared straight at her. "Helen, why don't they appoint superiors with a little heart and imagination? I know ours will be out of here in two months and back in the classroom but why do the sisters have to suffer through the likes of her? Abusing authority and making the sisters physically ill! Look at Little Falls. They had to transfer three nuns out of there last year and never touched the superior. Two were on the verge of a nervous breakdown. It's criminal."

"They think it's the way it's supposed to be. What about your headaches?"

"The doctor told me to teach near an open window, that the fresh air would help. The kids froze but it did."

* * * * *

The 'Wicked Witch' was transferred in June and our whole staff breathed a sigh of relief. My fourth grade teacher, Sister Boniface, a kind, spiritual but old time superior who believed in strict interpretation of the rule, was assigned. The migraines were over, but still there was to be no interplay with the parish, so I threw myself into teaching. We won prizes in the regional Science Fair, took first place in the Diocesan Music Meet, swept the Middle School Art Contest. At home, I volunteered sewing the sisters' habits, whipped up cuddly dolls for charity bazaars, learned to make an edible cream puff, all this plus juggling my fifty-six sixth graders. I loved my class but I still hungered for Van Olstaad and its opportunities. However, I had plenty of time to read and had followed the civil rights movement in the South carefully. Few people understood what Negroes wanted; they just didn't get it.

"They had a lot of nerve, tying up the whole city of Montgomery."

"How would you like sitting in the back of the bus...not able to eat in a restaurant? Where are their opportunities? And why can

225

Bunker Hill be so great if Montgomery, Alabama isn't?" Rosa Parks
had become a heroine of mine. Imagine the nerve of that woman, an
ordinary woman who risked all for what she believed in. Christian
witness had never been assigned to my back burner, and, since the
Church was on the move, I had great hope. Its eyes were turning away
from itself and towards its flock. Pope John XXIII had announced the
Second Vatican Council over a year ago, as ideas simmering for years
had come to a full rolling boil. Time to reorganize, to renew!

"Aggiornamento" he said. "Open the doors of the stuffy old
Church, sweep out its house and let in some fresh air. Out with the
legalisms that wrap us like mummies, tie our hands, dry out our hearts
and bury our spirits in cold tombs. "Open the windows," John said.
"Let in the fresh air." Unfortunately, most sisters here evidenced little
interest in the future. Their fate had always trickled down. Few faced
the responsibility they neither understood nor wanted. Virtue
depended upon conforming to decisions made for them by others so
they chose to ignore these precarious times.

The discreets who believed convents needed stability, order, and
routine, continued to appoint conservative superiors who could keep
an even keel. Superiors like 'Dead Eye' turned their backs on the dark
clouds brewing in the distance. But, dimly, the discreets knew the
cargo was shifting. We were the new breed and they were trying to
fathom our viewpoint. "I don't think the sisters realize what's
happening out there," I commented once to Perpetua, who nodded,
adding nothing. And you're one of them I thought to myself.

Was anyone paying attention?

* * * * *

"Look at this thing!"
"What?"
"This magazine." I held it up to my face, wearing it like a mask
and stared through the holes Sister Boniface had cut in the pages.
"The only readable part is the date, April, 1960. Like censored mail in
wartime. How can I find out what's going on when I can't read a

226

whole article? I'm taking American History this summer and Sister Rosaleen is a stickler. She'll make us read everything."

"You know how Boniface is." Sister Perpetua laughed at my antics and continued correcting her English papers. "She tears out all the underwear ads, anything with bare flesh...she fears for our chastity."

"Honestly, Perpetua, we're not children! The convent has to move into the sixties." I lay the magazine back down on the community room table and continued. "Today at noon, we had silence, reading and public penance during our meal. The children are supposed to go home for lunch, but you know some hang around the playground. They need supervision. While Clotilde read the Passion, and I knelt with my arms outstretched, Sister Anne had lunch duty alone. I could hear the seventh graders across the street cheering on a fistfight. These upper-grades aren't easy to handle, and each year, they're worse." I flipped through the laced pages of the magazine again.

"The eighth grade is wild and someone is going to be clobbered on that playground. We can't help with lunch if we're on our knees in the refectory." She didn't comment, so I casually asked, "Has the mail come?" I hadn't told Perpetua I might have plans besides St. Rose for the summer. My parents knew one of our sisters had toured Europe last August, a gift from her family, and asked if I would like to go.

"You left home so young," they said. "We'd like to give you something." Poor people don't fly to Europe, I thought. All that money, gone in two weeks. I came up with a better idea. "What about studying for an art major? The money you'd spend on my trip could send me to college for five summers." Art sounded like a vacation. Perfect, just perfect, I thought.

"What kind of a vacation will that be?" they hmmmphed.

"A wonderful one! I'll have five summers to draw and paint and carve! Wonderful! I'll end up with a degree in art! Everybody wins, including the community."

"Fine," they said, "anything that makes you happy," so last week I had confronted Reverend Mother. I wasn't supposed to refuse a gift that saved the community money even though the idea was unusual. But since the sisters had *me*, my parents weren't about to give them anything else. If the discreets did not approve, the deal was off. My mother and father absolutely refused to donate to the convent. The letter came. Permission granted. For the next five summers, I would attend a small Catholic college in Scranton, Pennsylvania, studying art. Perfect.

I needed some outside influence. This move might broaden my views.

CHAPTER THIRTY-THREE

"You're studying at Marywood?"
"You too? Oh! Bryand, I can't believe it."
"Business, I'm taking business."
"Art. We'll be together for six weeks." The summer assignment list had appeared on the bulletin board in the Motherhouse following Easter retreat, and Bryand and I had read it together. We were thrilled and all but danced a jig, right there on the first floor of the Motherhouse.

Marywood College was picture book, designed for seductive brochures. Mature trees shaded the stately brick buildings and walkways surrounded the sloping, grass carpet. Sisters from all over the country, dressed in flowing habits and imbued with their customs, peculiarities and ideas, came to the college during the summer and my real education began. Catholic University or Notre Dame it wasn't, but we had our moments.

The Democrats had nominated Kennedy and all the sisters sat glued to the TV in the recreation room. An Irish Catholic President at last! Harvard educated. An author, a war hero whose PT boat was destroyed and who swam to shore dragging one of his wounded crew with his teeth. He had a beautiful wife who spoke French, too. Was it possible? Had the image of Irish Catholics finally crawled out of grimy overalls and bars? These were heady times, hopeful times and we took advantage of any conversations we could squeeze into our busy schedules.

This particular Friday evening, a group from a German community, accompanied by a dictatorial superior walked the grounds saying the rosary after dinner. The eight of them, sweltering in brown and black wool habits, moved as one, in step, by twos, preceded by their superior. "They look like the drill squads I used to see at the Albany Academy," I noted. A crowd of us, squashed into the largest dorm room, members of seven different orders, watched their parade from the window as we stood, all showered and cool in our light nightclothes, sipping cold drinks and munching on whatever goodies our friends and families had sent us. One of the 'brown wools', Sister Bartholomew, was a real peach. We often chatted during class or at supper, but her every other minute was planned, leaving no time to socialize.

I found out all orders were neither as joyful nor practical as ours. And there was more. The demographics of many large cities were changing since the rush to the suburbs; huge churches and grade schools were abandoned to the poor, to children of different races and faiths. After 'the flight of the white,' some communities retained the convents, and the sisters assigned had to be strong characters able to handle change.

"Half my third grade class is black and Baptist."

"In Brooklyn? I thought Brooklyn was Jewish or Catholic."

"Years ago. Some public schools are lacking good principals and parents want their children disciplined. We don't care if the students are Catholic. If there's room, we take them. The tuition is nominal. However, they *must* study religion." Sister Bonaventure stretched out on the bed, hands under her head. "Last June, Aaron Goldberg won the eighth grade religion prize. Father Yalmokas had a fit." And she laughed. She was forty-three and observed her life, which was far different from mine, as if she were watching a movie. The children were in and out of her convent everyday after school, cleaning, cooking, anything they could be paid for. The community had money because they owned private academies, and found this a good way to distribute it.

One little four-year-old girl would come with her sister and stand up on the huge kitchen table, singing and dancing, entertaining the nuns as they prepared dinner. She ended up on Broadway, then Hollywood, playing the part of a deaf-blind girl. Bonaventure said she had given her her start.

No matter where our conversations began, though, they eventually turned to burning issues of the Church. There were Franciscans (two kinds: brown robed and Alleghenies), Josephites, Immaculate Hearts, Charities (black capped and white winged), a few Dominicans and

Sisters of Mercy from other dioceses, talking, talking, talking. Ideas, spinning like dervishes, flew around the room.

"The 'brown robes' are a perfect example," Bonaventure pointed out. "Look at them parading around in ninety-six degree heat, saying the rosary when they should be recreating. They've been slaving all week. We all say our rosary…we all say our prayers, but not like that." Bonaventure's voice neither rose nor fell. It stated. "It's going to go, that kind of structure."

"There can be no religious life without a prayer life," Sister Frances offered. "We're supposed to sacrifice."

"Of course, but we need to swim in a different channel," Bonaventure interrupted. "The world is dying out there. And taking on the poor is sacrifice. If you think dealing with them is a picnic, you've seen too many movies. Some who need help are desperate, and you can do so little to change their lives. Some are connivers, users who have no desire to change. Some keep making the same mistakes. Some resent your help. There's not much feedback except from the few whose paths you alter and they're worth everything. They all are. Who knows what grace filters through our words? If not now, maybe later. But, if you're really involved, working with them is exhausting. We have no right to throw penances at the sisters when they're flat out at the end of the day."

"In our convent, we still have public penance…"

"I don't want to change the life we lead now. Prayer is important and this life has existed in the Church for years and…"

"Our pastor won't allow the sisters…and I'm sick and tired of devoting my life to making him happy."

"And as the superior, it's time that I should be able to…without having to ask Reverend Mother…" and on and on.

"These habits are ridiculous. Think of the time it takes to starch the pieces when we could be…"

"What about the children we teach now? If we abandon the schools, who's going to teach them? They are the future leaders…"

Most of these women were in their early forties or older, two were superiors, none as young as I. We had fallen together: some from the business department, some from the art crew, some because they sensed life and a good time. (Last Friday night, a group of us let loose by the pool. Dubbed the 'Flippin' Flappers', we had dressed in Roaring Twenties outfits and entertained the sisters. Everyone roared watching us navigate the Charleston in rubber flippers.) However, most of us clung together because we talked about changes in the Church that might very well affect our lives forever.

I realized I'd led a sheltered life. I knew next to nothing about how other communities navigated and some of their priorities were enlightening. A few groups played politics big time; a sister's promotion to authority depended upon her family, and how well she knew the clergy. A monsignor as a close relative was nice. Or, and I could barely believe this one, her family's wealth. In other communities, Dead Eye and the Wicked Witch were the norm, not the exception. I learned that Lister, who rolled up her sleeves and climbed ladders to wash school windows, was in the minority; not all sisters scrubbed floors and prepared meals. If a pastor could not afford a cook and housekeeper for the sisters, some communities suggested he look elsewhere for staff.

Were they right, I wondered? More time to study and prepare schoolwork? More time to be a lady and saunter down cloister corridors bowing sedately to others doing the same? Or should we do menial labor because we took a vow of poverty?

What are our priorities?

"Hey, up there. What do *You* want?"

CHAPTER THIRTY-FOUR

Every August 15, following the summer retreat at the Motherhouse, Reverend Mother posted our assignments. The discreets sent the sister where she was needed, filling slots. Grade school sisters moved often because new parishes and elementary schools needed staff. High school teachers were more likely to stay put, but that had its drawbacks. Many, stationed at the same place for years, complained of stagnation. Among that group were the sisters at de Paul and after I returned from college and heard I was going to be stationed there, diverse emotions flooded in.

Bryand and I were at Crooked Lake, a few miles outside of Troy. Edna, Nancy, Timmy and some others were cleaning a decrepit camp the community had purchased the previous winter for the sisters' recreation. Reverend Mother had planned to have it renovated during the fall but Bryand prevailed upon her to open it from August through Labor Day. A few took advantage.

Two buildings, nestled in the woods on the lake shore, boasted a roof, indoor plumbing and that was about it. At night, the mice tracked over my wet oil paintings I had left drying on the floor, and the raccoons raised havoc with our garbage, no matter how we wrapped and buried it. The middle of the dock had sunk and lay, despondent, submerged in water, but in the evening, we perched on it, looking like dishes sliding off tables at sea, playing pinochle and roaring laughing because we all cheated. "Stop pointing to your finger, Bryand. It's a corny diamond signal." We feigned lovesick for hearts, dug a finger into our palms for spades, tapped the dock for clubs. Since we swapped partners after every round, we all knew the signals, so trying to alert each other without detection was the real game.

One night, Bryand brought out a case of beer, and after a particularly wild bout with the cards, we began singing old camp favorites, like *There's Potatoes in the Oven.* We crooned WW I ballads, *Whispering Hope* and *There's a Long, Long Trail A'winding.*

Other campers joined in and voices floated across the small lake. The harmony was close, sweet, beautiful. When we finalized our concert with the Ave Maria in Gregorian chant, we heard a little applause.

During the mornings, since Nancy and Bryand knew carpentry, they mended the screens, tacked up drooping shingles, and leveled old doorjambs. The rest of us scrubbed, painted and sewed curtains. While Nancy oiled and rescrewed all the brass hinges, Bryand rebuilt the front steps. What a scene! Whirring and pounding.

It wouldn't have been so bad, but next door, members of an extremely sedate order of nuns strolled around their manicured grounds in full habit, saying their Office, while we gallumphed about in whatever old clothes we could find, hidden in denim aprons, our night coifs tied behind our ears and perched on our heads like a clump of limp biscuit dough. We'd smile sweetly at their gardener, as he cultivated the petunias and he'd roll his eyes in disbelief.

He had a crush on Bryand. One evening, as she walked saying her Office, he came over to her with a beautiful bouquet for the chapel. His hair was slicked back and his hands were scrubbed and his jeans, pressed. He stood, hat in hand, and presented them to her in a courtly fashion and she blushed. Who'd believe? Bryand with all those brothers! We had a field day teasing her until she admitted she was shy with men.

Edna looked rotten. The R.M. had sent her out with us to rest, but she took on KP. "How do you expect me to sit around when you're all working?" And work we did, but at three, we quit and went swimming. I had designed my bathing suit, had practiced gathering fabric with thread in the top and elastic in the bobbin. "What do you think?" I asked Edna, parading around in the modest blue one-piecer with a gathered skirt.

"Stick close to shore. If you drown, we'll never claim you."

"I don't look that bad! I'll work on a tan." But Edna, who was fair, stuck to the shade, reading a copy of *Lady Chatterly's Lover* she had smuggled in from somewhere.

"How can you read that smut?" I asked her.

"D. H. Lawrence is not smut. If the girls in school are reading it, I read it. This book is over thirty years old. Like it or not, it has changed the way people think about sex. That's morals, Irene. I'm teaching them religion. Meet them on their own ground. If not, how are you going to lead them anywhere?" And she stuck her head back into her book.

What a crowd had opted to come out here! Everyone talked politics. A sense of euphoria surrounded Kennedy's possibilities and we claimed him as a close relative. An up time for Catholics, and I devoured the conversation because there was little of it in my branch house. But when Mercy arrived at the camp early Monday morning with the startling news that I was transferred to de Paul High School, I had mixed feelings.

I'd live with Bryand and Edna and Timmy and lots of good talk. Hooray!

At de Paul and all that gloom. Yuck.

But Dead Eye was back at the Motherhouse. Relief.

And I'd teach high school students? Uncertain. I alone remained skeptical while Bryand, Edna and Timmy were joyous. We sat around the kitchen table drinking coffee and Bryand exclaimed, "This will be great! What fun."

"What will I teach, Bryand?"

"World History, probably American, too," she mused, "Religion, English II, and General Business. Not a bad schedule."

"World and American History? And General Business? I never took one business course!"

"No problem," Bryand inserted. "Stay two chapters ahead."

"Is the discipline bad?" I felt panicky. Fifty-six sixth graders I had no trouble with, but fifty sophomores were another thing (plus study hall duty with one hundred rambunctious teenagers including the football team.)

Timmy laughed out loud. "Are you asking me? My own habit won't behave," and she laughed at herself. "The first month of school, the chemistry honor class had water gun fights in my room. They ate potato chips in front of me, scrunched them on the floor when I was at the board. Did they care what I said? They never listened." Those brats, I thought. Those beastly little brats! I knew through Edna about de Paul honor students, each of whom had a Ph.D. in boredom. They

yawned, sent notes, read books hidden in their texts, but still managed
to be A students. Good colleges seek good grade point averages. They
could not afford an F, but no one graded 'Taunting Teachers 101', so
they amused themselves with Sister Timothy.

"But Timmy, Bryand told me your discipline was great lately."

"Oh, it is. They all failed their first test."

"They failed? What happened?"

"Revenge was delicious. To a man, they came running up to the
desk, waving their notes, claiming they could find my exact words.
How could their answers be wrong? "I finally had their attention. So I
sat them down and told them this was a science class where they
could take nothing for granted. Why should I be right? Suppose my
notes were flawed, untrue. From now on, the ones who could discover
incorrect information would receive bonus points." Timmy sat sipping
her cooled coffee, oozing self-satisfaction. "It was war, and it still is.
But finally, I'm teaching students."

"Didn't their parents complain? How did you get around the
principal?"

"He loved it, and told the parents to mind their own business.
They were seniors, and they could handle me. As far as study hall
goes, the principal has enough sense not to assign me to the duty."
That night as I said my Office I thought, so, it's back to de Paul with
Edna, Bryand and Timmy. It would be a change. I loved sixth grade
and all the enthusiastic kids and their utter lack of sophistication.
Teaching high school was supposedly a step up, an involvement with
more challenging problems. History? A fabulous subject to teach now
because life was exploding everywhere.

I closed my Office book and stared at the tabernacle. Hmmm.
Could I set jaded teenagers on fire?

* * * * *

It was a blast. The girls slunk around, smoked in the lav, filed
their nails between classes but weren't bad despite their affectations.
They still crowded into the Madison Theater and Diner on Friday

nights, hung out at the Greeks, and batted long eyelashes at their boyfriends in varsity sweaters. Teenagers don't change much. We had wonderful times as the early sixties cantered by. Kennedy, his young family and riveting oratory regenerated the nation; the country appeared to return to the idealism and enthusiasm that had flavored the forties.

The Vatican Council progressed and patient scholars plodded through reams of Church Law and outdated traditions, separating needed from needless. The Civil Rights movement had captured the nation's attention; we could no longer ignore that racial differences and economic deprivation produced second class citizens who really weren't allowed to vote. Women began speaking out. Social justice as a topic moved out of the classrooms and into the dining rooms, while men flew around in space like Buck Rogers.

Everyone passed through these extraordinary times but some were lucky enough to experience them. "Edna, do you realize how blessed we are living now? I mean, look at the space exploration and the emergence of the downtrodden and now, Vatican II. It's all so heady." I waited for a response. "Edna, you're in the middle of this. How can you stay so removed, be an onlooker?" But she never answered me, just retreated to her books.

Edna would finish her undergraduate degree this summer and the discreets were considering sending her to Notre Dame or St. Mary's to study theology. Our community was planning to open a junior college but there were no doctors and only a few with master's degrees. The rush to educate the nuns beyond a bachelor was on.

The sisters also had more freedom with the students and their parents. Sometimes families invited them to dinner, a nice break. Excitement and steaming anticipation had snapped the world to attention and it was a great life…a great time to live, or so I thought, but I soon realized there had been little preparation for the slippery roads ahead.

The sixties, which burst upon us so joyfully, carrying baskets of flowers and bright promises, eventually cranked out conflict, discord and strife.

PART THREE

"Real life had blown in the door and sat among us, chilling our bones."

CHAPTER THIRTY-FIVE

"I'm in love with him."

"Well, he's in lust with you!" I snapped. "What are you doing, Bryand? Can't you see what's going on? Wake up! This isn't kid stuff!" It was Saturday afternoon in early November and we were in a parlor on the first floor of the hospital, waiting for Edna who had a doctor's appointment.

"I'm in love with him."

She turned her face from me, and I studied her profile as she gazed across New Scotland Avenue, her mouth a stubborn line. Cold, damp November winds swept October's brown leaves past the heavy traffic, gusting occasionally and dotting gray walls of clouds above. Wisps of Bryand's red hair had escaped from her coif, sparkling glints in a dismal scene.

I took a deep breath and lowered my voice. "So what, Bryand? So you're in love with him. So what?" How could anyone so practical, so business-like, so competent, be so romantic? She thought Guinevere and Lancelot were just fine. "What about King Arthur?" I inquired. "Those two were committing adultery."

Her relationship with Father Andrews had begun innocently enough. As senior class advisors at de Paul, they spent time together after school, at Saturday night dances and yearbook meetings. The relationship began to change and in other circumstances, if each were single, it might have worked. Maybe. But I didn't trust him, priest or not. He was slick. I didn't miss much, and as I passed his classroom on my way to the chapel each morning before school, I noticed the same senior girls draped over his desk and lolling around. It didn't look casual to me.

I nabbed them. "Go hunt elsewhere. What is wrong with you? He's a priest. And don't throw me those innocent looks. If the senior boys don't interest you, try the college mixers," and I stalked off, leaving them stunned. He should have had more sense than to allow their flirting but I guessed he enjoyed the flattery. Whereas Bryand had really fallen in love, I believed she was no more than another experience to him. Experiencing uncommitted love was big these days. I sighed and decided to try another approach.

"Bryand, have you ever been in love before? In high school? Wasn't there anybody? You used to go out."

"Not like this."

"You're older now. You're hitting your sexual peak. A frog could turn you on." Get her laughing. It's my only chance.

I saw her smile. "Come on, Bryand, let's talk. What are you going to do? So you've fallen in love with him. So what? Are you going to join the 'dish ran away with the spoon' contingent?" The community had suffered lately through some embarrassing situations. One sister had run off with a married man, father of one of her pupils; another eloped with a priest who had given us retreat. Instead of blaming it on unbridled passion, I chalked it up to delayed adolescence, ignorance and poor taste. At least I could take unbridled passion and true love seriously.

There was some of that, too.

Most sisters had entered religious life in their teens, had dated but had never been in love. The convent certainly didn't prepare nuns to work with the opposite sex. Neither the word, sex, nor its implications were ever alluded to. No one was supposed to feel anything, as if the vows and habits blocked off emotion and passion behind cellar doors, or obliterated both completely, like bleach on spots.

"Bryand, you have options. Are you still seeing him alone? How are you protecting yourself?"

No answer.

"And what are his plans? Marry you? Leave the priesthood? Where is this thing going?"

"I don't know. I don't *know*!"

"What are you going to do?"

"I've never felt like this before. My feelings are taking me with them. I can't think. I'm carried away. I'd do anything. Anything."

"Will you listen to me? Can you just listen?"

"I can listen but I can't promise. Besides, Irene, you don't like him."

"No, I don't, but so what? I'll overlook it. I'll even treat him as if he were someone I respected." We were both sitting now and I leaned forward toward her, my hands on my knees.

"First, you're both taken. Engaged. Vowed. So let's start with that. What you're doing right now is out of line. You're dating, for God's sake. It's out of order." I threw out my hands in frustration. "Does he want to marry you or just experience 'the great love'?" (Or a roll in the hay, I thought.) "A dispensation from vows would be easier for you than it would be for him, if that's what you want. But do you? And what about him? I should think you're far enough along to know what he wants."

She closed her eyes. I sighed, and lowered my voice even more. "Look, Bryand, these things happen. They happen to married women, men in offices, our kids in school. Venus is Venus is Venus. You didn't see it coming but you're in it now. The point is, what are you going to do? What does your vocation mean to you? I'll support you no matter what. You know that. But I want to be sure you know what you want."

Bryand began quietly, reflectively. "You entered the convent because you fell in love with God. You said so yourself. Well, it was guilt that grabbed me and dragged me, kicking and screaming into this place." "My falling in love with God had nothing to do with romance. It was a figure of speech." She stood and stared out the window. "We were poor, Irene. We lived downtown, and when we finally had enough money to move uptown to de Paul, I'd steal from my mother and buy stockings or a nice sweater, just to keep up with my new friends."

"Oh, Bryand," I said, soothingly, "she must have known, and not cared. It wasn't a matter of life or death…"

"I was such a sham in high school, Miss Goody Two Shoes. The nuns adored me, gave me all kinds of responsibility and honors. I took all the business prizes, was the first in my family to graduate from high school. They were all so proud of me." She began to sob. "And I was such a sham, such a sham."

I was not going to feed on this. "Oh, Bryand, that's over. You were a kid. You can't stay in the convent because you rifled the cookie jar. What a shallow idea of God. Please! You don't believe in all that nonsense anymore, do you? Are you here because you feel guilty? I can see doing penance for murder or genocide, but for a new sweater?"

"I just don't know," and she blew her nose, loudly.

"Listen to me. What you do now is your decision, and that's what it should be. But I can't see your staying here because you filched a few dollars from your mother's cache. And I can't see your throwing your life away because somebody is toying with you. You should decide right now what you want to do, which way you want your life to go and stop being carried away by your emotions."

She sat there, still staring at me. "Besides, Bryand," I added, "it's the chase that interests men, the chase. The catch isn't half as satisfying. When he has you, then what?"

"You can't stand him, can you?"

"No. He's taking advantage of you and you're my friend. If I believed you two were really in love, my heart would break for you both." I stood up. "But I don't. Can you deter the momentum? Are you too far gone?"

"Nearly."

"Okay, don't be alone with him. Keep the doors of his classroom open. Stay out of his way at school. The chances you're taking! Tell him the girls are talking. Tell him anything! Girls can be vicious and if you don't watch it, you'll be too far in and you won't be able to bail yourself out." I stood up, and grabbed my shawl.

"If you have the nerve, ask him what he thinks he'll be doing three years from now." I opened the door. "I'll pick up Edna and meet you in front of the lobby in ten minutes. We'll talk about this again, tonight."

I hurried through the gloomy corridors towards the elevator and up to the third floor, where Edna had spent the day undergoing tests. Two years ago, in 1961, the doctor had discovered diabetes; it was brittle, uncontrollable, regardless of her diet. That news was bad enough but now something else was askew and no one knew what.

My two friends had major troubles...first, Bryand and now, Edna. Timmy moved along and Helen remained the inscrutable rock.

But what about me? I hadn't examined my own life lately. I was plunged into readying reluctant minds for reform, suggesting books, listening to the conservative side with as much understanding as I could muster, rejoicing at good news emanating from the Vatican Council and preaching to the girls how blessed they were, living in such an exciting age. Was I enjoying this age as much as I claimed? It was all right for me to chide Bryand about her prayer life, but what about mine? Did the Mass still thrill me, offer me peace? Or had it become like my morning coffee, commonplace, but indispensable? Edna and Bryand were fighting for their lives while I was busy living in the future.

I knew Bryand would sort hers out, but I worried about Edna who looked awful. I loved Edna and relied heavily upon her; I relished our involved conversation…so vital, so spiritual, so absorbing, and now she was sick. Skin had tightened around her face leaving it drawn, but despite her exhaustion, she never complained, was never whiny or blue.

And I knew she was really sick.

But she'd get better. After all, she was only thirty-two. Nobody dies at thirty-two anymore. As I moved out of the elevator, I saw her sitting on a wooden bench near the nurses' station, reading the new issue of *America*. "Are you all right? Are you ready? Bryand's downstairs bringing the car around." I sat next to her. "You look so tired. Did they draw blood? Any new medication?" I could see she had been crying. She never cried.

"Oh, Edna, what is it?" I felt a cold raw fear. "What is it?" and I grabbed her hand, her small white hand.

"They want me to see Dr. Phelan."

"Oh, God, is that all?" and my heart began pumping again.

"Irene, he's a cancer specialist."

"I know, I know, but, so what? Looking isn't finding. He sees everyone. The community uses him all the time. Stop worrying."

So what! So what! Is that all I could say? So what? One of my friends struggles with a love affair, the other might have cancer, and that's my repertoire? So what?

245

"Listen, I'll go with you. We'll see him together. Come on, come on, you'll be all right."

But would she be? An iron vise gripped my heart. Oh, God, she would be, wouldn't she?

* * * * *

The four of us gathered in my cell that night because, on my way home from the hospital, I had begged a bottle of wine from my sister Pat, who lived a few blocks from our convent. When in the dumps, party, and we did. Considering Bryand's and Edna's dire situations, we were far beneath the dumps, but we had no other outlets.

Timmy hung out my window in the cold and simmered fondue on a camp gas burner so no one inside would smell the wine and Swiss cheese. A wild sight but I was beyond caring about what people thought. We sat on the floor like Girl Scouts, dipping crusty bread in cheese and sipping what was left of the wine.

I knew our lives were too raw for good conversation so I teased about our in-house spy, the Wicked Witch who had been transferred to de Paul and was living in the corner room on the first floor of our house, the extended convent. She had appointed herself 'acting superior', snooping every time someone came in the back door. When she heard Bryand and me laughing as we climbed the stairs earlier, our wine, pan and plates hidden in a full laundry basket, she had scooted out of her cell off the kitchen to check up.

Bryand had an idea. "Suppose we just kept coming upstairs but never came down? She'd go nuts!"

"Simple justice," Timmy concluded. "Who's first?" We were desperate to distract Edna.

"Oh! I'm first, but we need a strategy." My cell on the second floor, the former parlor in the converted two-decker, faced the street, not the back yard leading to the main convent. The front stairs were never used because, for safety's sake, the steps leading to the street had been removed. Bryand and I, with our laundry basket full of clean clothes, tiptoed down, climbed over the front porch railing, dropped into the rose garden, and sneaked through the back yard. Then we pushed open the back door, laughing and chatting on our way upstairs.

Timmy and I went next, carrying school bags.

"I didn't hear you leave," the Wicked Witch commented as we climbed up the stairs.

"Oh, no?" I tossed the words back over my shoulder. She couldn't bother me anymore because I had forgiven her years ago, and I would not give anyone that kind of power over me again, the power to ruffle my feathers. I was simply polite.

"We're mean," I said.

"Yes, but isn't it glorious?" Timmy asked. The party picked up. A few others stuck their noses in, amused by our antics. Even Edna seemed perky. "I'm forty years old," Timmy complained good-naturedly, wiping tears of laughter from her eyes, "and I should be listening to opera or watching French drama, reading the classics, not carrying on like a child. Instead, I'm sitting cross-legged on the floor like a Girl Scout and playing at pranks like a sixth grader."

"Well, it isn't as if we could go out to dinner at the University Club. This is all we have." We laughed some more, and finished up with candy bars for dessert.

No time to judge pranks. Real life had blown in the door and sat among us, chilling our bones.

CHAPTER THIRTY-SIX

I prayed for Edna's good health but it wasn't to be.

I talked about Lourdes but she wouldn't consider it.

I railed at God.

It didn't work.

Her diabetes worsened as did the strange disease bent on devouring her. Facial bones protruded against tight skin. Circulation was poor; sores would not heal. By April, Edna's fingers stiffened. She could no longer read, couldn't turn the pages. Two weeks after our crazy party, Reverend Mother stationed her at the Motherhouse. She was too sick to teach. Kennedy had been murdered before Thanksgiving, just after she left. The entire country went into mourning and nothing could alleviate my gloom.

The high school faculty shifted. Bryand had had it out with Father Andrews and had requested to teach at St. Matthew's. Helen moved in from Cohoes while the principal sought a new business teacher.

In March, they sent Edna to the hospital. Monsignor Fenner visited daily and the community did what it could, sending her to Cleveland and Pittsburgh, where specialists probed and probed. Helen and I could hardly bear it but Edna felt she had to make the effort. Finally, she informed Reverend Mother she was prepared for the inevitable.

The nurses at the hospital adored her and wheeled her around to rooms where those dying had no hope. Sometimes she had little jokes, sometimes not. Sometimes she comforted them, by saying nothing! Just being. Her presence said it all.

Members of the staff drifted into her room and aired their woes. Everyone had a problem. One of their sons was taking drugs, or a niece was pregnant and she was only fifteen and what was the world coming to? Everything's gone wild. Sometimes there'd be three or four nurses in her room, sitting on the arms of chairs or the floor, eating lunches and basking in her good humor and inexplicable attitude. Maggie Kamora, the head nurse, told me Edna was a holy woman. "She's a mystic. Look at her face. I've seen them come and go. I see people dying every day. But this one," and she blew her nose loudly, "this one is different."

"I know, Maggie. I think so too."

Edna's soul glowed from within her withering body. I was so jealous of my time with her that I bargained with the nurses. I'd walk over from de Paul every day and from four to four thirty, they had better see to it that no one interrupted us. When I wasn't there, other friends or Helen or Monsignor were.

We never discussed death. Helen unearthed jokes. Edna was corny and loved puns. I read her *The Little Prince* in French and she told me my accent was rotten. So I tried Oscar Wilde, cut out cartoons from *The New Yorker*.

Helen and I recounted stories about the girls we taught. I complained because I had inherited her religion classes. "What a rat you are! Leaving me religion classes. You're the theologian. Not me. The girls are clamoring. When are you coming back?"

But she was never coming back.

We'd always joked about the mystery of T. S. Eliot's *The Waste Land*, and the last day I saw her, I quoted from him. The words sounded marvelous but except for Macavity and his pals, a great deal of T. S. was over my head.

"I don't care what he means, Edna. I know what I mean."

It was written for her. All those years, living in gray, without any light. No light at all. I knew no other way to tell her I stood in awe of her inner battles and her astounding spiritual life.

And I read it to her.

"What have we given?
My friend, blood shaking in my heart,
The awful daring of a moment's surrender
Which an age of prudence can never retract
By this, and this only, we have existed, ... "

They talked about amputating her leg. Her LEG? Were they crazy? What good would it do? Prolong her suffering? Helen told me I chewed out the doctors, Monsignor, everybody. I don't remember.

The last thing Edna asked me was, "Are you going to be all right?"

"Am *I* going to be all right? Of course I am!" But you're not, my dear friend, I sobbed to myself. She died that night in her sleep.

Edna's wake was held at the Motherhouse and I knelt in chapel despite Helen's objection, keeping the vigil throughout both nights. I left in the middle of the funeral Mass and fled into the music parlor, the same parlor where we had received our habits years ago. I shut the door and keened, howled like a wild animal.

I couldn't stop.

She would read her books in the land of God now, and I would see her again, but it was no comfort and my heart split with grief and loss. They said later Clarissa found me, gave me something and put me to bed. I don't remember.

But I remembered the night before that, when I knelt before her poor faded body. "You promised! You promised me we'd grow old together," I sniffed. "You rat. Just wait until I see you again. You'll pay." I slipped a letter into her big sleeves, that she could carry with her and show to God, so He would know how badly He had wounded me. Then, I kissed her little hand and whispered, "Later, later."

A Poem

"I through all chances that are given to mortals,
And through all fates that be,
So long as this close prison shall contain me,
Yea, though a world shall sunder me and thee,

Thee shall I hold in every fiber woven,
Not with dumb lips nor with averted face
Shall I behold thee . . . in my mind embrace thee,
Instant and present, thee in every place.

eu'lo·gy

Yea, when the prison of this flesh is broken,
And from the world I shall have gone my way,
Wheresoever in the wide universe I stay me,
There shall I bear thee, as I do today.

Think not the end that from my body frees me,
Breaks and unshackles from my love to thee:
Triumphs the soul above its house in ruins,
Deathless, begot of immortality.

Still must she keep her senses and affection,
Hold them as dear as life itself to be.
Could she choose death, then she might choose forgetting,
Living, remembering, to eternity. "

St. Paulinus of Nola to his friend.

CHAPTER THIRTY-SEVEN

Edna's death forced me to re-examine my life. She had known she was dying and, heartbroken, I had observed her slowly embracing the inevitable.

Bryand also faced shattering decisions. Just as I thought, he was taking advantage. He felt she was wonderfully pleasant but had no intention of going anywhere. She opted to sort out her strong emotions away from him and de Paul. I suspected Helen had chosen her vocation at age twelve, bought a ticket for the train and would ride it blissfully forever. I had always thought my vocation was as clear as Helen's. I knew I wanted the God-centered life I had opted for in sixth grade. I couldn't see myself anywhere else.

I did want the sisters to be part of the world, though, free to move in and out of people's lives, helping them, aiding them as a friend, not coldly dispensing advice through grills or shouting it over high walls. Christ jumped right into the middle of the fray, enjoyed weddings, hob-nobbed with low life, reformed the wealthy, chatted with whores, slept in rowboats, lost His temper and threw the money changers out of the temple.

That's for me!

Some sisters didn't care what they did; they embraced either deep faith or deeper inertia, relying on the authority that had always ruled their lives. Some could foresee attitudinal changes but could not make the connection that their ways would be drastically affected. Those of us who sought reforms watched the Church scrutinize changing currents. Was it my vocation to force hands, to push for reform, no matter what, as Helen and Edna had always implied?

* * * * *

Helen had been appointed the superior of St. Matthew's, an old convent in a poor parish in the lower north end. It was late afternoon and we sat in one of the parlors in her convent, a beautiful three-

252

storied stone building. Hand carved mahogany moldings joined the twelve-foot high walls to coffered, paneled ceilings. The sultry sun joined us, languidly sprawling over the dark, velvet sofa. No one else was home and Helen and I had time to reconnoiter the place in peace and list necessities.

"I'm asking permission to go to my niece's Baptism."

Helen looked up. "Oh?"

"Why can't we go to Baptisms? My chastity won't be in danger if I see or hold a baby."

"You won't leave a stone unturned," Helen informed her notebook, without looking up.

"Edna said that to me once." My whole heart ached when I thought about Edna and I knew Helen felt the same.

I shifted my weight in the captain's chair then bent over to unlace my new oxfords and rub my chaffed instep. "Helen, I don't need to be protected."

Helen stood up, observing me quietly. "We should head back to camp or we'll run into traffic."

"Be with you in a minute," and I quickly tied my shoes. As Helen drove towards Averill Park on Rt. 66, battling the onset of rush-hour traffic, I continued our conversation as if it had never been interrupted.

"When I couldn't go to my sisters' wedding receptions, I accepted it, because nuns put guests on edge. That's understandable." I stopped at the light. "People freeze up and examine their consciences and twist their hats in their hands when they're with nuns.

"But the Nuptial Mass itself? A sacrament? My own sisters' weddings? What's behind it?"

"Umm." I exhausted Helen but her lack of enthusiasm didn't deter me.

"I wasn't snared, or led into this life, a schnook, with no mind, no sense, no backbone. And I don't feel the need to be protected from a sacrament."

Helen looked out at the sprawling farms, at the rows of ecru and green corn, at the shiny tar, oiled by mirage, at dry parched grasses, longing for rain. I gave her a rest and watched the road in silence all the way back to the camp. The Baptism was not the beginning of my campaign. The previous June, as a special present to the nuns, the bishop had hired an entire amusement park near Lake George just for the day, so all orders of sisters could enjoy an outing. But instead of being grateful, I wouldn't go.

"Does he think we're Girl Scouts, Bryand?" I complained one night after dinner as we put away the dishes. I was visiting St. Matthew's for the weekend. "Would the pastors spend the day out there? Like children?" I asked as I stacked the heavy white plates in the cupboard.

"Most of the sisters don't see it your way, Irene. It's a day out. They'll go, meet their friends, enjoy the picnic, and ride the rides. And be careful of those plates."

I ignored her. "And poor Sister Edmund! She has a week's work piled up on her desk, but she'll go, thinking it's her duty." I thought a minute.

"Bryand, next Saturday there's a Rembrandt Exhibit at the Met in New York. Want to take an early bus down?" Our feast day money was ours to keep now and the sisters stretched it to unbelievable lengths.

"What about the picnic?"

"What about it?"

Pause. "You're on." We sat a full hour on a shabby velvet bench in a room crammed with Rembrandts stacked nearly to the ceiling. After lunch, we visited the Modern Museum of Art. What an experience! I was grateful to Bryand. She liked picnics and the rides even better. When Sister Edmund's picture appeared on the front page of *The Times Union*, riding on a merry-go-round, I was fuming. As long as the laity could dismiss our antics as childish, they could dismiss what we said, too. Whew! I'm angry all the time lately, I thought as we turned down the dirt road that led to our Villa. I'm losing my sense of humor. This vacation would do me good.

* * * * *

Our new Reverend Mother granted me permission to attend my niece's Baptism, treating the request lightly. "I think you'll be the first in the community to go." Times were changing and I was doing my part to push them along. I knew we could respond to raw need, and keep our purpose intact. "The spirit of the community dwells within the sisters living at the time," Bertrand had said.

So, here I am, God. Here I am.

But, here I am to do what?

The answer wasn't long in coming. School had resumed in September and I suspected the girls in my classes thought we were dried up old relics who didn't have a clue about their problems or temptations. With morality evaporating at the rate it was, and 'Experience it, baby' rolling in on silver wheels from California, where did religion fit into their lives? Since I headed up the department, I could dispose of our outdated religion books that stressed judging how much and what kind of servile work we could perform on Sundays without committing a mortal sin. Bring religion up to date.

* * * * *

"Shut the door, Sister."

"Thank you, Father."

"I have a problem."

"I can see that."

"It's the religion book. It's an antique."

"I see." He sat back in his oak chair behind his office desk and his huge blue eyes quietly observed me. I amused Father MacKenzie, our principal, and we often joked together, but I was not in the mood today.

"Father, I would like you to consider new religion texts. You can't expect the girls to spend three days digesting the intricacies of Church Law regarding servile work on Sundays, when Carol Franks has hopped a bus to California with her older brother to join some crazy cult in Los Angeles." I had prepared that sentence, and Father seemed impressed. Carol's bolt was the talk of the school.

"Sister, I'd like to help you out but we're not able financially to purchase new texts. Besides, with the Council still in session, there are bound to be changes we can't anticipate at the moment. New books might be outdated before we can get our use out of them." He sounded prepared too. Someone must have warned him.

Catholic schools were poor and even our ditto paper was rationed. "Father, I understand but I'm scrapping this text and teaching the girls what is relevant to their lives." I had a class in three minutes and as I rose to leave, I added, "They'll pass the Diocesan exam, Father, but this text is in Limbo." He nodded, and I left. Why had I asked him? Out of habit? Afraid to move without permission? After all, I was the head of the religion department.

But what if he had insisted that I use them in the same old way?

* * * * *

"All right, girls, take out your religion books and lay them on your desk. From now on, we'll devote the first half-hour of this class to practical religion. Ask me anything you want, and if I can answer, I will. If I can't, I'll find out." (Raised eyebrows, suspicious looks.)

"During the last twelve minutes of our class, we'll read silently. You are responsible for the content of the book. The week before exams, we'll review, and if you've done your reading, you'll pass. Any questions?"

They stirred in their seats and I allowed them time to buzz. Why not? A girl from this group had been sent to her grandmother's in Nebraska last year to have her baby, while the father, a senior, played Varsity basketball and dated someone else. Where could they find straight answers? From each other? On the second day, the girls selected Cheryl spokesman and she bravely inquired, "Sister, is it a mortal sin to get a hickey?" They tittered but were alert, interested.

"Well, I'd be glad to answer that but what is a hickey?" We all laughed, some nervously, and as Cheryl struggled through her explanation, I realized the girls were serious. Some never took their eyes off their hands but since I wasn't embarrassed, we muddled through. I stood leaning against the desk, semi-sitting and remembered Sister Boniface and her martyrs. What would she think about this conversation? The girls had written their questions and most of them involved boys and sex. "What you're asking me is, how far can I go and still be a good girl? You'll have to let me read the questions. That's fair. I promise I won't hedge. Give me until tomorrow."

I was ready for them the next day. I assumed my leaning position and stared at my cards. "What do we have here? Can I give or get a hickey? How far can he fondle? What part of me is untouchable? Is under the bra off limits? How far up the legs? All right, girls, this is how I see it."

"It boils down to, why all these rules about sex? Well, it's one of our strongest appetites. But first, let's pretend that the Commandments don't exist." And I went on about the rush of passion, its absolute joy, BUT the need to protect oneself against pregnancy for the sake of the child. "There's where the rules come in. Other animals can mate at will, but human animals need protection for years and years. It's the bottom line. All the taboos about sex are for someone's protection, not to cramp style. Remember, girls, you're the ones who will bear that child and be responsible for it. And that's the reason the nuns are always on your case. The Commandments are guidelines, not barbed wire fences. They're rules we should follow to get us through life."

Nobody volunteered anything.

"No fair. I told you what I think. It's your turn."

"But you didn't answer any of our questions."

"But I answered *all* your questions. When you're locked in someone's arms, you're the only one who knows how far you can go!" I moved away from the desk and began gesturing. "Once you're into a passion, do you think you can turn it off like a faucet? And what about the boy? While you feel warm and fuzzy, or whatever, he's poised for the take. It's biological. The male animal in its teens is hot to trot," and we all laughed, as the girls exchanged knowing glances.

"Suppose, suppose he uses something so the girl won't get pregnant."

"You already know the Church doesn't sanction having sex outside of marriage."

"Why?"

"All right, again, let's pretend there were no Commandments. What do you believe? That having intercourse with just anyone is fulfilling or dissipating? Does that kind of intimacy mean something or nothing to you? If it means something, then you'll experience something. The Church happens to think it's something, too. That it's an expression of real love and especially, commitment. "But if you think it's no more than a physical thrill, that's what you'll get, the same as the dogs on the street. And the Church believes you deserve better than that. Besides, if people act like animals in that intimate area, what's to prevent the attitude from spreading to all segments of their act and thought?"

They had no comeback.

"Look, I'm no sex expert. Ask Mrs. Josephs, your business teacher. I'm not married, and I'm not sleeping around. See what she has to say."

"You know, Sister, you're real different. Are you talking about the Church or are these your ideas?"

"I'm trying to teach you that practicing religion isn't being stuck with a set of no-no's."

CHAPTER THIRTY-EIGHT

Chris Josephs, an old classmate, had replaced Sister Bryand in the business department. As I stood in my doorway doing corridor duty between change of classes, she rushed past me on her way to the typing room and asked, "What's going on in your religion class? I've been barraged during my shorthand period with questions about sex. You're breaking new ground." She stopped for a second, and peered at me over her half-glasses. "They're drooling over that new rock star, the dirty one with the stringy hair and black fingernails. I told them if that's what they want to wake up to in the morning, they're beyond my advice!"

"Someone has to talk to them. All they think about is boys." She dashed away to her class, laughing. As the weeks went by, the girls began trickling into my room after last period, goofing off, chatting, dancing around their problems with jokes. But there were plenty of things on their minds besides boys.

"My stepfather is putting the move on me, Sister, and I can't be in the house alone with him. Nobody believes me. What am I going to do?"

"My mother's a drunk, Sister. When I go home after school, she's passed out on the floor. I can't get her to the priest. My brother is fifteen. He's in trouble, I know he is. He stays out all night. There's only the three of us. I work part-time, but it's not enough. What am I going to do?"

"Sister, I think I'm in love with a girl. I've never had feelings like these for any boy. I think about her all the time. I think about holding her and kissing her. What's wrong with me? What am I going to do?"

Dear God, I thought, what am *I* going to do? I went to Sister Edmund.

"Sister, I know the girls come to you and that you've been listening to them for years. Can you help me? I'm over my head."

"Why don't you ask to study counseling? You'll be finished with your art soon, no?"

259

"I'll think about that, Sister," but I didn't leave. Her office, originally a storage room, was dingy, crowded but neat, and lit by one skinny window opening onto the grimy air shaft that rose, tenement-like, through the middle of the building. How did she work in here? Couldn't they find her an office, a decent office? Even the brave little geranium, battling for its life on the windowsill, couldn't dispel the gloom.

"Sister, you've been the principal here since I was a student. I know times have changed but have the problems changed? Are these situations new or was I that sheltered?"

"Probably a little of both." She took off her thick, wire rimmed glasses and cleaned them with a large man's white handkerchief. "We're living in turbulent times. Most of *our* roots are grounded in a very conservative era. We should be able to bend with these winds. But if adults are having difficulty adjusting to the changes, even with the advantage of a strong upbringing, imagine what it must be like being young with no solid frame of reference at all?"

* * * * *

I made up my mind about counseling and couldn't wait to talk to Helen and Bryand. "Helen, what do you think? About counseling, I mean."

"You'd never keep quiet long enough to hear what they have to say."

"Well, thanks a lot!" Helen looked tired. Interesting because her economy of physical movement always astounded me. She appeared to stand in the same place and accomplish everything without ever moving her feet.

"Come on, Helen, I'm *already* counseling without any official training. Besides, they'll teach me technique." This particular Friday night in early December, we were lounging in the front parlor in St. Matthew's Convent. Even though she was the superior, Helen took her turn getting meals claiming cooking relaxed her. We ate broiled red snapper with Mornay sauce and baked potatoes with sweet butter. Where did she ever find fresh asparagus?

"You should have been a chef, Helen," Bryand commented.

"Pooh to the chef business, Bryand," I chided. "Don't you care about *my* future?"

She laughed. "I love to keep you hanging. You're easy to tease."

"Well you know how things go around this place. We're always interrupted so I have to grab you when I can."

Bryand settled back in her overstuffed chair. "I do think you'd be a good counselor. When I needed you, you listened and didn't fudge. Have you asked Reverend Mother yet?"

"Yes, and she can't afford to send me this year, maybe next." I discussed the problems of the girls at de Paul and I knew by my friends' comments they had more savvy than I. Around ten-thirty, the doorbell rang, loud and uneven and someone was pounding hard. "What's going on?" I asked. We were the only ones up and since this wasn't the best part of town, I was alarmed.

Helen, never flustered, went to the window then hurried to the front door. "What in the name of God are you doing here at this time of ni...Oh, dear God, Vickie! The three of you get in here, hurry. You'll catch your death," and she shoved the three young Negro girls into the parlor.

The older one was a bloody mess, the right side of her face, gashed. Her lip and upper right arm were cut and bleeding; her blouse was ripped at the neck. The youngest was still in sleepers, wide-eyed but excited, and the one about fourteen was raging, but not hysterical. None of them had coats and it was below freezing.

"Sister Bryand, sit Vickie on the couch, and find a towel to clean her up. Vickie, lay your head back, and throw this sweater over you, honey." Helen turned to the fourteen-year-old. "What happened, Glory?"

"He raped her. That bastard raped her. I came in! He was on top of her. On the floor. He was drunk. And I hit him. On the back of the head. I left him lying there on the floor." Her eyes narrowed and she defiantly thrust her contorted face into Helen's. "I don't care if he is my father. I hope he's dead." I had moved toward the little one and put my arm around her. She looked terrified now, clutching her shabby stuffed cat that observed the world with only one eye. Vickie had been staring at the ceiling, saying nothing, as Bryand who had scurried back with warm water, gently cleaned off her face.

"Vickie," Helen said, quietly, "you'll have to go to the hospital." She stirred, about to protest. "I promise I won't leave you for a minute."

"I'm okay, Sister, I'm okay. He didn't," she looked down, "he didn't get in. Glory came just in time." She touched her face. "It hurts. I think he broke my jaw."

The youngest one didn't need to hear this. "What's your name, honey?" I asked, looking down at her.

"Keneesha."

"Do you want some hot cocoa and chocolate chip cookies?"

She couldn't have been more than seven. Keneesha's skin was much darker than the other girl's and her hair was thick and long, braided into two soft plaits. A beautiful child. Helen and I had been talking with our eyes, gesturing with nods, so I led her downstairs into the kitchen and began the chitchat I used to distract young children. I put her up on the stool and gave her three cookies. "We have a big kitchen and we have to walk around a lot to cook and we use all those big pots," I commented, tapping them all as I walked by. She watched me solemnly, and then tears began to run down her face.

"Oh, don't cry, honey," and I ran around the huge stainless steel worktable to comfort her. "Vickie will be fine. She's with the sisters and Glory. And you can stay here with me and we'll play upstairs. There're presents upstairs." The Christmas toy drive was on and the community room was littered.

The tears turned into a howl. "Where'll we sleep? We got no home. And Daddy's daid on the floor."

"No, no, no, no. He isn't dead, and you'll sleep here with us." I prayed he wasn't dead anyway.

Suddenly, Bryand appeared, rushed to Keneesha and gave her a big squeeze."We're leaving," she told me as she pet the little girl's thick hair. "Helen contacted Father McCullen and the girls' mother. She wants you to call Jim O'Neill and tell him what happened. Here's his number and Vickie's address. Someone has to go over there. He knows."

"Jimmy! What's he got to do with this?"

"Oh, I forgot you knew him. Good. He's our right arm. Helps us out all the time. Don't let anybody in. If there's noise at the door, call the police. "Keneesha, you're a lucky girl." She leaned down and squeezed her again. "You can play with my friend and all the toys we have upstairs," and she waved at us and hurried out of the kitchen, taking the stairs by twos to the front door.

Call Jimmy right now, I thought. Dear God, will it be awkward? He had dropped by when I was visiting Mom and Dad last year and we caught up on our lives quite formally but I hadn't seen him since."Come on, honey," I told Keneesha, "we're going upstairs and you're going to play and I'm going to use the phone and then we'll be together."

But Keneesha had settled her little back end on that stool, the only concrete thing in the world that she related to on this terrible night and nothing except that bit of stability enticed her. Her eyes widened as she grabbed the stool and her stuffed cat simultaneously, and murmured, "I don' wanna go."

"I don't blame you, sweetheart, but we can't stay down here. It's too cold and Cat will be sick." I examined the one eyed toy. "He doesn't look good to me at all. Tsk, tsk, tsk! He needs a blanket and you need a sweater. I think mine will fit. You don't want to take care of a sick cat down here all by yourself, do you?"

She decided not. Besides, I think trying on my sweater intrigued her. Jimmy was out playing poker when I called so I talked to his wife, Lois. "I always know where he is," she said, good naturedly. "Don't worry. I'll get hold of him."

The sisters and Glory returned after three, and since it was too late for coffee, Father had walked them to the door and left. Keneesha was asleep at my feet in the community room, clutching her toy on the makeshift bed the two of us had put together with sofa pillows. Around twelve, the cocoa had kicked in and she dozed off. The poor thing was exhausted, but I was itching with anticipation, laden with questions. My imagination was running wild. Had Glory killed her father? Is Vickie all right?

Glory had been determined to stay at the hospital but Helen persuaded her that Keneesha needed her more. Bryand and Helen brought her home and we put her into an empty guest cell with twin beds and carried in the sleeping Keneesha. Glory laughed and laughed at herself in the nun's long white nightgown, but she finally threw herself into Helen's arms and sobbed.

I was about to cry myself. The child was fourteen, her sister, sixteen. What a horrible thing to happen! Thank God they had a place to go! We were all exhausted but I stopped by Helen's cell before turning in. "I'm so glad she's all right. What about the father?"

"Come in. Don't wake the children." She shut the door behind me.

"This is strictly between us. Vickie's jaw isn't broken but he did rape her and if Glory finds out, Vickie is afraid she'll find her father and kill him. And frankly," Helen mused, "so am I."

"Is the father all right?"

"Yes. Jimmy has friends. They went to the house. The father was in a drunken stupor. Glory gave him a bump on the head, nothing more. He had no recollection at all of what he had done, and it's just as well.

"You know, their mother is a good woman. She works nights to support herself and the girls, but every once in a while, this character shows up and wreaks havoc. This will be the last time, I'm sure. Jimmy's friends have means of persuasion that I don't want to know about. He told me they gave him money and warned him to take the first bus out of town. Jimmy doubts if he'll be by again."

"What's going to happen? Will she press charges?"

"No. She's decided not to."

"Do you mean to tell me he's going to get *away* with it?"

"Vickie can do whatever she wants. There will be no records at the hospital. Maggie Kamora and I have seen to that." Helen swooped off her linens, hung them on a hook on the door and shook out her hair, running her fingers through it, pushing it out of her eyes. "Vickie wants no one to know, not even her mother. She says the story will follow her forever, and she's right. Glory on the other hand, wouldn't care. She'd wear the incident like a badge. But Vicki isn't Glory and that's that. Go to bed. You must be tired."

"Not as bad as you. I'll take care of Keneesha in the morning, fix her breakfast and play with her. You and Bryand sleep in. There's a funeral at eleven so you can go to that Mass tomorrow."

"All right, but when the mother comes to collect the girls, get me up. She was afraid she'd lose her job if she left work tonight. No one in the convent need know what happened. The story is, the father came home and started a fight. The girls left and came here. You know nothing more, right?"

"Fine," but I didn't leave. "Helen, what's going to happen to them now?"

"What do you mean? They'll go home to their mother."

"Just like nothing ever happened?"

"That's right. Just like nothing ever happened." Helen looked old tonight. "People lead difficult lives, Mary."

"Yes, I can see that." I went to bed but couldn't sleep. Good Lord, what a fright! I knew Helen would arrange help for Vickie on the sly but could Vickie recover? Would she? I felt so helpless. What would I say to her if I were her counselor? I didn't know but I made up my mind that somehow, I was going to find out.

As I dozed off, I thought that this could never have happened at de Paul. The last place the girls would have gone was to the convent.

Sisters at St. Matthew's did much more than teach school.

CHAPTER THIRTY-NINE

The reality of life at St. Matthew's enthralled me. I convinced a few of my de Paul honor students to help me run a Head Start program for the neighborhood children. During the following summer, we knocked on doors, disturbed family picnics, chatted with parents through iron fences if we spotted a four-year-old, stopped mothers in the convenience store…anything to collect pupils. We taught weekday mornings during July in St. Matthew's convent community room. In the afternoon, I gave sewing lessons at the high school and at night, supervised dances for the teens. Any spare minute I had, I spent at St. Matthew's.

One Saturday afternoon in early October, I was visiting for the weekend. Timmy was due in that evening to wind up our plans for a community newspaper, a bulletin to keep 'the girls' abreast of impending Vatican changes. Bryand, Helen and I sat on the rickety, wooden, sloping back porch off the third floor on an exquisite clear afternoon, waiting for the Notre Dame football game to begin on the radio.

Someone was burning leaves and the acrid smoke drifted idly across our trim yard. While Helen ran her fingers under her sheer silk veil, hunting for loose threads, a flock of chirping robins landed on the mountain ash below us. The birds stripped the tree of its bright orange berries, fueling up for their long journey south. Helen began delicately rolling and stitching the hem where the thread had unraveled.

"You won't be doing that much longer if the Vatican has its way. I can hardly believe the Council is pushing for modernization of the habit. How are you coming on your new design, Irene? You'd better make us look good."

"Not so loud."

"Don't tell me this is another undercover operation," Bryand exclaimed in disgust, "like that St. Rose lecture."

"Reverend Mother doesn't want the sisters agitated."

"You mean she doesn't want to stir up Dead Eye and her crew."

"Dead Eye is scared! I could never convince her or any of her cronies that reform is not dissipation." Helen had over-stitched the hem of the veil and knotted the silk thread several times. She clipped it with a manicure scissors, leaving no tail, and went on. "But there it is, Mary. In Dead Eyes' view, in all of the old guard's view, Vatican II is your fault, and the habit especially. The sisters are nervous. Some of them believe the loss of their habit strikes at the very meaning of their life. It sets them apart."

"But Reverend Mother *told* me to design the habit and that's where my obedience lies. Rome directed us to modify our habits. How authoritative can you get? Would you believe Edmund and Abigail are leading the pro-change brigade at de Paul? I let Sister Edmund sneak a look at the one I designed for Sister Rosemary and she loved it. It will flatter everyone and it's a snap to keep clean."

"Some of the older sisters are up for anything," Bryand mused. "It's more a case of attitude than age."

"You bet. I consider myself a young sister but I hate some of these new hymns and love the Gregorian chants. I know most of them. That's what's so crazy about this whole Church reform thing! The Council threw the Latin Mass out the window and nobody had a choice. All that history, all that magnificent music!

"But the sisters do have a choice about their habit. No one is going to have to change, just the ones who want to. So what's the big deal?"

"What does it look like?" Bryand asked.

"Rosemary modeled it last week for the R.M. It's simple, black, washable, light, just below the knee and looks good on everybody. If the older sisters want it long, they can have it long. The headgear is a white cap that waves slightly near the cheeks then over the ears, shows a bit of hair, and the veil...it's short, hits the middle of the back.

"At least," I continued, "we'll finally have peripheral vision. Some of the IHM's have lost theirs. So many years wearing blinders."

"Reverend Mother really hopes all the Mercies will go the same way. No Heinz 57 Variety like other orders who can pick and choose." Bryand fell back into her rocker and whistled softly through her teeth. "You know, she told me last week that when the day comes that she has to announce to all the sisters that the habit is going to change, she's afraid someone will stand up in the auditorium and shoot her. And I don't think she was kidding."

"She'd better frisk Dead Eye." Helen's hands rested quietly on the veil she had draped carefully over her lap. "The whole country is in chaos. Vietnam, race riots in Watts. The trouble is everything is happening at once and no one would believe it was coming. No one would listen. Now, instead of sensible change, the world is teetering on the brink of revolution."

"We've been in the community around sixteen years," Bryand said, "give or take. With all that's happened, it seems we entered centuries ago."

We sat quietly for awhile as a train whistle from the Rennselaer side of the river drowned us out, wailing from afar, moaning and moaning, announcing its purpose to speed off to places unknown. Helen had slipped her veil into a piece of tissue and wrapped it tightly in dark fabric to protect it from the light. I stared at the neat little black square as she lay it on the table next to her.

"Life is moving so fast," she said.

"It sure is," said Bryand, consulting her watch. "Pick up your veil, Helen, it's game time."

* * * * *

"It's game time! It's game time." The impassioned announcer reported the frenzied clashes of the 'Fighting Irish' while Bryand and Helen corrected papers. As I doodled with the draft of a logo for our newspaper, my mind wandered. It was game time all right. In more ways than one.

In October, 1964, the Vatican Council issued the Constitution of the Church, *Lumen Gentium* (The Light of the People). I never read beyond the first two chapters and was ecstatic, felt like a mystic.

The Pilgrim People! The People of God! All mankind, regardless of religious beliefs, trekking through this world, in it, but not of it, trying to fathom the mess, clinging to God and His love, to Christ's Gospel and its radical twist. Carrying the Light and seeking the Light!

I was inflamed by the Holy Spirit who led us, by the Sacramental grace that nourished us, as pumped up as I was when I was a novice or when I made my First Communion. The first section was inspired, poetic, and I dined on it, prayed from it. We are the 'Light of the World'. Yes, yes! But when Timmy, Bryand and I discussed the document last week, I found Timmy interpreted it differently. We were concluding our preliminary plans for our newspaper in the community room at St. Matthew's, and as Timmy shuffled her work into her battered leather briefcase, I wondered how she ever kept track of anything.

"We are the 'Light of the world' all right, the tail light."

"Come on, Timmy, the Pilgrim People? Embracing the world, all religions, all beliefs." Timmy never criticized.

"It's mystical, poetry." I turned to Bryand for support. "It's poetry. You love poetry."

"You haven't read chapter III yet. The document lapses into the old paternalistic routine. 'I am the hierarchy, able to interpret all things. Submit your mind and will. I'm always right. Revere me.'"

"Oh, Bryand, don't take the wind out of my sails," I moaned.

"Be prepared," Timmy warned. "The tone changes drastically in the third chapter. What a shame! I feel they missed their chance," and she snapped her leather case shut. To protect myself, I had delayed reading the section describing the roles of the pope, bishops, priests, and deacons, but eventually, I succumbed. I'll have to break down and read chapter III, I sighed, after supper while the 'old girls' are washing their hair.

On every other Friday night, I had volunteered to be the in-house barber at de Paul. The habit would change soon, revealing manes neglected for years. Sister Edmund's and Abigail's thick, gray waves were no problem but poor Sister Vincent's hair had thinned so badly, we were trying warm olive oil treatments and lots of massage. I laid a threadbare sheet on the infirmary floor in de Paul and rewashed the thinning shears and combs, then finally read chapter III. When I finished, I threw the book straight across the room. "Why? Why? WHY?" Sister Edmund, who had knocked softly and was just entering, barely escaped being struck. "Why what?" she asked and she picked up and handed me the book, then wrapped an oversized towel around her shoulders, and settled into the kitchen chair.

"Why what?"

"I just finished reading chapter III of *Lumen Gentium* and I'm raging!"

"Mary, Mary, Mary," she clucked.

"More and more rules, rules, rules! Obey, obey, obey! Not think, think, think!" Edmund didn't stir and I played with her thick, damp, hair, pushing in and coaxing out waves where I could, as I lowered my voice dramatically, slamming each word and wagging my finger, "If you don't do what you're told," I sing-songed, grimacing ferociously.

Edmund clucked a little.

I sighed and switched combs. "You know, I love the idea of the Pilgrim People. Why didn't they leave it at that?"

She squirmed in her seat. "Don't be angry at my hair, dear. I didn't write the documents."

"I'm sorry," and I combed more gently, "but will the Church ever learn from its mistakes? The Inquisition? Greed, torture and murder? How could that have flown? And the list of forbidden books, plus the Church's silence during the Holocaust? That was only twenty-five years ago! And now they're asking me to believe they're right about everything? Come on!"

"You sound like Martin Luther."

"He wasn't so bad." I had begun snipping tentatively, around her ears. "All he wanted were needed reforms. He was looking for a fair fight, and look at what happened. Hundreds of thousands of people without the sacraments for centuries because of bull-headedness."

"Mary," she asked, a bit alarmed, "don't you believe in the divine nature of the Church?"

"The Apostle's Creed? The sacraments? Matters of faith or morals, yes, but opinions? Opinions change every week, Sister. Can't the Church say," and I lowered my voice, dramatically, "We're exploring. This matter is under consideration. Can you help us? What do you think? If they had done that with Galileo, they would have saved face."

She handed me the razor and I trimmed the back of her neck carefully. "The Church should be seeking the Light not guarding the tomb. If I had been alive during the Inquisition, they would have burned me at the stake."

"More probably spontaneous combustion," Edmund commented as she stood and brushed off her towel. "Mary, don't upset yourself. The Church is human, too. It plods along just like the rest of us but God is divine and He sees that it will all turn out. Have patience." But she looked worried. I stuck the combs into soapy water.

"Don't forget to set those waves, Sister. Use Dippity Doo, or your hair will fly and you'll look untidy." Some of the old girls had no respect for vanity, so I pushed neat. They'd pursue neat.

Sister Abigail sat serenely waiting her turn. Without her hearing aids, she smiled all the time. The two of them, I thought. Would I ever in my life be that calm and accepting? Was I supposed to be? That was the question that dogged me. The Vatican documents had shaken up most religious orders. Besides the veiled expansion of the Doctrine of Infallibility, they made it clear that there were two distinct bodies in the Church: the hierarchy and laity, and nuns were not hierarchy. No way! Even though sisters semi-knew that in the past, the habit and their spiritual life had leant an aura of authority to religious that mirrored and sometimes superseded the authority of the clergy.

So, what were we now? Laity, with the laity's responsibilities, finally expanded and defined? Would the next document be more hopeful?

It was, sort of. After combing the Decree, however, I realized the paragraphs about the vow of obedience could have been taken straight out of Tanquerey, our novitiate book.

"After the example of Jesus Christ who came to do the will of the Fathe...religious under the motion of the Holy Spirit, subject themselves in faith to their superiors who hold the place of God."

I read it in the presence of the Blessed Sacrament, because I did not buy the Church's idea of obedience anymore.

My God, it was straight out of the Divine Right of Kings! Poverty and chastity I understood. Obedience? No. Not the way religious orders were still interpreting it. As hard as I tried to believe that Christ came only to do His Father's will, it left me cold. Always 'Christ was obedient unto death.' Was that the only reason for the Crucifixion?

Didn't Christ have anything to say about it?

Here is God, who values free will above all things. All the chaos and horror running wild in the world, the evil and injustice, God could stop with a flick! But He doesn't, because, above all, He values our free will.

Instead, He leaves us to each other's mercy as He was left to ours!

I looked up at the golden tabernacle, at the flickering sanctuary lamp, and meditated. "I can't see Your being sent down to earth to play the role of a puppet. I always believed You died for us because You wanted to show us we were worth something to You and that was the only way…not because Someone told You to, even if that Someone were Your Father.

That wasn't my God the Father.

"How do you expect me to swallow all this?" There had to be more to our life than blind obedience. On TV news last month, a driver of an eighteen-wheeler drove his tanker off the road and lost his life to avoid swiping a school bus. "Greater love than this no man hath than He lay down His life for His friend." The Crucifixion was a loving choice, not a command. Was control at the bottom of the Church's obsession with obedience, just as my father had always believed? I hated cynicism, but my mind was flowing in that direction.

What did I think the vow of obedience should entail? A lot less than everyone else, I was afraid. Lately, I sat in chapel for stretches at a time. Was the Church wearing two hats, giving lip service to reform while doggedly clinging to outdated customs? I had always had hope, but lately…

And what about our lights, our ideas? Aren't we responsible for them? Should I have to bow to an authority that oversteps its boundaries? Just like the Germans during the war? I wasn't up for throwing the Commandments out the window but doesn't inspiration apply to *us*? If not, how will things ever change? Are we sisters still at the mercy of the whims or stubbornness of the Wicked Witch and Dead Eye while the needy go hungry and wander the streets?

Where am I and where are You? I felt abandoned, as Edna must have felt all her life. Something was rumbling around inside my head and I didn't like the noise it made. Bryand's loud lament and moans from the radio announcer suddenly brought me back to the present, back into the game. "The 'Fighting Irish' aren't doing too well this season," she commented, as the enemy team marched down the field, regaining its territory.

You can say that again, I thought.

* * * * *

I aired out my feelings with Bryand one afternoon in the front parlor at St. Matthew's. "Let some of the sisters experiment, Bryand. It's how all successful reforms take place. A few people move out, the old, superfluous ways die, the new ones that are worthwhile take over."

"That's what the nuns are afraid of. You're fiddling with vowed life, Irene. Communities will never buy it. They like things the way they are."

"Not everyone has to change. Just the ones who want to," and I leaned closer to her. "Be real, Bryand. Look at St. Matthew's. What would have happened to Vickie and her sisters if it weren't for the nuns? There has to be room in the community for this kind of work and it can't be left to chance. "Suppose Dead Eye had been superior? 'I'm sorry, but it's the grand silence and the sisters are in bed. No room in the inn." I pressed on.

Dear God, won't someone agree with me?

"Stop exaggerating."

"All right. The sisters who want their life the way it is don't have to change but what about the rest of us? The community has to trust the sisters and let them loose."

"In your dreams."

I slumped into my chair. "Am I really that far out? Bryand, what am I going to do?"

"Join the Foreign Legion." And as I stood to leave, we laughed, but that's exactly what I did.

CHAPTER FORTY

A foreign mission! The Vatican II documents prodded religious communities to expand their horizons, open foreign missions and our community chose Beirut, Lebanon, under the protection of the Pontifical Mission Society. Although seventy of us volunteered, I had a hunch that I'd be chosen, and took it as a sign from God.

"You said you couldn't be sent further than Cohoes," Dad complained when I told him I was going. "Are you running away, Mary? Is anything wrong? Remember, no matter where you go, you'll take yourself with you." I protested as I looked at him, plopped in his old armchair, sad and dejected, not his usual spunky self. Mom crooked her finger at me, led me into the kitchen and backed me up against the porcelain drain board.

"If you want to go, go. I always did exactly as I pleased and so did your father. Why not you?" Dad was seventy-nine. Would he be here when I came home? And Mom might look great, but what about her? How did she feel? She'd never tell me. Here I was again, tearing up roots, leaving people I loved, my family, my good friends, my better friends for what I believed was the will of God. It weighed against my heart but I was adept at burying my losses and emotions. Enter Lady Mary, stage right, bowing, accepting admiring looks, posing for pictures for *The Times Union*, attending meetings with the Archbishop over a seven-course meal at the Four Seasons in New York.

Lady Mary spent a great deal of time with me lately.

* * * * *

The Pontifical Mission, fearing we might suffer from culture shock, surprised us with a long leisurely tour through Europe to introduce us to our new surroundings. The publicity and high living annoyed the four of us since we were supposed to be poor missionaries, but as an artist, I wallowed in the trip. Decorum dictated I remain calm, but this was a God-given gift and I was going to enjoy it. We flew over the Aran Isles at dawn and I pressed my nose to the window and gazed at round haystacks buttoning the stark lonely islands to the sea. We toured Ireland who offered us her soft greens and bright waters and sly grins and twinkling eyes, and oh, did I know where I came from. But best of all, letters were waiting at every hotel.

"Dear Sister,
What a day Saturday was! Kennedy Airport will never be the same. Imagine the R.M. renting a bus so we could see you off. I have one final comment — you get the part...
Affectionately, Helen"

"Dear Mary Bergan,
We are wondering if you really got some sleep before you started for the lakes of Kilarney and all the potatoes and cabbage. So the Irish are wonderful and Ireland is poor but beautiful! Can't wait to hear more about cousin Jo Dornan. I'm glad you left your Kennedy halves with Gerard and Francie, where they'll be appreciated. No letters from you today. For all I know, you might have stayed on in Tipperary. Don't remember me to dear old London.
Love, Mom"

We took England leisurely. The young men wore long, long hair. The young girls wore short, short skirts and everyone carried huge black umbrellas. I succumbed to the magic of Lourdes, the candlelight procession, the miracles, and in Paris, I hopped a bus to Chartres, alone, practiced my French on two older ladies and watched breathlessly as the Cathedral spires rose out of the far meadow. I later tried discussing the significance of gargoyles with the other sisters but, though they listened politely, it was lost on them.

The four of us were an odd lot with little in common except our mission. Our superior, Sister Rita, who had taught me in de Paul, was a lovable, feisty, conservative redhead with an endearing lisp, a hot temper and a closed mind. Ellen, a few years younger than I, had the disposition of an angel, appeared to glide through any calamity and made the best spaghetti sauce from scratch I've ever eaten. Stephen Mary, a strapping young woman from a small town, was the youngest. Rita had nervously confided to me that Stephen careened over perilous roads with one hand on the wheel, like a truck driver, her other arm resting on the open window. Although her blasé attitude made our teeth chatter, we all had to agree she was an excellent driver. However, Stephen despised trying to learn French and observed each of Europe's glimmering capitals through indifferent eyes. "Seen one big city, you've seen them all."

Early on, I had abandoned discussing 'the changes' with these three who were to be my companions for the next six years. Talk about renewal upset them, and loneliness, with its heavy baggage, moved into my waking hours, rustled around the edges of my nights. I wrote in my journal, "Perhaps, when I get to Beirut, my work will fulfill me. Wish I could cry for three days and get it over with…God knows it's been long enough coming." I prided myself that I could snap off any emotions, snare them in a steel trap, ignore them when they clamored for attention, but lately, repression wasn't working. Could I possibly be homesick, for the first time?

"Dear Irene, ol' bean,

How was Paris? I'm sure your postcards would be marvelous if anyone could read them. We have no address for you in Athens. Are you sleeping among the ruins? Don't give the Holy Father a hard time in Rome as the cardinals are meting out enough trouble. We convinced Reverend Mother to allow us to see the ballet in Saratoga last Friday night: Firebird and Irish Fantasy. I thought of you and wept. We miss you so already.

Love, Sister Timmy"

As planned, we eased ourselves into another world and stopped for a private visit with the Holy Father at Castle Gondolfo, his summer home. I wasn't excited, only determined to have him speak to me, to give me direction.

That day, Rome was at its best. Sunny, not too hot, sparkling. When I first saw the Holy Father, a little African girl sat contentedly on his lap, fingering his white cape while he spoke to her parents who were draped in startling bright silks. The huge room soon cleared leaving the five of us, plus two monsignors standing behind the Holy Father and a photographer, who served as an usher and escorted us to the throne. The moment's solemnity was interrupted by the red headed monsignor standing behind the Pope, frantically waving his right index finger high in the air. He caught my eye and mouthed the words, "Who's number one?" I nearly laughed out loud but nodded towards Rita, our superior, instead.

He was American, of course, and began rattling away at the pope in pleasant Italian. As I stared straight into the eyes of Pope Paul VI, he glanced at me, then at the others, then back at me. My eyes grabbed his. In halting English, our eyes still locked, he began, "I bless you, the children of your mission, the congregation, everybody. I pray for your service in religion and your glory of Christ." And then, he reached for my hand and held it, looked straight at me with his dark soulful eyes and said, "You pray for me."

Pray for *you*? I was struck. His eyes were nearly black, penetrating. Dear God! Imagine his responsibility. Sorting out all that wrangling and the diverse views of the cardinals at the Council, orchestrating chaos and succeeding the beloved John XXIII to boot.

And I thought I had troubles.

The next morning at Mass, I prayed for us both and before we left for Athens, I ran up the hill from our hotel to see Bernini's statue of St. Teresa in ecstasy. As I knelt at her feet, in my own little ecstasy, I thanked God for this amazing opportunity, this romp through the splendors of Europe, and fantasized about disappearing for months and running around Rome looking at buildings and fountains, praying in churches and eating cannelloni in outdoor cafes.

I slapped my worldly self on the wrist for relishing such thoughts but on our way to the airport, I insisted we stop at the Trevi fountain and throw in our coins. Why should I feel guilty about enjoying life? Christ wasn't dour. Most of these glories were built to honor Him, anyway. Back in London, when the four of us were wandering around the mews, I had confided to Sister Stephen that I had yearned to bicycle through Europe during the summer of my senior year in high school, but the adventure didn't thrill her.

"Not for me. Where would you shower?"

* * * * *

In 1966, Beirut, Lebanon was the jewel of the east, a little Switzerland. Oil rich Arabs from Saudi Arabia deposited money in its banks. Commerce boomed. Shining buildings, with windows guarded by intricate ironwork, sprang up everywhere...bustling, bursting, streets torn up, a city in progress. Since our convent in the mountains wasn't ready, the P.M., or Pontifical Mission had rented us an apartment through November in the heart of the city. Some sheik's son from Saudi, who had escaped the constraints of the desert, was living it up next door with belly dancers, pipes and zills, music and revelry until four every morning. While the other sisters longed for the peace of the convent, I found the whole situation fascinating.

The noise was deafening, but all Beirut was hopping. Huge trucks overran the streets and hauled bundles of thick metal cables, rebars that covered the vehicle. Plunked on the hood, tied with wire that wove through the windows, they draped over the front windshield and dragged on the ground behind. Drivers peered anxiously through them on the lookout for goat herders, poised to cross the wild roads. Slapping a ram on the back end to get him moving, the shepherds would grin through missing teeth and shrug, "I mean, what could I do?" as the herd ambled across the six-lane highway, holding up traffic that screeched to a halt.

Lebanon, and its Christian population in an Arab world, captivated me. Beirut, teeming with shops, expensive apartments, hotels and restaurants, was bordered by a sandy beach that was lapped by the Mediterranean. The terrain slowly ascended, revealing its heavenly views. As the mountains rose, the levels were divided by altitude, the seventh usually ensconced in clouds.

Many French-speaking Lebanese Catholics were well-off and since English was becoming the language of commerce, they cried for an English-speaking school. We had been assigned to design, build, and staff it in the suburbs using the plan most French Canadian sisters had adapted. Whatever the shape of the building, the architects divided it into two separate schools; the playgrounds were walled off from each other as were the children who wore different uniforms. One school, geared to the wealthy, paid a hefty tuition; the other, supported by the first, was free to the villagers. However, the sisters who taught both groups showed no discrimination. Seeing children again made us more anxious to get started.

Nuns weren't used to leisure.

As our initiation into this exotic land began, we learned protocol was all. We met: the Papal Nuncio, who looked like John XXIII and peeled us ice cold cactus fruit under a cool grape arbor; the President of Lebanon and his entourage, who invited us to pose for pictures with him in his palace; and the office staff from the Pontifical Mission, who relayed vague messages about buying land, arranging permits, where to go for our driver's license, and by the way, here's your mail.

A secular religious community of women staffed the office and I sensed the one in charge, though cordial to the teeth, had little use for us conventual sisters, who she thought spoiled and pampered. However, we became great friends with the young ones, even though I never adjusted to their receiving our mail.

One night, I realized I had fifty-seven letters to answer and decided to run them off on a machine.

"October 9, 1966
Hello and Happy Columbus Day to all!
I have much more respect for Christopher since I've seen a storm at sea.
I heard about Sister Kenan's snide remark that my typing was as bad as my writing. Hmmpphh.
First impressions. The city looks as if it's been bombed. Old structures gutted, new ones popping up all over. Imaginative

architecture. No grass, just beautiful, deep rust colored sand. Flowers everywhere. Our apartment is a minor botanical garden.

We visited two Palestinian camps last week. The second one made the South End look like Park Avenue. A boy who works for the Pontifical Mission brought us to his home…three rooms, one a porch, and all a good deal smaller than the second floor utility room at the Motherhouse. Six people live there: three men, a teenage boy, a five-year-old boy and the mother. No lav. No doors on public toilets. I truly hope our teaching here will give them skills to move out of this poverty.

I love the people. The children all came running out of the houses and hugged our legs. By the time we left, a little girl could say, 'I Angela, she Teresa.'

One man stood off, glowering at us. Finally, as he approached, I expected to hear, 'Die, Christian dog!' But he stated flatly and with difficulty, 'My brudder, ee leev een St. Loo ees,' then turned on his heel and proudly walked away.

In the eyes of the others, he could speak English.

We met Father Roberts, a Dominican who lives among the clouds in the seventh level with deaf boys he has literally gathered off the streets and snatched out of asylums, because they're thought to be crazy if they're deaf. He has taught them sign language and to speak, read and write Arabic. One seventeen year old lip-read and wrote on the board as Father dictated. He's learning English as a second language. Father uses music and rhythm and the older ones tour Europe, singing and dancing in native costumes, to raise money to support themselves. What wonderful work!

I'm itching to get going.

I took 38 shots of Greek temples, 3 showing the evolution of the Ionic column from the ram's horns. Sister Stephen is enthralled. Ha, Ha. We are all well.

In Christ, Sister Irene"

* * * * *

We continued to explore the country. Sister Stephen expertly tore over narrow, mountain roads and hairpin turns in our station wagon while Ellen and I hung on for our lives. Rita stared out the window, pale, nervously fingering her beads. In late October, we visited the Roman ruins at Baalbek, then watched Haile Selassie parade through town. In November, when we moved to our new convent, a remodeled villa on the third level, different orders of religious sisters began swarming around, because everyone wanted to meet the American nuns. We were invited to or had guests for dinner six nights out of seven, and Ellen merrily turned out scrumptious meals as effortlessly as a hen turns out eggs.

Before Christmas, we toured the Holy Land and trod on ancient cobblestones that paved the cold damp alleys. As the school children, dressed in their uniforms, shouting and laughing, ran up and down the curved narrow streets, weaving past robed Arabs, serious shoppers, and reverent tourists, we made the original Stations of the Cross.

"December 18, 1966
Dear whoever is reading this,
We spent last week in the Holy City and its environs, and I'll take it from two angles.

From a devotional point of view, as far as the sites, ceremonies, and artistic endeavors go, forget it. The places where jurisdiction is shared are catastrophes. There is no electricity to speak of and candles function valiantly, to little avail. Being artistically inclined doesn't help either. Aside from the looks of things, there is the sound. For the next eight years, the Holy Sepulcher will be under construction and the stone cutters will provide an anvil chorus from seven-thirty a.m. to sundown.

However, the shrines in the Franciscan's jurisdiction are truly beautiful...Gethsemane, Bethany and more. You might think I reek sour grapes but what is, is...a big aspect of the Holy Land. Some pilgrims could not get beyond it. For a while, neither could I.

Then, suddenly, the Gospel pops up... like the first general view of the City from a height. We stood where Christ wept over Jerusalem. We saw the magnificent Moslem Dome of the Rock, built over the old temple ruins, dominating the city. We saw no-man's-land, sandbags, barbed wire and various Christian rites divided over this or that. Add the Crusades, a few recent incidents and you begin to get the picture of why God sent the flood and wonder why He ever sent the rainbow.

Outside the city, the rolling hills, the black Bedouin tents sprinkled about, the curves in the winding roads, the women walking to the wells carrying heavy water jugs on their heads... all made the Advent liturgy live! We drove to where John the Baptist preached, to Jordan, Jericho, the Dead Sea.

Sister Rita insisted we make the Stations of the Cross, though the three of us weren't so keen on it. The city streets are narrow-narrow and donkeys doing the heavy work are ever present because cars can't navigate. The passageways are steps, cobblestones, dark corridors. They're flanked by open markets covered with stone arches, and crowded with Arabs clothed in long robes and inscrutable looks. I kept thinking, could I face this? It served me right because, you guessed it, a spirit came upon me, the same spirit that prodded me to send home 64 bottles of Lourdes water.

The scene hasn't changed much since the time of Christ. Police and traditional guards, who wear heavy cloaks and carry whips, precede the procession. Some stations are corners of buildings, a plaque in a wall, a mini chapel. The pilgrims kneel in the street. At the sixth, seventh and eighth station, the route passes through the open market, going against traffic at that.

Seymour and Hanratty couldn't have done better in the footwork department. I zipped in and out and hung close to the heels of the priest leading the prayers, the one with the megaphone, and I completely ignored the eastern tradition of 'men first'. At the last station, Brother Francis ushered me to a prime spot along with two other brothers. I could look in and see the three candles I had lit earlier in the day. I prayed for everyone.

Summation? 'God so loved the world...'

Merry Christmas, Sister Irene"

In January, we had guests from home and the four of us braved icy roads and wild French snow-mobilers on our way to the noble

Cedars in the mountains, then had early supper with John Gill and his wife from the embassy on a veranda that overlooked the Mediterranean. Young men swam in the sea as we sipped Turkish coffee.

We did everything except make progress with the school, and although we deeply appreciated our opportunities, we yearned for solid work. Each morning, Mr. Dabaghi taught us Arabic; I practiced French with anyone who would cooperate. In between all this, we worked on plans for the school late into the night. Busy, busy, busy but no real action, and although not sophisticated in worldly ways, we sensed a run-around. We were American nuns, used to getting things done.

The school situation wasn't a happy time for any of us, this pushing boulders up hill and although we laughed whenever we could, we felt we were fighting windmills, running on wheels like gerbils in a cage and so far from home, unable to move on our own.

We were prepared for French bureaucracy, but this was ridiculous! Sister Rita couldn't open bank accounts or transfer money without someone's permission. Planning to remove a closet or enclose a corridor on rough blueprints took months to approve; some people at the Pontifical Mission who had no business interfering, did. Even for Beirut, the situation was questionable. Our Jesuit chaplain, the French nuns, and our Greek advisor could not understand the delays. We could. The superior had all the responsibility and none of the power.

At least the renovation of the convent provided comic relief: no chapel, walls out, foot wide ditches in the kitchen, and mice pouring in to escape the cold. Appliances were moved because to open the oven door, we'd have to sit in the refrigerator.

Inconvenience didn't bother us. If nothing were ready, so what? The question was, would it ever be, was it supposed to be? Something had switched us 'on hold' and I had my doubts. We felt like invited guests who, once they reached their destination, found themselves pests and unwelcome. Despite our frustrated efforts to become involved, it was also becoming apparent that what I saw as our mission and what the other three sisters pictured were two different things. While I had hoped to become part of the village, friends of the shopkeepers and neighbors, their mission was to establish a convent and find their community with the other sisters and clergy in the diocese.

We had a tennis court and swimming pool on our premises. Could we give the children lessons while we learned the language? No dice. The convent grounds were private and off limits. One afternoon, some village girls had stopped at our door and we invited them in and fed them snacks and the following week, they reappeared at our gate. The sisters felt they might become pesky, dropping by all the time, and sent me out to tell them we were at prayers.

They never came back.

Here we go again! Van Olstaad versus de Paul. Oh, Lord, what have I done?

If I had wanted de Paul, I could have stayed there. Convent life, even in the Middle East, was straight out of the fifties when I had expected fewer restrictions and more freedom. I've moved myself half way around the world, full of hope for a real apostolate, left my family, friends, my special little community, all my interests. For what?

I could feel the floor slowly sliding out from under me.

* * * * *

Anything, let's do anything! "Why can't we open a small summer school in the convent for the village children," Rita asked. "We could teach mornings." So we delved into plans and composed flyers. The Canadian nuns had offered us extra room at their school next fall. Was life looking up? No! The Pontifical Mission said we must spend our time planning our own school. No moving in with the Canadian or French nuns in the fall.

What was going on? Were they driving us out, hoping we'd give up and go away? Why did they ever ask us here? Was it a good idea gone bad, or had the timing gone wrong? If that were the case, why didn't they tell us? I couldn't forgive their deception. We had a right to know! Finally, in April, when Reverend Mother visited, we learned the entire project had been ill planned and an exercise in futility.

I was unforgiving! How could they sit and watch our growing frustration, hoping we'd tire ourselves out and go home? Sister Rita had left a dying mother. Me? My sick father. All of us left friends, family, everything familiar. For what? This didn't smell like the will of God to me. It reeked of whitewashing bad judgment, authoritarian hanky-panky, playing with people's lives. Spiritually, the situation was desperately confusing. Do I fight like a tiger to fulfill need or sit placidly and wait for God to perform His miracles? I felt like a pawn one minute and an ingrate the next. But watering the stick was never up my alley. I believed God gave us our brains to use. Otherwise, we'd still be in the cave.

My migraines came back.

Besides my personal inner battles and our joint disillusionment, the political scene in the Middle East was heating up and the age-old enmity between the Jews and Arabs festered like a pesky sore that would not heal. Nasser, the Egyptian president, made big noises about regaining parts of Israel. He had recently blocked the Jew's access to the Suez Canal and they, long after the Holocaust, were feisty, itching for a fight to prove they were spineless no longer. Was that it, war? Did the Pontifical Mission fear war? Why didn't they say so? Well, it wasn't here yet and we were. Maybe we could find other jobs and move out on our own, out from under the thumb of the P.M.

I went to the superior.

"I can't see sitting around every afternoon this summer, Rita. The sisters in the hospital need volunteers. I could practice my French and Arabic."

"How could you get there? We'd still need the station wagon."

"I'll take the mountain bus down in the afternoon."

"You'd have to wear two girdles with stays," she sighed. "Your habit won't protect you. Pinches. You're young. And the bus, so crowded." She looked tired and distraught. The worst of our swimming in molasses fell on her head. "You don't need anyone's permission except mine to do this. You may go."

I sat down across from her at her desk in the small stark office.

"You're worried, aren't you?" Besides the stone walls we faced trying to establish the school, we couldn't ignore the conflict brewing. Wednesday night, a Franciscan priest, who had barely escaped with his life from his mission in Yemen, had arrived at our door asking for help. Our reputation for hospitality had spread because the Beirut taxi drivers had heard the American nuns were generous, and it was a long lucrative ride from the airport to our convent. All kinds of travelers were dropped at our door. We'd fed the Franciscan well and after dinner before two of us drove him down to the Jesuits, he told us the Arab world was about to explode. We already knew. Last Friday night, in the middle of an open-air concert outside Beirut, the families of the oil companies' personnel were rounded up, given two hours to pack and were shipped home.

"They could send us back any time," Rita sighed.

"Could we go with the Canadian nuns into the mountains? They said they'd hide us and we'd be safe. Or maybe a couple of us could teach at Mrs. Johnson's school in Ain Anoub this fall."

"We can't do it, Irene. I don't want to leave any more than the rest of you. We have no choice. We must be evacuated for our safety if there's a serious incident. Mr. Gill called from the embassy yesterday. We're American citizens and the P.M. insists," and she threw me a wry glance.

"The Pontifical Mission must have prayed for this mess. Convenient for them, isn't it?" She sighed and took off her glasses, ignoring the barb. "And he's right. We would be in danger." She leaned back in her chair and fiddled with a round glass paperweight she had brought from home, the snowy kind. The complacent scene immediately clouded, obscuring the figures and peaceful little house.

"I know the P.M. didn't start this mess but what really gets me, Rita, is our being treated like children. I'll never get over the fact that we don't receive our own mail. The total lack of respect!"

"They don't think we're as knowledgeable as they are."

"We aren't, but whose fault is that? Why didn't someone think of sending us to Maryknoll for a few months, or to some other group of missionaries to learn the ropes? That's just one more example of their arrogance, or misplaced faith, or abuse of authority, or…"

"You're terribly upset about this, aren't you?"

"We all are. People in charge are going to have to make up their minds what they what want from us. The sweet little cloistered witless 'nunnies' they've cherished in the past or competent professionals who know what they are about. You can't hold two hands in one game, Rita."

"No, no you can't."

"Lay people are just as bad. Even DeGaulle is complaining about the habit change. He said he'd rather see the tricolor leave France before the white wings of the Sisters of Charity. Obviously, he doesn't have to iron the darn things."

"Irene, Irene," she finally said, pushing her night coif back on her head. "Make plans for the hospital. You could volunteer all day if you want to. You might as well know the P.M. has cancelled our summer school, too."

"Not the summer school? Oh, Rita! what's going on? Can't they be honest? Are they trying to drive us out?"

"I wish I knew." I stood to leave.

"Maybe nothing will come of it. Mr. Gill told me that in the fifties, the Marines landed in full uniform with bayonets drawn. The vendors waded out to meet them with ice cream and Cokes." We both laughed. So typical.

"Could I start Monday at the hospital? After we finish shopping?"

She sat there watching the murky water, shaking it now and again, then looked at me vaguely. "Fine, fine."

CHAPTER FORTY-ONE

Sunday afternoon, the four of us attended a cookout at the University, given by and for the American community who stuck together for moral support. Most were good-hearted people but some found the Lebanese second rate simply because they weren't Americans. As I wandered around, I realized I didn't fit in with that group, who never ventured into the souks or markets which fascinated me.

"And the meat markets, my dear, whole lambs out in the open, hanging on hooks. Ugh."

"And the bargaining. No set prices. I don't like to argue. It's upsetting."

"One has to wash everything, everything...even the oranges."

"The children never leave the compound and...

Talk about attitudes.

I moved towards a group of oil executives who had recently returned from 'walking the line', examining miles of pipes strung across the desert. They were tall lanky men making easy conversation; their gaunt faces, long thin arms and long thinner legs suggested tight jeans and ten-gallon hats.

"How are things coming, Sister? Any progress with your contractors?" Both the Pontifical Mission and sister Rita had warned us not to allude to the school, nor anything else important, like the Arabs in the camps, their poverty, the injustice of it all. I had plenty of opinions, but too bad for me. It annoyed me but I nodded and smiled as prescribed and moseyed along. I tried to toss off my anger at these dumb restraints. I was thirty-five years old and still treated like a child. Everyone indulged us.

"Don't you look sweet in your new habits with a little hair showing." Pooh! This mission was tricky, an adult situation and no place for a group of inexperienced 'little nunnies'! I strolled towards the buffet table that was laden with bowls of tabouleh, mountain bread and hot kibbi, ground lamb and rice wrapped in grape leaves.

Might as well eat my way through the party. I ended up with the young dishwashers. The boys were strong. Muscles bulged beneath their white T shirts and dark skin. Showing off for giggling young girls, they stacked heavy wooden cases filled with empty soda bottles against the stone walls that bordered the garden. Until dusk, they practiced English and I practiced Arabic, describing American teenagers, mostly through mime and smiles. The afternoon floated by on wafts of soft laughter and barbecue smoke.

In Beirut, the sun doesn't set. It plops unceremoniously into the sea, dragging down cool breezes that hold hands with the dark. Late afternoon signaled our departure. Traveling over mountain roads to the convent by day was bad enough. By night, nearly impossible. After polite good-byes, I stood alone, waiting for the others near the gate and observed the scene. "Right out of an English period movie, isn't it, Sister?" Professor Hillman, a theology instructor, had ambled over to me, placidly smoking his pipe. "Could have been filmed in India in the thirties…the children racing about, just a bit out of hand." He looked at me kindly. "Beautiful women in sheer summer dresses…attentive servants in starched white coats." Was he reading my mind?

He blew some smoke in the other direction, and I heard Mrs. Snyder's confident voice. "But John, why should we worry? Nasser won't do anything, and even so, the Lebanese love us. This will blow over." She sipped her cold drink. "The American University has survived one hundred years without incident. We'll never be disturbed. Why should we worry?" Professor Hillman knocked his pipe on the garden wall, and as all its contents fluttered to the ground, he mused, "We *should* worry."

* * * * *

Later that night, unable to sleep, I grabbed my pillow, a light blanket, took to the roof, and spread myself out on a lounge chair. It was a beautiful starry night. I looked down at the sparkling city below, at the moonlight skating across the Mediterranean, then up at the glittery stars, the same stars that shone on all my friends at home.

I had never been so lonely in my life. I was washed out, desolate, drained. Everything had caught up with me, and I was bone tired: tired of restraint, of living under a surface, of hoping for change. Tired of getting up every morning and putting on an acceptable self the same way I put on my habit. Tired of being told to keep my opinions to myself. Tired of pushing for new attitudes that no one wanted but me. My ideas were at odds with everyone's, a situation that would forever be. I couldn't deny it anymore.

I felt the Pontifical Mission was working against us, hoping we'd go home. Shifting in the chair, I tossed off the blanket, and asked myself, was I losing my faith? Where was the young girl who floated through the stars on the palm of God's hand? I always had such strong faith, but where did His work end and ours begin? I didn't know anymore. Sometimes I felt like such an ungrateful brat. Here I was in this magnificent place, meeting world leaders, hob-nobbing with golden people. But it wasn't the work I wanted, not what I came here for. I wanted to run down to the village and talk Arabic with the old people, invite the young girls in for lunch in the convent. This was a mission, not a suburban cloister. I had more freedom as a J.P. in Van Olstaad.

Well, if my surroundings wouldn't cooperate, I'd do it myself. It wouldn't be the first time. At the hospital, I could engage the floor sweepers, the nurses, sick children in their wards. I'd be out working from nine to five, mainly on my own, the way I did at Van Olstaad. Maybe I could visit the gypsy camps below us, where people lived in one-room shacks with flattened oil cans for roofs. I'd ask Haseeb, our caretaker, if I'd be safe. If the bus proved too dangerous, I could borrow Haseeb's donkey. What was wrong with a donkey? I could ride a donkey. Lots of people did. Nothing had ever stopped me before and God always provided. It was the only answer. Strike out on my own. I knew I could serve God here if they'd let me. I would help with the school plans but not grind my wheels over them. I would go and find my place.

Again.

I stood up, folded the blanket and moved to the railing, staring into the night. It was late and cloudy now. Light had fled and the twinkling city retreated, fading into the murky sea. My old ideals and hopes clattered around my feet. I had finally left my spiritual house, the house I had wandered around for years, unable to find my room. As the night had changed, so had I. I had shut a heavy door behind me and ventured out alone.

I was sad, hopelessly sad. I finally admitted I could never expect guidance from the Church or community again. I could only find my own way and hope for tolerance.

CHAPTER FORTY-TWO

The next morning, as we drove down to the open-air markets to buy our fresh produce, I was determined to start again. I quietly peered out at the scenery, the goat herders and their flocks. I loved the warm, friendly Lebanese and the country itself. The area near our convent was Biblical and I believed God had snatched me by the hair of my head, carried me half way round the world, then installed me in this ancient place inhabited by people and sprinkled with customs unchanged since the time of Christ. Wild beauty, drenched in orange blossoms and dotted with poppies, surrounded us. In early spring, I had gathered fresh flowers for the chapel: roses, as big as my fist, and anemones and daisies, giant cyclamen that flung themselves from rocky walls.

Our neighbors, who showered us with fresh chickens and vegetables by day and filched our building supplies by night, didn't perplex me. It was a different land. The thought of the view of the woods from our convent roof, of ancient Roman aqueducts and the sparkling Mediterranean comforted me. I could close my eyes and see Christ walking among meadows of purple and red poppies. "Consider the lilies of the field." I concluded my vocation lay in Beirut, that this was the place for me. I'd find a real mission and apostolate. Yes, this afternoon, I'd finally begin. This afternoon, I'd gird my loins and do battle with the mountain bus.

But another battle had already begun.

* * * * *

"Sisters, Sisters, go home, go back home," the Lebanese shopkeeper warned softly. A huge, usually happy man, he padded over to us quickly, "You're not safe on the streets. The Jews, they've dropped bombs."

"Where?"

293

"We don't know. They say Americans are involved! Made an umbrella of planes that protected the Jews and they destroy everything."

"Oh, Daoud, that's silly. We don't do things like that!" But he looked around, then lowered his voice. "We love you, you know that, but go back to the convent. Stay there and don't let anyone in. You're in danger, real danger!" And he shooed us out, looking everywhere at once while nervously patting his brow with his white cotton apron.

On our way up the mountain, we passed the International Airport and sighted small fighter planes flying so low we could see the pilots. Some waved.

"This is hard to take seriously," Rita said. We'd had no word from the Pontifical Mission so Ellen began baking a pie, while the rest of us rummaged half-heartedly through our things, just in case. The phone rang. It was the embassy. We all crowded around and Rita held the phone away from her ear. "You have two hours to get to the University. Pack no more than forty pounds. You might be evacuated on an Army transport."

"What about the Blessed Sacrament?"

"Eat it or give it to the Village priest."

"The car?"

"Drive it down."

"The convent?"

"Lock it up and get out of there! You're not safe. You're too near the airport. We have no reliable news, but the situation is bad, serious. All American civilians are on alert, possibly the English too. We'll meet you at the University compound."

"Aren't we being a little dramatic?"

"Sister, this isn't the Marine invasion of the fifties! You have two hours," and he hung up .Rita turned and faced the three of us who had lined up in front of her like ducks at a shooting gallery.

"It will blow over," Ellen offered tentatively.

"Nothing in this part of the world ever lasts more than five minutes," Rita added.

"What should we pack?" Stephen wanted to know.

"What you can't replace," and I moved quietly into my bedroom. I didn't want to believe it but I knew in my bones it was over. They could patronize us, pretend our evacuation was temporary, pretend everything. It had all been pretense anyway.

Ellen came by and leaned against the doorjamb. "What are you taking? Your wood carvings?"

"No, too heavy." I had begun emptying drawers, tossing everything on the bed. "I'm taking my carving tools, my record collection, my paints…and my white habits. The present I bought for Mom in Paris, you know, the delicate ceramic." I was talking to the empty suitcase. "And my copy of Guardini."

She sidled up behind me and gave me a big squeeze. "We'll be back. Don't be discouraged." So typical of Ellen, always thinking of everyone else. Our departure was a blur, a movie run amuck. Haseeb, our caretaker, his wife and their daughter Sousan cried as we drove the packed station wagon out of the driveway, three sisters waving and trying to smile, all except me who carried the Blessed Sacrament in a ciborium on my lap. We left it with the village priest, who solemnly blessed our group; then Stephen drove us safely to the university. I tried snapping pictures and my camera snatched every scene the minute we slowed down. I had rolls of film and was determined to use them all.

The compound was in a tizzy. Some women had reasons to worry. They had to leave. Their husbands had to stay, and some were 'out on the line'. No reliable information had reached the embassy. Teenaged messengers, high on excitement, scurried round, laughing and talking in nervous groups. Everyone decided to lighten a dark time by being cheerful, and we barely escaped hysteria.

"Hang those dark blankets on the windows," Rita ordered, face tight and arms akimbo. So Stephen clowned around, half falling off the chair, doing her best aping one of the 'Three Stooges'. I don't remember what we ate for dinner. Later, in our bedroom, we peered through edges of blankets at what we thought were Syrian planes flying over a city submerged in a haphazard blackout. The last I remember before I fell into an exhausted sleep was Stephen murmuring disgustedly, "If they wanted to bomb this place, we'd be sitting ducks."

The next morning, the ladies planned a lovely luncheon to distract us all from stark reality. "We need to normalize, normalize," Mrs. Snyder chanted to no one in particular, fanning herself with a linen napkin. The women carried in platters of turkey and freshly sliced roast beef, and salads left over from our party Sunday night. We had just finished grace when the phone rang. Dr. Hillman calmly reentered the room. "It was the embassy. A group of students and rioters have crashed through the gates. They want us all off the bottom floor, up to the top. David is chaining the staircases and we'll leave the elevator door ajar upstairs. Hurry. Everyone on the elevator. The Special Forces are on their way. We're not in serious danger." He smiled encouragingly.

"What about the food?" I called after him and tossing my camera around my neck, I lined my arms with platters and everyone grabbed something and we were off. Mrs. Snyder fanned herself with wads of napkins and Mr. Hillman packed his pipe.

"This has never happened at the University," Mrs. Snyder complained softly to herself. "The University has always been safe, you know." Rita patted her hand, and no one spoke again all the way to the top floor.

"I think we should eat. The police will be here shortly," Dr. Hillman advised. A balcony surrounded the upper floor, a penthouse, and I scooted outside with my camera. From the north, tanks were rolling towards us, ever so slowly down the wide boulevard that flanked the peaceful Mediterranean which, for want of interest, yawned in the noon sun. The building to the immediate south, separated from us by a narrow street, was the British Embassy. I could hear shouts and glass breaking. The back yard, where we had recently partied and which I feared was the scene of the fracas, was walled out, not visible.

I could hear Rita inside. "Way-ah's Iween?" (Stress strengthened her lisp.)

"Maybe the ladies room."

I owed Stephen.

A young Lebanese student joined me, leaned his arms on the railing, and we watched the show.

"Why don't I feel danger?" I asked him.

"Because we don't. Sister, You will be protected. No harm will come today. Just noise. See? Look. They are finished. They have made their statement." I couldn't believe it. The young men were pouring out of side streets, stripping off their shirts and trousers and diving into the Mediterranean, swimming leisurely on a beautiful summer afternoon. I started taking pictures furiously.

"Why didn't the police stop them?"

"They are young men. Why should we kill our young men? Or maim them for broken glass? See? They're moving in now, gathering them up." The red berets, an elite force, were herding the stragglers into wagons, and not too gently, clearing the streets. It was over. As I stuffed film cartridges into my pocket, I heard Rita's alarmed voice from the doorway.

"Iween, what ah you doing out hee-ah?"

"I'm fine, I'm fine. It's all over. There were no guns." I could tell Rita was upset with my exposing myself to danger, but I was saved by the appearance of Mr. Gill and we all went inside. He stood there, addressing us, one arm around his wife who didn't look as calm.

"The only casualties are the windows of the British Embassy. All those soda bottles from Sunday afternoon. Every rock in the garden that wasn't cemented down. They threw everything, even the wooden cases." He turned to us.

"Sisters, you have to leave. The last Pam Am flight out of here is at three-thirty. Women and children. No men. Headed to Rome. You can stay there until this blows over.

"There are four empty seats left and I want you in them."

* * * * *

"What do you mean *he* can't go? *He's* a *she*! Her name is *Sister* Stephen. *Sister. Soeur, Soeur.* Sisters take men's names." All this was said in halting French to two officials who were adamant about the name, Stephen. So many were trying to smuggle themselves out of the country that taking a passport literally was all these two could do. Rita had argued with officials who weren't blind but kept insisting that the rules were the rules. She switched to slow English, and they continued to rattle back at her in rapid French. A small man with a thin mustache joined them as Sister Stephen's patience evaporated.

"Look," she said, as she dropped her bag to the floor and slowly and purposefully, began to unbutton the front of her habit, all the time staring right at them.

"Mon Dieu, ma soeur, mon Dieu," the thin one gasped, slapping a flat hand over his eyes, and commanding the other two to stamp her passport.

"Hummmph," complained one in French. "These American nuns, with their short skirts and hair showing. They don't even look like our French nuns."

"Deo gratias!" I shot back at them in Latin.

We were in Rome that night. The four of us sat in the taxi, comforting each other and as we careened towards our hotel, we passed the Trevi fountain. I remembered my coins and chided God. Rome again, yes, but not like this. We'd be back in Albany Wednesday night.

"Oh, Lord," Ellen exclaimed. The pie, the pie! I never took it out of the oven." We laughed until tears ran down our faces. But tears ran down my face because I had lost hope. I knew we all doubted we would ever return to Beirut, but I had left more than the pie. I had left my dreams of fitting into a new community and I was on my own.

PART FOUR

"My eyes filled up as we gazed at each other across the table, across Edna's death, the death of part of my life. We stared at our youth, our escapades, the not so funny, the truth, the change...all of it."

CHAPTER FORTY-THREE

Things weren't much better at home. The late sixties, violent, wild-blind years destroyed without judgment all levels of life. The price of revolution was everything out, good or bad. As the stability of our society jumped on the fast train or dissolved before our eyes, the footings of my personal life eroded out from under me.

In January 1968, my father had a crippling stroke.

Bobby Kennedy, whom I had met and chatted with at the Palace Theater, was shot to death in June in a hotel kitchen in California.

I discovered my friend Sister Bonaventure had left her order.

The community had split into very conservative and very liberal camps.

I began to wonder if I would ever fit into the community.

In late spring of sixty-nine, Jimmy O'Neill proclaimed his undying love to me on a beach in Gloucester.

I opted for a leave of absence in June to study for my masters in counseling at Boston University.

It fleshed out something like this.

* * * * *

After I returned from Beirut, Helen, who was the superior of St. Matthew's, arranged my transfer there where I began teaching high school in September. The shenanigans of the Pontifical Mission in Beirut had dealt a blow to my vocation and my zing had evaporated. So, to clarify my ideas then rid my system of turmoil, I doggedly composed a thirteen page letter to the Chapter, outlining my opinions about the vows, the apostolate, and the future of the order. Everyone had been asked to contribute, but Sister Edmund informed me later that I was the only one who did.

"Bryand, read this. I'm submitting it to the Chapter."

"Now, what are you up to?" She stared at the papers and without looking up, asked, "Do you have a sharpened pencil?" I smiled and thought at least some things never change. Bryand would never tackle a theme without two sharpened pencils.

THE IDEA OF COMMUNITY AND THE INDIVIDUAL

Community consists of individual sisters joined together by vows, with similar ideals, who rely on each other for mutual support in order to live a Christian life. However, because of background, temperament and culture, the expressions of each sister's ideals differ one from another. This has always been true. Nothing in our past, however, acknowledges the intrinsic worth of this variety of expression. On the contrary, variety has been discouraged and suspect in our past training.

This is deadening.

Perfect freedom should be given to each sister to express her own peculiar charisma within the community. Imagination and initiative should be fostered and, if the community values these things, there should be a written expression of this in the rule and constitutions.

If a sister can rely on the support of the ideals of the group, she can withstand the lack of sympathy or interest of the individual members. The changing of each sister's sense of values and the accepting of people different from herself are the responsibility of each sister and cannot become a matter solved by legislation.

But if a sister has no mutual support either ideally or in reality, then no community exists for her. She could just as easily lead her life as a secular, for there, she would still have God.

In the past, the sister who could best find peace within the community was the conformist. She was not the 'disturber of settled ideas'. We can not afford to perpetuate this error. In justice, if this is the only type person who will in the future receive the approval of the individual sisters and the community as a whole, then other types wishing to join with our community should be refused entry. The waste of psychological energy because of the conformity phenomena has been appalling, especially when the energy could have been channeled into fruitful apostolates.

Only the barest essentials of structure should be imposed on the sisters from without in order to see what vitality lies within each individual. This would produce a truly living spirit.

The sisters themselves make up the community. If each sister could approach her life using her own lights and ingenuity, if she could approach problems thinking in terms of, "What is possible?" not, "What has been done before?" In fact, if she could approach the apostolate with the sense of possibility, then the subsequent renewal might surprise us all.

"They'll never ask who wrote it." Bryand said.
"It's my swan song, Bryand. I'm through talking. If anyone wants to know what I think, let her read this."
"You'll never shut up."
"Watch me."
She did and I did. I had nothing left to say.

* * * * *

Mom and Dad were in Nassau on vacation when Dad suffered a serious stroke. After he came home, I minded him on weekends to give Mom a break.
"He won't eat," she sighed, "I can't make him eat."
"He probably can't see his food, Mom."
I knew stroke. When I was a novice, I looked in on old Sister Benedict, a stroke victim who talked gibberish. A big powerful woman, she could be frightening when her frustration boiled over. Usually, I could discern what she wanted and Mother Patricia called on me occasionally when the nurses were frantic. One visiting Sunday

when I was a novice, she appeared in the front hall in her nightgown and night coif, flailing her arms, obviously distraught. I ushered her up to the second floor as fast as I could and found that one of the old sisters hadn't made it to the bathroom and the floor was a smelly mess. After I cleaned it up, and calmed them both down, Benedict patted my hand and wouldn't let go. Dad was no problem compared to her; he only slurred his speech. "He can't see out of one eye, Mom. I'll get him to eat." I found a platter-sized plate and put small portions on his good side, a trick that worked with Sister Benedict.

"Doesn't look like much," he'd complain.

"It's only a little, Dad. There's more if you want more." I'd always give him more and he'd lap it up and then he had his ice cream.

I handled him like a child.

It was so sad.

A quiet gloom settled inside me. A sense of loss colored my good times. Of course I knew no one lived forever. But still.

* * * * *

When Bobby Kennedy was shot in late spring, Sister Bryand and I left our eighth period classes early and took the Greyhound bus into the Port Authority. We hopped a cab to St. Patrick's Cathedral, sat at his wake for two hours and prayed for the repose of his soul. In the station, the two of us ate sandwiches we had packed, sipped on a can of warm soda and took the late bus home.

We were grief-stricken. John Kennedy, Medgar Evans, Martin Luthur King. Death after death after death. It was too much.

* * * * *

In August, my old friend from Scranton, Sister Bonaventure visited me but she wasn't Sister Bonaventure anymore. She looked well dressed in a quiet tailored suit.

"I left last June," she explained between sips of iced tea, which I had brought upstairs to the parlor on a pretty tray.

"Why, Bonnie, why did you leave?"

"I didn't want to do it anymore." That simple, I thought. "Look, Irene, you've changed your habit and we had changed ours. But the essence of religious life isn't going to change. A vowed life is an obedient life."

"Some sisters are taking jobs in colleges," I protested, "and they're moving into the world…"

"…and are still wearing their habits and under someone's thumb. Too much red tape for me, Irene. I'm principal of the Public Elementary School in the Bronx, down the street from my old school, Blessed Sacrament, which the diocese finally closed. I applied to the city. Nobody else wanted the job."

She bit into a homemade raspberry tart. "Ummm. Good." I waited. "Two of the other sisters who also left are teaching with me now and we have a bang-up faculty, even if it is combat duty. The three of us go where we want, attend night meetings, visit the homes, anything. Act like normal women. No restrictions. No pastors. No bishop."

"Do you miss it? The convent, I mean? The community? The prayer life, you know…?"

"Yes and no. We attend Mass when we can. I'm not angry with anyone and I haven't left the Church. The three of us live in a big apartment, which offers some community. I'm not sorry, Irene. I'm doing what I think I should." She wiped the crumbs of the tart off her fingers with the small linen napkin and looked at me.

"I didn't have the stomach for it anymore."

* * * * *

St. Matthew's was perking; I was finally involved in the kind of life that made sense to me. Besides teaching, we did a lot of rescuing. During the summer, an eight-year-old girl tried to burn down the school so she could go live with her sister in a 'home for wayward girls'. "Jolene, she got a room of her own, with heat!" Helen argued with judges and social workers, had her removed from an irresponsible family and properly placed with a good one.

The sisters threw a surprise birthday party for sixteen-year-old Hiram from Bryand's homeroom, who lived alone in a crummy apartment and supported himself by driving an ice cream truck to Utica on weekends.

One of our seniors who was black had played pool in the wrong place one Friday night and had been unjustly accused of drunk and disorderly conduct. Father Hubbard, the South-end priest, and I sprang him from the Albany County Jail. The experience made my bones itch: noise and shouts and locks and slamming iron gates. And the echoes. Chilling. The judges, mostly family friends, were sick of me, warning my relatives to keep me out of their hair. "Tom, not one more time do I want to hear from her, nun or no nun." In the meantime, some members of our community looked at our doings with alarm. While we were out throwing block parties on steamy summer evenings, learning the shag from our neighbors in Afros and wild colored muumuus, they were watching our antics and praying they wouldn't be asked to do the same.

I met Sister Rebecca at the hospital one afternoon, and she asked, "How do you like it down there, Sister Irene? I'd be scared to death."

"It's a challenge." Sometimes, however, I wondered if we were no more than goodwill ambassadors, the 'Belles of St. Matthew's' as the kids referred to us at times. Prejudice, social justice and integrated education were serious issues, requiring a great deal of understanding and delicacy and we sisters, except for good instincts, were not prepared to deal with any of them. I had just returned from the Beirut fiasco, where we had been sent totally unprepared to face the realities of a mission.

Was our work at St. Matthew's to be more of the same? Good-willed but spotty?

I decided to ask Reverend Mother again about my counseling degree. I could minor in race relations.

* * * * *

Jimmy O'Neill had succeeded amazingly well in real estate and had the leisure to volunteer part-time at school two or three times a week. He had met the pastor in the army and had adopted St. Matthew's, donated equipment, coached the older teams, and refereed an occasional game. We sat together and chatted about our families during the basketball games.

"Your parents were awfully good to me, Mary. Encouraged me to go to college. Your Mom always built me up. Did you know she wrote me every week when I was in Korea?"

"She didn't tell me. Probably forgot." Mom was always cagey about Jimmy.

One afternoon, Helen and I walked home from school, down the hill to the convent, past the church, a miniature cathedral over one hundred years old. A small park, girdled by a wrought iron fence fronted the edifice that reigned like a queen over the once charming square. Most of the old brownstones were run down now and it was pitiful, especially since this had once been one of the loveliest streets in the city.

I interrupted our companionable silence. "Jimmy is such a bonus this summer for me, Helen. I still miss Edna dreadfully and talking to Jimmy fills an empty hole. I feel so comfortable with him, as if we were back in grade school."

"Be careful, Irene. You're seeing too much of him."

"Really, Helen! You know we've been friends since sixth grade! We're not romantically involved."

"Are you sure that's the way he feels?"

"He's married, Helen, and has three children. And I'm committed, a nun! He's a good friend and that's it."

"Do you think his being married and your being a nun are protection enough?"

"I think our vows clearly mark out our possibilities." Was Helen questioning my judgment? Jimmy and I weren't clandestine. We weren't running around, meeting behind closed doors, panting into each other's faces like frustrated teenagers.

"The trouble with you is," she continued, as we crossed the street, "you don't see things the way they are. You think people want life the way it ought to be."

"Isn't that what I'm supposed to think? Keep pushing for the best?" What did she mean?

"Sometimes. But down underneath, you believe people should rise to something better, should see a better light, a better way to be. That's what makes you such a great teacher, but it can be dangerous."

"I'm supposed to look for the best in everyone, the untapped. What do you mean, dangerous? I don't think that's true, Helen."

"I know you don't." She paused. "Look, I see life as it is. You see it the way it ought to be. Jimmy loved you once and I believe he still does. You and your family took him in when he was young. He felt he was part of your clan. You love him as a friend and you want him to feel the same. I don't think he does I don't think he ever sorted it out.."

I felt hot, insulted. "I think you're wrong, Helen. I'm not going to get carried away. Don't you think I can read signs?"

"Hmmm, well, it's not you I'm worried about. I'm telling you to be careful," and on that note, she opened the huge oak door to the convent and we disappeared, gratefully, into the dark, cool building.

CHAPTER FORTY-FOUR

In February, some of our teachers and Jimmy signed up at SUNY for a seminar involving race relations. In late spring, the class finalized its program with a consciousness-raising weekend so popular at the time. Jimmy drove the pastor, Helen, Bryand and me to an old mansion on the Massachusetts North shore between Gloucester and Rockport. We laughed most of the way.

Two psychologists ran the conference. The Saturday session ended at six and since the workshops had exhausted us all, Jimmy offered to treat our faculty to a lobster dinner. As soon as we returned to the mansion, Father had gone right upstairs, but the four of us were still wound up. After chatting a bit Bryand said, "I've had it. I'm going to bed."

"Me, too," Helen dittoed and they left Jimmy and me together still talking and laughing in the huge lobby.

"Let's hit the beach. I'm stuffed. We'll walk it off."

"Not much beach, Jimmy. We could climb down the rocks a bit." I'd feel safe anywhere with Jimmy.

"Meet you back here in ten minutes."

"It's a deal." The sisters were wearing secular clothes on occasion and this was one of them. I changed into sneaks, jeans, a big cotton sweater and a rubberized plaid raincoat I'd picked up for a dollar at the Thrift Shop. I felt and looked like a schoolgirl, off to go fishing at Norman's Kill. This was wonderful! I'd never been to the shore before. Imagine! To sit and look at the ocean, and at night, too.

When I met him in the lobby, he had a paper bag and in it were two plastic glasses and a bottle of ice cold Great Western Champagne. "A little celebration won't hurt us," he said as we left the building, crossed the road and climbed up onto a huge rock. We settled down and listened to the waves rhythmically chant their monotonous tune. I was completely comfortable. The mist and dank smell of seaweed and salt air clung to my hair, which flew around my face and into my eyes. I gazed at the foamy water and into the thin spring wind, shuddered, and wrapped my arms around my knees.

"Have a sip of this, Mary. It will warm you up."

"Yummy." We sat companionably while the winds and water whispered their evening messages to the starred sky.

"How many kids from St. Matthew's will ever see this, or anything like it, Jimmy?"

"Nobody I know. I wish it were different."

"At least you work at it." He refilled my glass. "Jimmy, would you ever have guessed when we were kids that I'd be bailing someone out of the county jail? What a dismal place! It still gives me the willies. Jails aren't like the movies, are they, Jimmy?"

"You always wanted life like the movies."

"Yes, like all the sweet times when we were young, remember? Remember Norman's Kill?"

"Remember the Canteen when you tried to teach me how to dance? I'm still no good at it. Just lumber around."

"Remember when we took the bus to Altamont and climbed the rocks, and we saw the red fox...?"

"...and nearly got lost in the caves?" He reminisced about the hospital and how he used to love to run the elevator up to the nurses' floor and watch the girls scurry around in their underwear. "At fifteen, it was as good as sex." I jostled him with my shoulder, and we laughed.

"I always wondered, Mary, how you lived without sex, how most of you did, but you especially. I used to dream about you and me, all those years in high school, and when I was in Korea, I always thought maybe you'd leave."

I skirted around the last part. "I think it's harder for men, Jimmy. They're built differently. Different drives." Jimmy had had a couple of cocktails before dinner and he wasn't about to be put off.

"I've always loved you, Mary. I guess I still do."

"I love you, too, Jimmy," I answered, purposely misinterpreting him. "You're my closest friend."

"I don't mean it that way."

"But I do." I turned and looked at him squarely. "Jimmy we're so lucky we can talk. Let's not ruin it. You think you love me, and you've carried a torch, but it's romance. Men always want what's just out of reach. I might have been the first girl you ever loved. No one ever forgets his first love. But it was a first. And the second can't be a first. You're married to Lois, and she adores you. I watch her come into the convent for dinner, wearing galoshes and carrying her shoes in a paper bag. You put your arm around her when you're talking at the dinner table. Don't you know how comfortable the two of you are together? You owe it to her to bury this fantasy."

"It's no fantasy."

"It is, Jimmy! It's nothing but a warm memory. If I left the convent tomorrow, you'd never leave Lois because you love her, not because you're noble. Lois has given you everything you ever wanted, a wife, a family, a home. I'm the warm blanket my family and I wrapped around you when you needed it. And that's all it's ever been. Don't go and get maudlin on me now."

Damn, damn, damn! Helen was right after all. "Jimmy, I've never meant to lead you on. You've been the only brother I've ever had. So tonight, you're feeling romantic. It's only the night, believe me." I shivered and began to get up. "We really should go in. I'm getting cold."

He took my hand and pulled me down. "Don't go yet. If you leave now, it will all go bad." I sat back on the rock and hugged my legs tighter. The silence was long and not comfortable.

"Have I ruined everything between us?" he asked, staring at the water. I know you're right and I'm sorry.

"You've just had too much champagne."

"I had to. I've got something to tell you you're not going to like. You might as well know. St. Mat's is closing. This June."

"Oh, no!"

"The diocese can't afford to keep it open any more. The pastor's done everything he can, pulled every string." He sighed. "Have some more champagne. It might help."

"Oh, Jimmy!" I was near tears.

"I've been trying to find a way to tell you."

"I'm trying not to cry."

The sounds from the county jail flooded my mind, the huge metal clanging doors, confining, shutting out, shutting in; I heard caretakers' voices, "Please sign in. Don't go beyond there, Sister. Wait here, Sister. You can't go in there, Sister." I sat in a beautiful, wild expanse, and suddenly felt bound in chains, listening to every door around me slam.

"What will you do when they close the school, Jimmy? Where will you volunteer?"

"The pastor will find me a place. What about you?"

"I don't know. First Beirut and now this. There's nothing for me but closed doors, closing me in or closing me out." I didn't care if I cried in front of Jimmy. It wouldn't be the first time, and I blew loudly into my handkerchief. "After St. Matthew's, what would satisfy me? I can't go back to de Paul again, forget everything I've learned, turn my back on responsibilities and retreat into that shell. There's no room for me, and I'm really scared when I think about it." I turned and faced him. "What am I going to do, Jimmy? What am I going to do now?"

"Why don't you go back to school, go for your masters? You've been hankering after it. Go to a big city like New York or Boston. It would broaden you out. Try Columbia, N.Y.U., Boston University.

"You've plenty of choices, but forget about a Catholic University. Your mind is too filled up with the Church. It would do you good to think about something else." He pitched a small rock towards the ocean and it skittered down, clicking and clicking and clicking over rocks until it chipped off the side of a huge boulder and sailed into the ocean.

"I don't know if the community has the money."

"Go on furlough. Didn't one of your sisters go on furlough last year? You're always complaining you've had no experience, that you've been sheltered. Rent an apartment. See what it means to be on your own. Have bills you have to pay. Go out for a year. Get a job teaching. See the world. Go to school."

"You mean take a leave of absence, go on ex claustration?"

"If that's what you call it."

Ex claustration was unusual but granted to a religious who needed time, as a secular, to reconsider her vocation. During that one or two-year period, the religious was excused from the obligations of her or his vows. "Jimmy, I've never thought about it. I could get permission for that. They have to give it to me. You're a genius!" We sat and watched the water rush in, watched it smash against unyielding rocks, then quietly withdraw.

"Mary, are you really happy? Lately, you're going at St. Mat's like a drill boring through wood. You're keyed up all the time." I was about to retort but his hand silenced me.

"Sister Margaret, Helen and the other sisters, they run around and they gripe occasionally but they're comfortable, peaceful. Whatever comes their way, they'll do. But there's something different about you. Even Lois mentioned it." He tossed another pebble at the water. "You're not peaceful."

"It's a hard time for us all, Jimmy. Worse for me, I guess. I never see things the way the others do. My friend Sister Bonaventure is teaching in public school in the inner city, but she had to leave her community to do it, and I don't think she wanted to. And as we sat under the stars, I told him about the priest-workmen in the forties and fifties and I told him how I thought the life of Christ was lived out in the open, among the people and not under someone's thumb.

"You'll always be under someone's thumb as long as you're a sister, Mary. It's the way it is."

"Maybe that's what has me nervous. I don't know whether I buy it anymore." I couldn't believe I was saying this to Jimmy, of all people. "How can I give witness to a life I think is wrong for me that won't change. Yet, this life is the only one I ever wanted. I keep trying to find a place."

"Well, no one wants to hear from you, that's for sure. I watch them in the lunchroom. If you say green, they say purple. Even small things. You'll never be right about anything, Mary. You're wasting your time." His long hand hunted through the small rocks, sliding over the cold stones. "Why did you ever nail yourself to rules anyway, and become a nun? Everybody thought you were crazy, including me."

I sat up straight on the rocks, shifted my position on the stone. "I had a vocation, a calling! I thought this life was my way to do good and that I should do it. I thought I belonged to God!"

"Don't you think everybody does?"

I ignored him. "Now, the times are different. Who could have expected Vatican II, this uproar, this social twist, and these needs? But if my superior told me to sit on my hands for the next twenty years, I'd be bound by my vows to obey. I can't do that anymore, Jimmy. I see other ways."

"You and I, we have different ideas about callings. Imagine me, an English teacher or an astronaut. We're supposed to do what we're good at, Mary. Isn't that why we're all different? That's what the pastor says anyway.

"You're not good at taking orders. You've always had your own ideas. The other nuns, they're nuns. You? You're a free spirit in a nun's habit. And it shows. You're frustrated, tight, strained, and you still bite your fingernails." He picked up my hand and looked at it. "I never understood it and I still don't...how somebody like you could stay in a place like that for as long as you have. Not that it's wrong for everybody but it was never right for you."

"Oh, Jimmy. I don't know what to do. What's more important? Doing what I think I should, or hanging on because I said I would. I don't know what God wants! Is it all a temptation? Would I be losing God or finding Him?" My voice cracked. "I keep going over it and over it."

Jimmy clicked two stones together and finally said, "I've got a joke."

"A joke, a joke, Jimmy, NOW?"

"Yeah, a joke. About a priest. There was a flood but he wouldn't leave the church. He stood on the roof. The Boy Scouts came in rowboats, then his neighbors, and finally, the police. And each time he said, 'No, I must stay. God will take care of me.' Of course he drowned. And when he met God in heaven he asked, 'Why didn't you take care of me?'

"And God said, 'I kept sending people for you but you wouldn't come.'" He paused awhile, and polished a flat stone in the palm of his hand with his thumb. "What do you want, Mary, a stroke of lightning?"

"I don't want to leave, Jimmy. I just want some room. I want things to change."

"I know that, but you can't always have what you want."

"You sound like my mother."

"I don't feel like her." We laughed and sat silently a while.

"You're not decided and I don't want to influence you. Take some time. Go to Boston, Mary, or New York. When you came back from Beirut, you griped a lot that you felt out of place over there, dumb because you had no experience or savvy. So, get a job. Go to school on the side. If you don't tell anyone you're a nun, believe me, you'll learn plenty. And things might change around here."

"If I go, will I come back?"

"This move doesn't mean you won't come back. Take time to think it out. It's the only way."

I squeezed his hand. "I *do* love you, Jimmy. You're my best friend." We sat a long time, the both of us, listening to the drone of an endless ocean as it wore away the rocks.

CHAPTER FORTY-FIVE

Iopened my eyes and came out of my reverie. Where was I? I felt light-headed and took deep breaths while I looked around the motherhouse chapel. My head spun from unearthed memories, surprisingly not threatening at all. And why should they be? Those twenty years had been part of my life, a part that had been clamoring for recognition but buried for years. My back was beginning to bother me, sitting on the hard pew, waiting for Helen. Besides, I was hungry. I could eat. Why hadn't I had another bagel at Katie's? How long had I been sitting here? Twenty minutes? At that moment, Helen stuck her head in, genuflected, and beckoned me out of the chapel.

"I'm ready. Here's your coat."

As I struggled into it, I asked, "Are you up for Italian?"

"Sounds perfect." We retraced our steps and were out the door on our way to steaming manicotti with ricotta cheese, garlic, parsley, fresh ground nutmeg, and homemade red wine.

"I'll cut over Manning and Hackett," I said as I opened the car door for her. "How about Scarlozzi's? Do you mind?"

"And what if I mind? What good will it do me?"

"You could walk to McDonald's I suppose." I shut her door, laughing, and let myself in the opposite one, settling behind the wheel. Driving away from the Motherhouse, I turned right at the hospital.

"I do miss you," she drawled. "There are too few left to banter with."

"And I miss you. I really loved sitting there in chapel this afternoon, an extraordinary experience. I relived all the old days with all my friends. You know, Helen, when I left to teach in Boston, I wanted to be treated like a person and I never told anyone I was a nun. Pretty soon, I began to believe it myself. It was as if those years never happened. But those years knew they had happened. Coming here today was like meeting an old friend I'd been on the outs with for a long time. They weren't easy years, Helen."

"No, they weren't."

"How is Bryand? I see Jimmy occasionally when I come back for weddings. His oldest daughter is an engineer, you know. He's so proud of her."

"You know Bryand left a few years after you did and is married. I see her occasionally at the old Brady Hospital. Believe it or not, Sister Mary Ann adopted an AIDS baby from there a few years ago."

"Adopted? Legally adopted?"

"Things have changed since you left. Sister Augustine is in St. Louis counseling drug addicts, runs a clinic, and Rebecca still works at St. Peter's Hospital."

"What about Timmy? She must be in her seventies."

"She is. She works part-time at St. Peter's. Sister Kenan's the pastor in Grafton. There's no priest." I stopped at the light on Academy Road and took a right. The streets were nearly empty, but warm lights glowed behind curtained windows. Did women still make dinner while men read the paper? Was anything familiar left?

"How do you feel about woman priests, Helen?"

"I don't see anything against it. Our sisters in Alaska are ministers of the Church. They read the epistle and gospel, deliver a short sermon, distribute Communion, run the parishes and do everything else except say Mass and administer other sacraments, like Kenan. But you, of all people, know what the Church is like."

"Do I ever! Slow as a three-legged turtle on wet tar. The hierarchy would rather see the faithful go without Mass and the Sacraments than change. It's not as if the male priesthood were a matter of faith and morals. It's only traditional. Why can't the nuns fill in for them in a pinch?"

Helen stiffened; her voice hardened. "Why should they sweep up the pieces and be called in when the primary labor force is depleted? Only one more way we'd be used as second class citizens. 'Bring in the peons.' No!" she stated emphatically, "women should be ordained on the same level as men." She set her lips and stared straight ahead.

"Well, don't get *me* started! I think the greatest sin of the Catholic Church is its failure to treat women as equals. We can't rewrite history, but today? How can the Church continue to ignore the message of the Redemption and its implications?

317

"People can rave on all they like about religion being dead, but as the Church goes, so goes the world. The good and the bad of it. I'm telling you, Helen, I would never want to answer for the Church's attitude today." I took a left at Whitehall Road, and slowed down, stretching our time together. The car was virtually crawling over the vacant street. Prodding Helen into verbal exchanges had never been easy, but now, in her position, she had few to confide in. How much she must have missed Edna and me. Heaven had better end up eternal conversation or I might have to rethink the whole thing.

"How many sisters are left?"

"A little over one hundred. Nearly half the community left during the early seventies...and deaths..."

"Are you getting any vocations?" I felt I already knew the answer.

"A few. No young people. Widows, women in their forties who are trained and responsible. You know the young don't have that spirit anymore.

"Individuals want to do their own thing. It's another age. People can understand our doing good works. They'll always appreciate that. But the laity has never understood a vowed life. Respected it, yes, but understood it, no." She turned as if to shake off her gloom. "We're all sad to see religious orders disappear. It's natural to want others to continue in the path one's chosen. It lends credence to the life. It's not easy to be the last in line."

I said nothing.

"We're beginning to concentrate on our Association. We're new at it and not so sure we're running it right...it's not an easy transition. It will take time."

"What's the Association?"

"A group of lay women and men, married or single, who want to do more. They don't live in community or take vows, but they make public promises to affiliate their lives with the order. They provide witness to the works of mercy wherever they are...a lay apostolate, sort of. Certainly not a new idea."

"Go on."

"It cultivates a sense of community and provides a way to develop a spiritual life while performing good works. We call it Mercy Corps, and some Protestant ladies are joining, if you'd believe that one."

We pulled into Scarlozzi's parking lot.

"With so few vocations to the community itself, Helen, are you folding up your tents?" She turned and faced me.

"I don't know. Ironically, Mary, as I look down the road, I find myself turning around and looking back. And believe it or not, I've concluded our solution may lie with Mother McAuley's original idea: a group of dedicated social workers…women living together, leading a spiritual life, able to join and leave the community at certain times of their lives.

"What would hold it all together? What would keep it from falling apart?"

"I'm sure some of the women would elect to take permanent vows. But I simply don't know. It's difficult to foresee the future. Active orders of sisters are relatively new in the Church. When they were approved by the hierarchy, it was the men, not the women who had the last say. Men went for the cloister, and I'm sure cloistered orders won't change. But active communities?

"It's the sisters' turn to make the rules now, isn't it?"

"I guess, but you know, Mary, we're getting old. I think what's left of the community simply wants to live out the life it chose. Who are we to tell the young what to do? They'll have to learn new ways to serve God and each other and solve their own problems. We whacked away at ours. Now, it's their time." She took a deep breath.

"Anyway," she sighed, "it's all in the hands of the Holy Spirit."

* * * * *

Scarlozzi's was crowded. However, the maitre d', who knew Helen, was delighted to see her, and ushered us to a booth next to the windows facing the lighted street, just far enough away from the fire that roared in the gray flagstone fireplace.

the children who watched us. Living without prejudice was one of my mother's finest gifts to me, one I appreciated the most." I warmed up.

"I took Jimmy's advice and never told anyone I was a nun. We'd all go out drinking in Roxbury on Friday afternoons after school and let loose. What a time! And I learned plenty, learned to work and play with other races without overcompensating."

"The inner-city schools were in bad shape, Helen. No materials, no books. The Christopher Gibson School was over one hundred years old and in poor repair. We started a faculty senate and we took on the school committee. The Roxbury Neighborhood Association was pushing to alleviate racial tensions, so I worked as the school volunteer. Came in to the meetings on Sunday afternoons. I knew the neighbors, joked with the mothers. They involved me in some Oyster Club where we took bets on which one had the pearl. For the first time since I entered the convent, I was able to move by my own lights. I felt with it, competent."

"You worked in Boston a long time."

"I worked with disadvantaged kids until I retired, and loved it. Oh, Helen, we had so much fun! I applied for grants and we took the children all over the city: to Chinatown for lunch, to the North End for spaghetti, to St. Margaret's for St. Patrick's Day, out to Southborough to the farms and to the shore in Southie. It was great. One day, a mother tapped me on my arm and said, 'Hey, honey, do you know you're the only white girl on this bus?' I hadn't realized it. Why should I?" I leaned back in my chair. "One time, my Mom stood up for the only black woman on the bus. I'm sure that woman realized it."

She sat watching me. "As much as I miss you, Mary, for your own sake, I'm not sorry you left. You know, when your two year leave was up, I hated being the one to break the bad news to you... that your request to come back and continue doing what you were doing was not granted. "It was the priest-workman thing, Mary, operating undercover. Every one of the sisters who was working outside the community was doing it as a nun. They couldn't allow you to act like a secular. Cross-purposes. What a shame."

I looked towards the fireplace and stared at the open fire, snatching a moment to regain my composure. It had been a hard day. "That was such a bad time, so painful to admit to myself that I was in the wrong place. But my conscience wouldn't allow me to live that life anymore. I didn't want to go back to de Paul or any place like it. I had to do what I had to do." I sighed. "And it cost. You're probably the only one who knows how devastating that decision was. You know, Helen, so many people think of us who left as quitters, like we deposited our ideals and spiritual lives along with our habits on the doorstep. What a crock! Our vocation simply changed residence! The fidelity we vowed was to God. Where it roosts is something else.

"Besides, what kind of people did they think we were? Here were women who had devoted the most productive years of their lives to their community. What could prompt them to give up their way of life, their friends, security, their vocation? They left with nothing. For what? A powder blue suit and a tube of lipstick? Please!" Helen sat very quietly for a minute, staring out the window at cars inching their way over patches of black ice, as the waiter served our food.

"Mary, you were always leaving."

"That's not true, Helen," I snapped. "I..."

"Hear me out. You were on a collision course with values you couldn't accept. And the more that truth rose to the surface, the more frantic you became, the tighter you clung. You wanted the life so badly so you hung on. Underneath, you had to know, but you wouldn't admit it."

I can't cry, I thought. Not here. I leaned across the table, leaned towards Helen.

"I know you're right. You and Edna and Bryand, you made a home for me. You marked off places where only I could dance. I went off and fought my battles and limped home and you tried so hard to help me make it work." I reached across the maroon linen tablecloth and laid my hand on hers. "It was always hopeless, Helen, wasn't it? I suppose in some way, I knew but I didn't think I was supposed to give it up. I couldn't face leaving because I didn't want to. The ironic twist was that no one could tell me what to do. Since the day I entered the convent, I had touted the importance of individual decision. And the day that the 'big one' landed in my lap, I didn't want it."

I leaned back in my chair and the two of us smiled at each other, the kind of smiles seen only on faces with crow's feet, and laugh lines and little creases around mouths, mouths that turn up in repose, faces that belong to people who know how to lay things to rest. My eyes filled up as we gazed at each other across the table, across Edna's death, the death of part of my life, the agonizing uncertainty when I decided to leave the convent and finally, the peace. We stared at our lives, our youth, our escapades, the not so funny, the truth, the changes, all of it.

It was a moment I will cherish until the day I die.

"My fettuccini's getting cold," Helen drawled, blowing her nose unceremoniously. I laughed out loud. "I've known you over forty years and that's the most emotion I've ever seen you show," and we dove into our food.

CHAPTER FORTY-SIX

I dropped Helen off at the Motherhouse and headed to the drugstore across from the hospital. I needed some aspirin. CVS was crowded and I had to wait longer than I would have liked. Thank heaven Katie had decided on a casual buffet, on finger food and lots of hors d'oeuvres. I might make it on time for dessert.

I'd better drive carefully. I'm emotionally drained, dead tired. How am I going to face this gathering? All those people? Visiting hours were over at the hospital, but New Scotland Avenue was bustling with Saturday night traffic. I could see two nurses, the only customers, drinking coffee in a booth of the Dunkin Donuts. As lonely as a Hopper painting, I thought. I knew that feeling, isolated, in the midst of bustle. During the years before I left the convent, I felt unanchored, drifting downstream, away from busy crowds who ignored my shouts and alarms. A frightening dream. As I pulled up, I couldn't believe I found a parking spot right in front of Katie' house. I was late and people must be leaving, but I needed a minute.

Heaving a great sigh, I took deep breaths, and closed my eyes. Somehow, this day had erased all that pain I had attached to leaving the community and replaced it with warm memories. I had chosen to enter the convent and I had chosen to leave the convent. I never thought it was a mistake either way. I never felt guilty leaving my parents, despite the cost to them; I never felt guilty leaving the convent though there were those who hoped I would, those who thought I should.

I still treasured those years, a rare place to have been young, a place where I built deep friendships, developed a strong sense of prayer, a stronger sense of God, a sense of what was important.

I opened my eyes. This was the first time in twenty years I had allowed myself this review. My life had gone on. I eventually married Ed, a widower with five children, four of them teenagers. A few years later, Ed and I had a son of our own. I made a mental note to call the both of them as soon as the relatives left tonight.

It had been a long day that was not over yet.

As I pushed myself out of the car and shut the door, I looked up and commented to the Almighty, "What a ride! You're full of surprises, aren't You? I remember so well the day I promised You my undying devotion, and You promised me a great adventure.

"I just didn't expect the one I got."

* * * * *

I left my boots in the hall and tossed my coat over the nearest chair in the living room. I spotted Marilyn Kennedy standing near the couch talking to two of my nieces. "So, I'm addressing the chief of surgery at St. Peter's Hospital? You're the first woman to hold that position. It's wonderful, Marilyn."

"Thank you, Mary." Marilyn wasn't a favorite of mine but she was one of Katie's friends.

"Sister Helen told me Sister Edmund was working in the front office part time. Do you ever see her? An amazing woman. She's over eighty."

"I avoid her whenever I can," Marilyn snapped, sipping her drink, tossing her blond pageboy and lapping up my nieces' attention. "She was never one of my favorite people." I ceased smiling, and headed for the kitchen. I liked Sister Edmund. I liked her a lot.

"Hey, Aunt Mary! How are you holding up… ?"

"Oh! Aunt Mary. I'm so sorry. I know how close you were to Nana."

Guests were still hovering over the buffet. After hugs from my nieces and nephews, I found Katie, fussing with canapés. "That Marilyn might be a wizard with a knife, but she has the personality of a porcupine!"

"Sshhhsh, she'll hear you." I filled a glass with ice, splashed it with C.C. and added seltzer. As I walked back through the living room, I heard her raving on about the rotten time the sisters had given her at de Paul, especially Sister Edmund.

Wrong night.

"I don't know, Marilyn, I lived with her at de Paul convent for years and she was no battle ax. She was cheerful, had a sense of humor. I remember she'd fix the nuns their supper on pick-up nights." I sipped my drink. "The younger ones too. Helpless by design, you know the type, and she was the high school principal." I sipped again. "I found her kind and generous and never put-on."

"Well, I can't remember one nice thing she ever did. She'd make us take off the boy's varsity sweaters and the corridors were cold, and she was always raving on about make-up and she never smiled..."

I'd had three glasses of wine at Scarlozzi's. My face was flushed and Pat, sensing action, had inched her way from the game table towards the couch behind Marilyn.

I was my father's daughter.

No one criticized the nuns.

"What you remember, Marilyn," I continued, "is the time she chewed you out in front of your boyfriend on the third floor and called you 'Missy'. How can you consider that incident so important? Get over it."

How could anybody her age with her experience be involved in adolescent thumb sucking? But Marilyn wasn't about to let go. "She was so miserable and mean."

"Come on, Marilyn, don't be such a baby. Don't you think nun bashing is a little silly at this stage? She was no principal. She was a *teacher*. She gave being a principal her best shot. Think about her responsibilities. And the bishop was a bas...he was difficult."

"You, of all people! How can you defend the nuns?" Her face looked cold, chiseled. "I don't have one decent memory of Catholic schools. I won't even give to the Bishop's Fund."

The C.C. and seltzer had done it.

Nice was out.

"How terribly convenient," I sneered. "You know you wouldn't be where you are now if it weren't for the nuns. You had a fantastic education, almost free! At the expense of people you don't respect. And you couldn't conceive of the cost to the sisters! Even if you don't like them, at least you could be grateful."

The room had gone dead quiet when Katie walked in from the kitchen, with a plate of crab canapés and a big smile.

"Crab, anyone?" she asked brightly.

"Marilyn, you've hit me on the wrong night and you're lucky I'm a guest in my sister's home, or you'd be wearing that crab, and I'm SURE it would become you." I turned on my heel and stalked into the kitchen, Pat two feet behind me.

"Well," cried Pat, "you can still boil over after all these years! Thank God there wasn't a pail of water handy. She *wouldn't* have looked good in that."

Katie rushed in, setting down the empty plate.

"Marilyn just left. What happened?"

"The crab is gone, the crab is gone," Pat and I chanted and were laughing so hard we couldn't talk.

"I have more," Katie began, staring at the empty plate, "but what happened to Marilyn?" Pat was roaring and beating the table with her hand. Katie knew she had missed something.

A sudden commotion at the front door brought us to our feet and drew us out of the kitchen. My niece Cailin rushed in and I could hear the word, Fire!

"It's the Motherhouse! The big convent on New Scotland! It's on fire."

"Oh, no!" My hand went to my face.

"Come on, come on, Aunt Mary," she mouthed over Katie's head. I grabbed my coat, boots and hat, and the two of us ran out the front door before anyone could ask us where we were going. "I just heard about it," she told me as we galloped down the front stairs. "I thought I should come get you."

CHAPTER FORTY-SEVEN

Cailin was covering the fire for *The Times Union* and, between conversations on her cell phone, she filled me in. She guessed that sparks had eaten through the cracked wires and devoured the brittle wood. The fire was hungry. Fueled by old newspapers, stuffed furniture, and musty trunks, its ravenous appetite had transformed the attic into an inferno. Tongues of flame had leapt out the small windows, and licked at the doors of a few makeshift cells.

Thank God it was early evening! None of the sisters had been in bed. There had been no sign of fire when I dropped Helen off. When did it start? Cailin had been talking on her phone non-stop since we pulled out of Katie's driveway. My head was filled with horrifying pictures. What about the infirmary? She was sure the nuns were all out, but how did they move the old sisters? Couldn't she drive faster?

We sped past Raft Pond and reeled around the corner of Euclid Avenue, onto New Scotland. Part of the street was taped off. Fire engines, ambulances and neighbors blocked the road. An elderly couple Cailin knew waved us into their driveway. They huddled together, the old man's arm draped over his wife's shoulder. "We've lived across the street from the nuns for over thirty-six years," the woman said.

"Anyone hurt?" Cailin interrupted.

"No. The attic's gone, just the attic. It seems under control." I broke away and promised I'd be back with news as soon as I could.

The street was a pool of wet ice. I slid down the sidewalk in my flat, furry boots, and noted that the trees, bushes and grass seemed drenched with sparkling gems.

Didn't nature have any sense? Don't sparkle tonight! The fire was out but the pungent air stung my eyes. When I picked my way through the crowd to the catalpa, where most people were gathered, I sensed no feeling of tragedy. No mourning, just relief and some tears.

Where was Helen? I spotted her, read her expression, and knew the building was safely evacuated and no one was hurt. Oh! God, thank you!

The immediate concern was, where were the sisters to go? Some ambulances and vans had taken most of the infirm to the Holy Names convent up the street. Friends and family were collecting nuns, leading them to cars and nearby houses, wrapping them in blankets and men's overcoats. "We have two spare rooms. We'd be honored." Sisters from nearby convents were herding a few into cars; reporters stood everywhere, stomping their feet in the cold, questioning the older nuns who patiently answered their questions, much to the firemen's annoyance. I saw Sister Claude with reporters.

"It's freezing out here!" A big, black fireman was scolding the reporters. "Where's your common sense, man? Get these nuns out of the cold, for God's sake." And he stomped off in his huge rubber boots.

People are wonderful! Thermoses of hot coffee appeared from everywhere, because some of the sisters wouldn't leave. I spotted Sister Martina, away from the crowd, staring up at the fourth floor, now a big smoking icicle.

"How much damage?" I asked Helen. "Do they know?"

"The fourth floor is gutted. Water damage on the third. The firemen aren't certain yet, but they think the slate roof saved the building. The main part is fine. Those huge fire doors worked." She shivered with relief. "No damage in the central building. Not even smoke. We'll be able to use the offices and the chapel. Your mother's funeral is still scheduled for Monday. No problem." She turned away from me to talk to a short, bald policeman who had been waiting patiently during our conversation, hat in hand.

The excitement was over. It was time to take stock, to thank God for no injuries, to accept and mourn the passing of an era. I crunched over the icy grass to Sister Gonzaga, who stood by herself, surrounded by loss. "Sister, where will you spend the night? Are you going over to the hospital? Cailin and I will be glad to take you."

She wasn't listening.

"I'm so sad for you, all your things..." I offered, lamely. Nuns never had much, but whatever they did have, now, was gone... pictures of their parents, little holy cards, sweetly inscribed by friends who had died years ago. Some of the senior sisters had kept parts of their old habits, the huge rosary, the crucifix that had hung around their necks.

All gone now.

"Sister, can I move you out of this cold?" I offered. Helen had walked over to us and put her arm around her.

"Why don't you go to the hospital, Sister? The firemen promised me we could search the third floor in a few days. If anything is salvageable, we'll get it." Helen signaled one of the nuns who was waiting quietly behind us. She threw another sweater over her and led her off, with soft warnings,

"Watch your step, now, watch your step."

Helen and I shoved our hands into our pockets, crackling the frozen grass as we slowly walked around towards the front of the building. "Well, the decision is made," she said. "We clean up the attic, renovate the third floor and add the new wing."

I said nothing.

"I think God could have been a little less dramatic, though," she drawled. "He didn't have to go to all this trouble. A simple inspiration would have done it. A meeting where all the council agreed. Or perhaps, during prayers."

"Oh, Helen, how can you joke?" Then I saw the tears in her eyes.

"I can't believe this has happened," I murmured. "All in one day! It's like a soap opera. Who'd believe it?"

The fire chief came over to speak to Helen. "A miracle no one's hurt! Such a damn close call. Sorry, Sister, but if it broke out in the middle of the night? God, I don't know what might have happened!" He stamped his feet in the cold.

"But you'd planned to renovate anyway, right Sister? The old wires must be all shot. This way, the whole building will be safe, and you can add the new wing while you're at it." He grinned at Helen. "Oh, come on, Sister. It could have been worse."

But Helen and I stood, staring up at the remains of the old chapel, of the old dormitories, of the dreary old cells, of poignant memories, of a way of life gone forever. We grieved for a piece of ourselves that most people in this world could never understand.

EULOGY

A clear shattering morning, cold and brittle. Our whole clan stood in front of the Motherhouse, waiting, shuffling our feet, stomping, blowing puffs of frost from chapped lips. The firemen had cleaned up as best as they could. The front of the building near the chapel was pristine, the older section, in disarray. Several men in ski masks and yellow slickers, breathing balls of cold mist, hauled rickety furniture and burnt trunks, the remains of sisters' lives, and threw them into huge dumpsters parked on the frozen lawn. I couldn't look.

Danny gave the signal. Cousin Eddie grabbed my arm, squeezed my hand, while the pipes keened their ancient agonies. Oh! Mom! you'd love this. You and your pipers. We were ushered into the first pew. I noted the discreets' stalls were empty. Helen knelt with the other sisters, who wore suits, or pieces of their habit as it suited them.

My eyes roamed, my spirit settled and I realized how much I loved the chapel, the space, the glow. Its austerity had faded, softened by the monotony and warmth of the nuns' presence, nuns familiar with the human side: whispering together in the back pews, tending the old and sick in their wheel chairs, tossing a pink cardigan over the back of a stall, setting flowers in surprising places. The God who lived here knew Mom well. The nuns and Mom led different lives but their thrust was the same. They believed that life owed them nothing but they owed God everything.

I sat up straight in the hard oak pew, fumbled for my handkerchief. Who would take their place? Who could? The world had changed. I wasn't going to cry. I would be fine. I had to be.

The Mass began. My nieces read the word of God; the priest introduced me. How many times had I glided out of those upper stalls and into the middle aisle to intone the Office, cocking my ear for correct pitch, adding a stately genuflection? Old graceful rituals. All gone.

I left the pew, walked to the lectern and turned, facing my family and friends. I found Pat's and Katie's eyes and began my eulogy with a quotation from Proverbs.

"Who will find a valiant woman?

She hath opened her mouth to wisdom, and the law of clemency is on her tongue.

She hath opened her hand to the needy and stretched out her hands to the poor.

Give her of the fruit of her hands: and let her works praise her in the gates."

Terms

(as used in this book)

apostolate — the mission of a religious person to do God's work.

branch house — any convent other than the Motherhouse.

canon law — a body of ecclesiastical law governing the Roman Catholic Church.

canonical- first year novice who studies canon law, the spiritual life and no secular subjects. Her visits from parents and friends were limited.

cloister — the covered porch attached on one side to the Motherhouse and open to the inside of the courtyard. Also the parts of a monastery or convent reserved only for nuns or sisters.

discreets — four nuns elected by the finally professed sisters to head up the community. Reverend Mother, Mother Assistant, Bursar, Mistress of Novices.

finally professed — a Sister of Mercy who has taken perpetual vows of poverty, chastity, obedience and service of the poor, sick and ignorant.

hopper — storage closet with large sink used for emptying pails of dirty water and storing wet mops.

junior professed — sisters who have taken temporary vows for three years and are usually performing duties of the community in branch houses.

monstrance — a golden, sun-burst vessel in which the consecrated host is exposed for the veneration of the faithful.

Motherhouse — A large building housing discreets, novitiate, retired sisters, sick and infirm and nuns teaching in nearby schools that had no convent. The place where sisters gathered for jubilees, feast days, ceremony days, elections, retreats and scuttlebutt. Headquarters.

novice — one who has been accepted into a religious order on probation. Usually two years.

novitiate — the time or place where one is a novice.

order — a religious society united by common rules that have been approved by Rome.

postulant — a candidate awaiting admission to the novitiate of a religious order. Usually a six-month period.

press — chest of drawers. Dresser without a mirror.

sacristy — room off the chapel that housed sacred vessels and vestments. Where the priest vested for Mass.

set — a group of sisters who entered the convent at the same time.

BIBLIOGRAPHY

Burns, Robert A., O.P. *Roman Catholicism Yesterday and Today*. Chicago: Loyola University Press, 1992. Simple but solid explanation of the Church's positions today.

Degnan, Sister Mary Bertrand, RSM. *Mercy Unto Thousands*. Westminster, Maryland: The Newman Press, 1957. A definitive biography of Mother Catherine McAuley and her times, a must for Irish scholars. Author deceased. Reprinted with permission from the Sisters of Mercy Albany Regional Community.

Eliot, T. S. *The Waste Land*. New York and London: Harcourt Brace Jovanovich, 1971.

Gonzales, S.S.P., Reverend J. L., compiled by. *The Sixteen Documents of Vatican II*. Boston: Daughters of St. Paul, no date.

Guardini, Romano. *The Church and the Catholic and the Spirit of the Liturgy*. New York: Sheed and Ward, 1935. A classic, especially in the days of clanging guitars.

McAuley, Mother Catherine, RSM. *The Rules and Constitutions of the Religious Sisters of Mercy*. Dublin: Brone & Nolan, Ltd. Re-edited edition. 1926.

McBrien, Richard P. *Catholicism*. San Francisco: Harper Collins, 1994. A tome from one of our great modern American theologians. Reference.

McNamara, Jo Ann Kay. *Sisters in Arms*. Cambridge, Massachusetts: Harvard University Press, 1996. A scholarly, 376 humorous, feminist account of nuns throughout the ages, their trials and contributions. Thoroughly researched by a delightful, respectful author. Reference, though great reading in small segments.

Roche, Douglas J. *The Catholic Revolution*. New York: Paperback Library. Revised edition. 1969.

Tanquery, The Very Reverend Adolphe, S.S., D.D. *The Spiritual Life*. Westminster, Maryland: The Newman Bookshop, 1948. The Bible of Mistresses of Novices during the forties and fifties.

Teilhad de Chardin, Pierre. *The Phenomenon of Man*. New York: Harper Colophon Books, 1959.

Yves de Moncheuil. *For Men of Action*. South Bend: Fides Publishers, no date. Still relevant.

MARRYING ED

CHAPTER I

MAURICE, WHO ARE YOU, REALLY?

It was a dark and stormy night. No cliché intended. I wasn't keen on driving from Back Bay out Rt. 9 to Southborough to a singles party where I didn't know anyone and I didn't care to. I was warm and cozy and safely tucked in on this Sunday night. "But you're the only one with a car," my friend needled, "and Judy and Vivian have just come back from Europe and we all need to meet new people and you should get out too. Our work is so serious etc., etc., etc."

So I said yes.

I was chauffeuring three women. The two I didn't know were expensively put together. Anne, a colleague from school whom I had recently met had conned me into the evening.

"The girls have just returned from Paris!"she exclaimed "They taught in primary classes for a year. They might have a fresh approach to Early Childhood education," she offered encouragingly. That intrigued me. I was currently teaching Kindergarten in Boston and organizing a new curriculum.

Unfortunately for me, they weren't interested in children.

I collected them on Boylston Street across from the Pru, and after hurried introductions, Anne settled in the front seat with me and the other two's conversation immediately turned to men.

"I just want to meet men who speak English, who are looking for more than sex, widowed or divorced, no young children, good looking, professional and well off," Judy began.

I wish you luck, I thought. You are about to encounter some stiff competition. I'd been to these gatherings before.

"I'd love to meet a widower with grown children, but no divorced man," Vivian continued. "Some exes never let go. Even if they lived in Tahiti, they'd keep their finger in the pot…especially if they have children. I don't blame them. I just don't want the hassle."

Anne said nothing. I uh-hummed a great deal, trying to navigate the wet, dark roads and ignore the dancing wind-shield wipers. We finally passed Framingham, were in Southboro and I took a right and we all began searching for Lover's Lane.

"Who'd believe anyone lived on Lover's Lane?" I asked no one in particular but there it was.

I drove at least a quarter of a mile under a canopy of pines, past stables, an Olympic-sized swimming pool and a guest cottage before we reached the main house. The rain had let up by the time the four of us arrived but I had worn a lime-green cape with a huge Vogue stand-up collar that I happened to look good in. I kept it on. The evening was chilly for early May.

A tall male was leaning against the front door, highball in hand, giving us the once-over and not being coy about it either. He didn't move so I quipped, "Are you checking I.D.'s?"

"No, I'm Maurice the butler. Can I take your coats?" I doubted his explanation but, why not? I'd have to relinquish the rain cape sometime.

"Certainly," and in we went. The house was large, rambling, and inviting. The walls were mahogany, the floors were polished hardwood, the kitchen was industrial and the library was beautiful. The house was packed with flowers, food, drink and fortyish singles making a great deal of noise. I grabbed a chardonnay and a plate of munchies as Maurice came downstairs and singled me out.

Here we go, I thought. Let the games begin.

"Well, Maureeeeece, are you from Boston?"

"No, I'm a widower."

I turned and looked up at him. "I'm sorry, I asked you if you were from Boston."

"I thought you asked me if I was divorced."

"How rude," I exclaimed. "How could anyone ask such a thing?"

"You're the first person here who hasn't asked me…such a thing." He laughed a nice easy laugh. I liked him.

"Maurice, who are you, really? I doubt if you're the butler."

"I'm not. I was looking for something to do. I'm Ed Blanchard. I'm a widower and I live here in town. Who are you?"

"I'm Mary Bergan and I live in Back Bay. Shake."

We moved into the library and I sensed he was relieved to escape an unfamiliar scene, a scene I had become used to. He wasn't fishing. He hadn't asked me if I were divorced or had children. Very polite. I liked that. He told me why he had accepted Ruth's invitation and about his misgivings.

"This is a singles party for college graduates. That's not me. I hated school. My mother wouldn't let me quit so I got my high school diploma at night. After I came home from the service I took courses at Clark in accounting but no degree." He studied his drink. "Most of these people are lawyers or doctors. I've always been in business. But they *are* people. You have to talk to somebody. I don't want to turn into a hermit."

The library was crowding up with couples who had paired off so we ambled into the kitchen and sat on the high stools near the counter. Ed continued where we left off. "When your wife dies, you're the one left and your married friends disappear, people you've known for years. It's bad enough that so much of your life changes but there you are. Alone. So I came. Why not?" He turned and smiled. "But who wants a man my age?"

"Plenty of women," I answered," including two out of the three girls I drove here with, especially if you own a house like this." We both laughed.

"I don't, but my house is a nice colonial that overlooks the reservoir. We had it built. Wanna see it? It's less than a mile from here." He stood up and said, "Don't worry. I don't own any etchings." He dramatically put his hand over his heart and recited, "My heart is pure and your virtue is safe with me."

"I believe you," and I laughed again. No way he'd be invited here if he were a serial killer. It was a small town and people knew each other. Besides, I liked his eyes. I checked with my passengers who had connected with partners and had rides home so we left.

We entered his sprawling colonial through a side door that led into a family room, the only room in the house I saw that night. We settled down and eventually sipped Galianno from a ceramic Italian soldier with a cork in his head.

"I suppose you wonder what I do for a living," he commented as he settled into the arm chair next to me.

"Not really." I lied.

"Well, when Jean died, she was only forty…and it hit me. It could have been me. And I thought, what do I really want to do?" He was staring out the window into the dark. The rain had turned to an occasional drizzle and the moon had little chance of performing tonight.

"Like, what was your dream if you could do anything you wanted to?" I asked, breaking the long silence.

"Yes, like that," he said "And I decided I wanted to own a tavern. They were fun. I liked the idea of working for myself. I was a distribution manager at the time, Narragansett beer…New England area. I knew the business. I've been in small business all my life." He was staring out the window again. and seemed so far away.

I wondered if he were talking to me.

"The day I went back to work after I buried Jean, I upped and quit. Just like that. I didn't like my boss anyway and he was nagging me for paper work. I didn't need anyone pushing me around right then so I threw the papers at him, right across the desk." Ed laughed at the memory.

"If he wanted the job done, he could do it himself, I told him. I stayed home for six weeks and built the shed out back. You can't see it tonight in the dark. In the meantime, I looked around and bought the bar, renamed it Ed's Place and that's what I do. I run a tavern."

"And do you like it? Was it worth it?"

Here's someone who doesn't fool around, I thought, waiting for an answer. How many people in this world take chances like his and really go for what they want.

"Yes and yes," he answered, finally, and he was smiling.

We continued chatting about this and that and it was after two a.m. when he led me as far as the Pike, drowned me in specific directions, told me how to get off at the Pru and made a date for a Red Sox game Tuesday night.

CPSIA information can be obtained
at www.ICGtesting.com
Printed in the USA
FSOW02n0538281215
14844FS